# The Sovereign Prerogative

THE SUPREME COURT AND THE QUEST FOR LAW

. . . *inasmuch as the real justification of a rule of law, if there be one, is that it helps to bring about a social end which we desire, it is no less necessary that those who make and develop the law should have those ends articulately in their minds. I do not expect or think it desirable that the judges should undertake to renovate the law. That is not their province. Indeed precisely because I believe that the world would be just as well off if it lived under laws that differed from ours in many ways, and because I believe that the claim of our especial code to respect is simply that it exists, that it is the one to which we have become accustomed, and not that it represents an eternal principle, I am slow to consent to overruling a precedent, and think that our important duty is to see that the judicial duel shall be fought out in the accustomed way. But I think it most important to remember whenever a doubtful case arises, with certain analogies on one side and other analogies on the other, that what really is before us is a conflict between two social desires, each of which seeks to extend its dominion over the case, and which cannot both have their way. The social question is which desire is stronger at the point of conflict. The judicial one may be narrower, because one or the other desire may have been expressed in previous decisions to such an extent that logic requires us to assume it to preponderate in the one before us. But if that be clearly so, the case is not a doubtful one. Where there is doubt the simple tool of logic does not suffice, and even if it is disguised and unconscious, the judges are called on to exercise the sovereign prerogative of choice.*

OLIVER WENDELL HOLMES, JR., 1899

(in "Law in Science and Science in Law,"
*Collected Legal Papers* [1920], pp. 238–39)

# The Sovereign Prerogative

THE SUPREME COURT AND THE QUEST FOR LAW

By EUGENE V. ROSTOW

NEW HAVEN AND LONDON, YALE UNIVERSITY PRESS

1962

FOR VICTOR, JESSICA, AND NICKY

# Acknowledgments

I OWE MUCH to the generosity of colleagues and other friends who patiently read various drafts of these papers, kindly trying to save me from error, and to Jan Deutsch, a fourth-year student at the Yale Law School, who helped prepare these pages for the printer. As always, I was greatly aided by my wife, who first proposed the idea of this book and contributed to its development in the bracing spirit of The Union.

Thanks are due as well to many friends, hosts, universities, and publishers for the invitations which led to the preparation of several of these papers and for permission to reprint them. I gratefully acknowledge amiable indebtedness to President and Mrs. Quigg Newton of the University of Colorado, to Dean and Mrs. Edward C. King of the University of Colorado Law School, and to the editors of the *Rocky Mountain Law Review*, in connection with Chapter 1; to Christopher Morris, Fellow of King's College, Cambridge, Arthur L. Armitage, President of Queens' College, Cambridge, Professor Ronald H. Graveson, Dean of the Faculty of Laws, King's College, London, Professor Arthur Phillips, Dean of the Faculty of Laws, Southampton, and to Professor C. J. Hamson, Editor of the *Cambridge Law Journal*, with regard to Chapter 2; to the Houston Bar Association, Judge John R. Brown, Lloyd F. Thanhouser, Esq., and the editors of the *South Texas Law Review*, with respect to Chapter 3; to Dean Joseph O'Meara of the Notre Dame University Law

## Acknowledgments

School, and the editors of the *Notre Dame Lawyer,* for Chapter 4; to the editors and publishers of the *Yale Law Journal,* the *Harvard Law Review, Harper's Magazine,* and *Fortune,* for permission to reproduce Chapters 5–9. And I acknowledge with gratitude the compliment of Attorney General William P. Rogers for his invitation to be the guest of honor at the ceremony referred to on p. 263.

EUGENE V. ROSTOW

*New Haven, Conn.*
*March 1962*

# Contents

# Introduction

THESE PAPERS treat two related subjects. They concern aspects of the work of the Supreme Court of the United States, and they examine some of the sources from which that Court, like other judicial bodies, draws its competence, its ideas, and its authority. I have ventured to bring these scattered articles and speeches together because their point of view is the minority position in the war of words now swirling about the Court's more important modern decisions.

In the lively literature of the Supreme Court, there are several themes. We can put to one side those know-nothing critics who regard the Court as the corrupt tool of class or political interests, and, equally, those who express, in Holmes' phrase, no more than "the unrest that seems to wonder vaguely whether law and order pay."[1] A good deal of what remains, both in popular and in technical books and articles, is in danger of being confused by the divisions of the Justices. In many of their cases, the Justices disagree. It is tempting to concentrate all attention on these disagreements and vicariously to share the joy of the judges' battles. The risk in that course is twofold: writers often tend to become partisans of one or another of the Justices, at the expense of their general view of the constitutional process; and the public comes to believe that the main constitutional issues of the day are exclusively represented by the problems

1. "Law and the Court," in *Collected Legal Papers* 292 (1920).

xi

on which the Justices divide. Thus the idea spreads that the Court consists of two incompatible factions, "strict" and "loose" constructionists, "activists" and believers in "judicial restraint," "liberals" and "conservatives," judges who "follow" the law and those who "make" it, "good men" and "bad men," according to one's taste and predilections.

The task of judging the Supreme Court and its work cannot be solved so simply. It is a useful corrective for such facile views to recall that the school segregation case, *Brown v. Board of Education*,[2] and many others of capital importance, were unanimously decided. It is equally chastening to realize that distinguished spokesmen for opposing schools within the Court criticize each other occasionally for exactly the same error—that of substituting their personal views for those of the community and the constitutional tradition in interpreting the language and policies of the Constitution.

The more serious writing about the Court, like the opinions and other essays of the Justices, concerns two sets of problems. The first involves differences as to the nature and function of law, and more particularly differences as to the duties and responsibilities of judges, as compared with other lawmakers, in the legal system we have inherited. The second turns on differences in weighing the relative importance of the various elements affecting the decision of particular cases or groups of cases. It often happens that differences of the second type—differences as to the significance attached to one feature or another of a problem before the Court—derive in turn from differences of philosophical position about the functions of law and the duties of the judge in the legal universe. In other instances, they represent the differing convictions of the judges as interpreters

2. 347 U.S. 483 (1954).

of the Constitution or the statutes, and of the values and feelings of society which lie behind them, as they are invoked to resolve highly charged social and political controversies.

The position exemplified in this book considers law to be the means through which social policies become social action. It views law as an integral part of the process of social change. It accepts as normal the fact that judges have a limited but inescapable duty to make some of the decisions through which law develops, in response to changing social notions of policy. "I think it most important to remember whenever a doubtful case arises," Holmes once wrote—and almost all cases which reach the Supreme Court, or other appellate courts, are doubtful to some extent—"with certain analogies on one side and other analogies on the other, that what really is before us is a conflict between two social desires, each of which seeks to extend its dominion over the case, and which cannot both have their way. . . . Where there is doubt the simple tool of logic does not suffice, and even if it is disguised and unconscious, the judges are called on to exercise the sovereign prerogative of choice."[3] It follows, in this perspective, that lawyers, judges, and academic students of law cannot meet their responsibilities to the legal process unless they devote as much thought to the reasons for a rule of law as to the rule itself—unless they understand the social ends law is designed to serve, and the movements and aspirations which determine the future of the law, and of the society it must organize.

Law shares the worlds of thought and action. The crucibles of law are courts and legislatures and the places where elections are fought and won; prisons, welfare agencies, and police stations; international conferences, the meeting

3. "Law in Science and Science in Law," in *Collected Legal Papers* 239 (1920).

rooms of labor negotiation, and every other forum where decisions of social policy are reached. Equally, law is made in libraries, classrooms, and studies. The law is bookish in its most active moments; yet the learning of law, however abstract, is tinged by the consciousness that legal ideas must sooner or later be put to the test by practical men responsible for the conduct of affairs.

As law is the all-embracing social institution, so is the study of law the universal social science. An understanding of the goals of law necessarily draws upon all other bodies of systematic knowledge about man's life in society. One cannot study the law of property, of contract, or of inheritance without investigating their social and historical purposes, or the theories of economics, ethics, and politics which give them coherence. It would be self-defeating to approach criminal law or family law today without using the insights of psychiatry, psychology, and the literature of social relations. The case is the same in other branches of law, and emphatically with constitutional law, the subject matter of these pages. In no part of law are the elements of social policy so evident and so frequently considered.

Law is not, however, a compendium of facts and thoughts drawn from other branches of knowledge, nor simply a mirror of history. The law helps to shape history, as it is influenced by it. Social experience emerges in legal form only after it has gone through a process of transformation. Emerging social forces are examined in the light of some of the key propositions of law itself, which in its turn acts powerfully upon them. In the end, the law is molded by a central body of its own ideas—peculiarly legal ideas, based on a long and maturely considered history. These cardinal ideas of the law—ideas about justice and order, and about procedures for seeking them—have great stability. Legal institutions change, as they should, in response to changing social pressures and changes in moral attitude. Yet behind the movement of change there is a body of norms, or aspirations, to which our law and our people are tenaciously loyal. These basic ideals of law must be reinterpreted and achieved anew as they are used by each generation in seeking to solve the problems of its own experience.

Our generation is no exception to this rule. The growth of the law inevitably reflects the forces and ideas which are transforming our society and world society. In one area after another, the law is going through natural processes of change—often of rapid change, corresponding to the violent rate of change in the world around us. New problems preoccupy the law, problems unknown a generation ago, or known in a different form, with a different degree of importance. Old problems take on new dimensions when seen in a setting that is steadily altered by the tide of events. As always in the evolution of law, the contemporary movement of change in law is also one of continuity. The law grows now, as it has in the past, around a firm axis of its own values.

The concept of law recapitulated in the last few paragraphs lacks an accepted name, although many have been applied to its variant forms. Part I of the book explores its content in some detail, and its implications are the subject matter of the entire volume. This view of law and of the judge's task in law might be called Sociological Jurisprudence, or American Legal Realism, with a strong orientation toward a jurisprudence of values. In identifying it, labels are not particularly helpful. Its ancestors are Montesquieu, Ehrlich, Pound, Holmes, and Cardozo. For many years, it has represented the prevailing approach to legal studies at the Yale Law School to a greater extent than has been the case in any other law faculty of the world. It also constitutes a significant, though not always a dominant part of the intellectual matrix in which almost all modern lawyers, judges, and scholars of law have been formed.

The chief differences among the Justices of the Supreme Court, and among the academic students of its work, stem in considerable part from variations of emphasis on the relative importance of the several factors I have sought to identify here. Some, like Judge Learned Hand and Mr. Justice Frankfurter, are still closely linked with the tradition of legal positivism.[4] They find a sharp separation between "the law that is" and "the law that ought to be," and tend to regard this second aspect of law as not quite the legitimate business of judges. Therefore they seek to limit the judges' historic role in making law. They fully understand that law is not a static body of fixed precepts, symmetrically organized only according to the aesthetic principles of logic. They know that law must change as society changes. But they would prefer law to be altered not by judges, but by legislatures, chosen, they believe, more democratically than judges are. They are especially doubtful about the propriety of the Supreme Court's extraordinary power to declare unconstitutional acts of the President, the Congress, or the state governments. Confining that power to the narrowest possible range, they would cabin its exercise by a series of rigid rules. They are among the many who have sought in vain to impose Euclidean forms on the non-Euclidean universe of law. Still, both Judge Hand and Mr. Justice Frankfurter have exercised the judge's "sovereign prerogative of choice" on many occasions, despite their eloquent concern over the legitimacy of their role.

4. Some of Judge Hand's essays are discussed in chapters 4 and 5, particularly at pp. 128–37, and 161–70. Justice Frankfurter's views are well summarized in his "John Marshall and the Judicial Function," in Arthur E. Sutherland, ed., *Government under Law* 6 (1956).

# Introduction

At first glance, it may seem paradoxical that Mr. Justice Black, popularly viewed as the antithesis of Mr. Justice Frankfurter, and as one of the leading exemplars of judicial freedom in constitutional interpretation, also opposes the principle of judicial lawmaking, both in his opinions and in his extra-judicial lectures.[5] He urges that the judges view those parts of the Constitution stated in categorical form, and especially those treating the liberties of the citizen, as having fixed and absolute meaning, so that society will be protected against the arbitrary exercise of judicial power. Clear rules, he has repeatedly urged, should keep the judges from declaring their private value preferences to be the ideas of the Constitution they are charged with construing in behalf of society. For Justice Black, too, his announced code of judicial philosophy has not proved to be a workable rule of judicial action. Law, like life, cannot achieve logical certainty nor avoid the dilemmas of judgment. Justice Black's career as judge attests the creativity of the judicial process in a changing society, and the futility of regarding legal rules as immutable. In many memorable votes and opinions, he has in fact followed the course indicated as inevitable by Justice Holmes' comment on the necessity for judicial choice. And he has thereby helped to write into the law many of the libertarian views he and others find immanent in the policies of the Constitution and in the polity of contemporary America.

5. "The Bill of Rights," The James Madison Lecture at the New York University Law School, Feb. 17, 1960, 35 *N.Y.U.L. Rev.* 865 (1960), sympathetically construed in Charles L. Black, Jr., "Mr. Justice Black, the Supreme Court, and the Bill of Rights," *Harper's Mag.* (Feb. 1961), p. 63. See also Adamson v. California, 332 U.S. 46, 68, esp. at pp. 75 and 90–92 (1947); Rochin v. California, 342 U.S. 165, 174 (1952); Green v. United States, 356 U.S. 165, 193, at 197 (1958); Uphaus v. Wyman, 364 U.S. 388, 389 at 392 (1960); Smith v. California, 361 U.S. 147, 155 (1959). On his view of the First Amendment as an absolute, see pp. 132–37, infra.

## Introduction

The survival power of positivist ideas about the nature of law and of the judge's work in law makes a difference, however. They affect the results in particular cases, and they color public and professional thought about what is happening and what is at stake. The strain of legal positivism which appears in the powerful opinions and papers of both Justice Black and Justice Frankfurter tends to impair realistic thought about the work of the Court and the development of the Constitution. It tends as well to divert attention from the genuine differences of constitutional policy which have often led these and other Justices to disagree. Both academic and popular thought have suffered in consequence. Scholars of influence have reinforced and developed Judge Hand's attack on the foundations of the American system of constitutional law.[6] Debate has been dominated by the issues thus posed, at the expense of efforts to delineate a more adequate and more affirmative constitutional doctrine of judicial action for our time.

## II

Before we can trace the interplay of these competing ideas about law in the work of the Supreme Court, it is essential to place the Court in its setting as part of the American

6. Several, who disagree with Judge Hand about the legitimacy of judicial review, would so encumber its exercise with rules and principles of exegesis as to accomplish nearly the same end—that of limiting the judicial influence in the formation of the constitution. See, for example, Henry M. Hart, Jr., "The Supreme Court, 1958 Term, Foreword, The Time Chart of the Justices," 73 *Harv. L. Rev.* 84, 98–125 (1959), Herbert Wechsler, "Towards Neutral Principles of Constitutional Law," 73 *Harv. L. Rev.* 1 (1959), discussed at pp. 24–39, infra. A basis for views of this order is cogently outlined in H. M. Hart, Jr., and Albert M. Sacks, "The Legal Process: Basic Problems in the Making and Application of Law" (tentative ed., mimeo., Cambridge, Mass., 1958). Cf. Lon L. Fuller, "Reason and Fiat in Case Law," 59 *Harv. L. Rev.* 376 (1946). And, further, among many recent books, Wallace Mendelson, "Justices Black and Frankfurter" (1961).

constitutional system. For the Court's job in American government can be defined only in relation to those of the President, the Congress, and the state governments; and its work can be appraised only as a part of the effort of American public life to realize—and to resist—the goals and values of modern democracy, within the framework of its constitutional methods. My purpose in these paragraphs is not to present constitutional law in a nutshell, but to recall certain salient features of the constitution—with a small "c"—as background for the comments on the work of the Supreme Court which comprise the book.

One difficulty with much of the writing about the American constitution is that it is confined to those of its features which come before the Supreme Court—that is, those which are customarily compressed into the form of law suits. It therefore leads to a foreshortened and misleading sense of the whole and to an unrealistic view of the Court itself. The Supreme Court is an important participant in the making of American constitutional law. But it cannot deal with all aspects of the constitution, nor even with all its most fundamental aspects. The risk in concentrating exclusively on the work of the Court is to leave some basic constitutional problems—including several affecting the work of the Court—entirely in shadow.

The American constitution is an evolving pattern of usage governing the exercise of public authority. The written Constitution which went into effect in 1789, and its amendments, are an integral part of the living constitution. But they are by no means all of it. And in the interpretation of the written Constitution—as in the development of the unwritten one—political and social experience, history, custom, and memory play a role far more important than the syntactic analysis of sacred words. For the rest, the constitution inheres largely in certain fundamental statutes which have nearly constitutional standing—like the Sherman Act and the Judiciary Act—and in the balance of political and social force and ideas within the American community and within the Supreme Court of the United States.

Many of the words used in the written Constitution, and many of the constitutionally decisive practices of our political system, derive directly from our British past. Sometimes there are mutations. But the forms are recognizable. The organization of Congress and other legislative bodies, for example, their privileges, their powers over contempts and over the qualifications of members, their procedures in debate, and the status of their presiding officers—all these structural elements of the constitutional order are drawn from Westminster. So is the most fundamental constitutional habit of all—that of electing members of the House of Representatives by majority vote in single-member constituencies. Senators and Presidents are elected according to the same principle, which tends to exaggerate the size of majorities in the interest of effective and responsible government. Our constitutional practice differs from that of Britain in one far-reaching way, in that members of Congress are required to be residents of the districts or states they represent. We do not drag the Speaker of the House unwillingly to his chair, as the British do, nor do we elect him for life. But the few spare words the Constitution uses to sketch the Congress, its simple references to "the judicial power," and many other aspects of the system it instituted, come to us with a gloss of historical experience extending in both directions from 1789.

The written Constitution is a brief and elegant paper, composed in the accents of eighteenth-century rationalism, with a stiff-necked republican flavor as well. It prescribes, for example, that all public officials, state and national, are to be bound to support the Constitution "by Oath or Affirmation"; that no religious test shall ever be required as a qualification to any office or public trust under the United States; that neither Congress nor the states can grant titles of nobility; and that without the consent of Congress no public official can accept any present, emolument, office, or title of any kind whatever from any king, prince, or foreign state. The Constitution manifests a fear of standing armies, for the history of the Roman republic, and of many later republics, was much in the minds of the framers. Thus the Constitution makes the President the Commander in Chief of the armed forces and stipulates that no appropriation to raise and support armies shall be for a longer term than two years. The Second Amendment, viewed as an integral protection of the civil liberties of the citizen, provides that the right of the people to keep and bear arms shall not be infringed, since "a well-regulated militia" is "necessary to the security of a free state." The Constitution guarantees each state a republican form of government. And it seeks to protect the people against the designation of political opposition as crime—that favorite weapon of ancient and modern tyrannies—by its extraordinarily strict definition of treason, the only crime defined in the document.

The written Constitution consists of a preamble and seven brief articles.

The preamble is more than a flourish. In the language of social contract, it embodies a theory of sovereignty which dominates the Constitution, providing a foundation for the practice of judicial review and its acceptance as a democratic institution. This theory—that the Constitution was made by the people, not the states—is discussed in Part II, particularly at pp. 91–92, and pp. 118–22. It leads directly to the conception of the Supreme Court as the agent of the people in enforcing constitutional limitations of power on both the states and the nation.

The most important characteristic of the American constitution derives from this view of its origin: that it represents an indissoluble union of the people, not of states. The contrary arguments of John C. Calhoun, appealing to the plausible principle of self-determination, were authoritatively rejected, not by the Supreme Court, but by the armies of Lincoln, and by his second election. The rule of indissolubility is drawn from history and the clash of arms, not from the persuasive power of words alone.

The written Constitution, and the constitution of experience which is forever crystallizing around it, establish three separate branches of the national government: the Congress, embodying the legislative powers granted to the nation; the Presidency, in which "the executive power" is vested; and the Supreme Court, and "such inferior courts as Congress may from time to time ordain and establish," as the repository of "the judicial power of the United States." This tripartite division of authority, the celebrated system of checks and balances, dominates the organization of state and local governments as well as of the national government.

The constitutional development of the Presidency has been a matter mainly of custom and politics, although a few of its vital features have come before the Supreme Court for adjudication. The Constitution provides in the main that the President is to take care that the laws are faithfully executed; to be the Commander in Chief of the armed forces; to appoint subordinate officials; to receive ambassadors and make treaties; to grant pardons; and to report from time to time to the Congress on the state of the Union, and "recommend to their consideration such measures as he shall judge necessary and expedient."

The great powers of the Presidency are most imperfectly reflected in these provisions. The President bears Lincoln's duty to preserve the Union, a duty nowhere mentioned and once strenuously denied, but inherent in the office now by force of history. No American President today could "let the erring sisters go in peace," as President de Gaulle has done. Secondly, he represents the nation abroad—a task which has been an active one throughout our history and is now of overwhelming weight. On this subject, the Constitution remarks only that the President is to receive ambassadors, and requires that treaties be ratified by a vote of two-thirds of the Senators present. Yet from the beginnings of the Republic, the President acted for the nation abroad in instance after instance which established a far-reaching reservoir of authority. He could and did make executive agreements with foreign nations, as incident to his conduct of foreign relations, even though the distinction between such agreements and treaties is sometimes difficult to ascertain. As Commander in Chief, he has ordered the armed forces into combat from the shores of Tripoli to Korea, although Congress has the formal power to declare war.

Under modern circumstances, the increased importance of foreign affairs has required the President more and more to appear the representative of the nation, beyond the strife of party combat. These transformations, and the growth since 1887 of national legislation regulating economic and social affairs, have greatly increased his capacity to form opinion and to speak to the nation on a host of topics as its political and moral leader. In the hands of a vigorous man, this feature of the Presidency is crucial. As President Theodore Roosevelt once said, the White House is "a bully pulpit." National leader or not, however, the President can never cease to be an effective party chief. If he fails in this role, he fails in everything else. Congress is always eager for power, and always pushes into a vacuum left by a weak President.

## Introduction

History, and the courts, have established certain limits on the formidable powers of the Presidency. A hostile congressional majority can harass and frustrate a President, although it can never fulfill his function of governing. And even a Congress strongly loyal to a President, of the kind we have not had since 1937 and have almost forgotten, has never been easy for a President to deal with. The inherent frictions of the system guarantee an almost equal contest for authority between Congress and the President. That contest has been embittered by the modern revival of old fears that the President can become a tyrant above the law.

The advantages of the President in his struggles with Congress are minimized in another way. The Washingtonian tradition that the President should not have more than two terms in office, much debated during the nineteenth century, was challenged by President Theodore Roosevelt and finally breached by President Franklin D. Roosevelt. The response of Congress and the nation was the Twenty-Second Amendment of the Constitution, codifying the two-term tradition as law. While there have been rumblings of criticism that the Amendment denies the people their democratic right to choose whom they will as President, neither party now seems likely to propose its repeal. President Eisenhower voiced doubts about the wisdom of the Amendment as a fixed rule, and many Presidents are bound to feel as he does. But the capacity of a modern President to become an overpowering national figure is equally threatening to both parties, and to the powers of Congress. The Democrats generally believed that President Eisenhower would have won a third term easily in 1960, if he had been nominated. Short of a prolonged national emergency, it is hard to visualize a combination of forces which would now alter this aspect of the constitutional position of the Presidency, as it has been re-established by the Twenty-Second Amendment.

Certain other features of the Presidency have occasioned constitutional controversy, both before the courts and in the forum of politics. The President's powers in war and other emergencies, a crucial problem for all constitutions, are discussed in Chapters 7 and 8. Where the exercise of emergency powers touches the freedom or property of individuals, the courts have accepted jurisdiction, although their treatment of such problems has sometimes betrayed an overpowering sense of the weight to be given the national interest in overcoming the emergency, at the expense of the individual's claim to the protection of the Constitution. The President's control over the executive establishment has occasioned litigation, with regard to his power to remove Cabinet officers and less august officials,[7] and to deny congressional committees access to papers or testimony deemed "confidential."[8] Similarly, Presidents have claimed the power, as incident to their responsibilities for the conduct of foreign relations, to deny citizens passports and the right to travel abroad, or to certain troubled places abroad. An important recent decision of the Supreme Court suggests that Presidential (or congressional) power in this regard, if it is ultimately conceded to exist at all, will be severely restricted in the name of the liberty to travel.[9]

7. See, e.g., Wiener v. United States, 357 U.S. 349 (1958); Humphrey's Executor v. United States, 295 U.S. 602 (1935); Myers v. United States, 272 U.S. 52 (1926). On Stanton's attempt to remain in office despite his dismissal by the President, see Milton Lomask, *Andrew Johnson: President on Trial* chs. 20–23 (1960), and Benjamin P. Thomas and Harold M. Hyman, *Stanton* 581–94, 600, 613 (1962).

8. Discussed in J. W. Bishop, Jr., "Executive's Right of Privacy: an Unresolved Constitutional Question," 66 *Yale L.J.* 477 (1957).

9. Kent v. Dulles, 357 U.S. 116 (1958). See Comment, "Passport Refusals for Political Reasons: Constitutional Issues and Judicial Review," 61 *Yale L.J.* 171 (1952).

## Introduction

These comments on the Presidency have necessarily involved some reflections as well on Congress as an institution. The most basic rule of the Constitution determining the place of Congress in the constitutional order is that no person holding any office under the United States shall be a member of either House during his continuance in office. This guarantee against parliamentary government goes far to fix the structure of American politics. Article I of the Constitution (after defining the House and the Senate, and prescribing their different modes of election, the privileges and immunities of members, and the requirement that they meet at least once a year, keep journals, and record their votes) consists of three sections. Section 8 lists eighteen fields in which Congress has the power to legislate, subject to certain qualifications and limitations. Section 9 enumerates eight subjects on which Congress' power to legislate is restricted or denied altogether. And Section 10 declares three sets of prohibitions upon the powers of the states. Together, these three sections of Article I outline the map of American legislative powers and establish some of its boundaries. But neither these sections, nor the rest of Article I, do more than hint at what was in fact to occur.

Nowhere does Article I mention, for example, the possibility that Congress may decide to proceed through committees. Yet our Congress, building on Elizabethan models, developed its methods of work through committees into the most effective device known to modern democracy for the surveillance and control of the enormous bureaucracies which everywhere characterize contemporary government. Although Congress, like most institutions, doubtless requires reform, we need not share the concern of other democracies that our legislative branch is withering away before the growing power of the executive. The committee system serves another purpose of equal importance to the reality of democratic government. Despite occasional abuses, it constitutes a remarkably flexible means by which Congress can remain in close touch with the community, receiving ideas and proposals, enquiring into situations which may call for governmental action, and generally acting as the Grand Inquest of the nation. Through these means, and through its debates, it contributes powerfully to the formation of public opinion: the classic primary function of parliaments.

Similarly, the provisions of Article I do not in themselves give the reader a real sense of the ways in which legislative powers are in fact distributed between the states and the nation. True, Article I mentions the federal legislative "specialties"—that Congress has power to coin money; establish post offices; encourage the progress of science and the useful arts by securing limited copyrights for authors and patents for inventors; establish uniform rules of naturalization and uniform laws on the subject of bankruptcies; regulate the armed forces; declare war; constitute tribunals inferior to the Supreme Court; and regulate commerce with foreign nations, and among the several states, and with the Indian tribes. It prohibits export taxes, bills of attainder and ex post facto laws, and preferences among ports; and it delicately mentions one of the compromise provisions on slavery which were indispensable to the formation of the Union.

It would be hard to imagine, from a reading of the text, that commerce, railroads, banking, insurance, and many other subjects would in fact be regulated in the end both by the states and by the national government, in a pattern which is sometimes one of cooperation and at others one of conflict; and that federalism in action would become not a neat and clear-cut division of exclusive authorities, on one side or the other of the lines drawn in the Constitution, but a tempestuous and cumbersome hodgepodge of multiple controls. Modern procedures, like the grant-in-aid and some of the cooperative arrangements of the Social Security system, have their legitimate source in Congress' power to tax and spend "for the common defense and general welfare of the United States." But the actual pattern of federalism, a most difficult and sensitive issue for our law and our politics, defies simple formulation. One aspect of the problem is considered in Chapter 9, another in Chapter 3.

Suffice it to say here that in regulating the federal division of powers between the national government and those of the states, the unwritten constitution of political practice has proved to be as important as the decisions of the Supreme Court. Acting as umpire of the federal system in settling controversies about the boundaries of state and national jurisdiction has been one of the most important tasks of the Supreme Court throughout its history. Disputes of this order involve intensely felt issues of politics. The Federalists of the first generation of the Republic supported the national power against the Jeffersonian defense of states' rights. Many of the men in our politics who claim descent from the early Federalists have come in time to resist the nationalist views of Marshall and Hamilton. Their opinions are now upheld most vigorously by the political heirs of Jefferson and Andrew Jackson. The relative strength of these forces, in Congress and in the country, determines the way in which national powers are in fact used. It is notable that in many areas Congress does not exercise all the authority in regulating business affairs or social welfare which the modern Supreme Court, following Marshall, declares it to have. For the moment at least, the real constitution of usage has a pattern quite different from that of the formal Constitution interpreted in Supreme Court opinions.

## Introduction

The separation of the three branches of government is not airtight. The President has massive legislative power, through his Roman capacity to veto and through his influence over public opinion. Elected by a national constituency, he normally appeals to popular opinion and tries to mobilize it in order to persuade the Congress. Equally, the Congress has considerable power over the President, beyond its legislative authority and its control of the purse. Public officials, for example, cannot be appointed by the President without "the advice and consent" of the Senate, save where Congress has authorized such appointments by the President alone, the courts of law, or the heads of departments. Early observers thought that the power of the House to impeach, and of the Senate to try impeachments, would make Congress supreme in the end, both over the President and over the Supreme Court. But the political habits of the American people, rallying to the manifest idea of the Constitution, frustrated this possibility. Congress was not to become a Parliament, with the President its Prime Minister. The final confirmation of the nonparliamentary independence of the President was the attempt to impeach President Andrew Johnson. The experiment was never repeated. And impeachment has not been seriously invoked, after an early attempt, against the independence of the judiciary, which the draftsmen of 1787 had sought to protect by providing life tenure for the federal judges. But Congress does have power to determine the number of members of the Supreme Court, and power also over its appellate jurisdiction. President Franklin Roosevelt's campaign to change the views of the Supreme Court by enlarging it collapsed, under dramatic circumstances, in 1937. And thus far all further efforts by members of Congress to qualify the independence of the Court by limiting its jurisdiction have similarly been defeated. The decisive factor in these battles was the ultimate repugnance of political feeling for attacks on the integrity of judges, and the general acceptance of the Court and its role as a valuable feature of the constitution. There have been many such efforts in Congress over the years. The threat they represent—and particularly the traumatic recollection of President Roosevelt's violent attack on the Court—have a place, no doubt, in the Justices' thoughts, particularly among those who lived through the Roosevelt "court-packing" fight as mature men. For these attempts symbolize and measure the ultimate political boundaries of the Court's power and the extent to which its independence is qualified by its place in the constitutional order.

The position and powers of the Supreme Court and of the lower federal courts are thus unintelligible save against the background of the Presidency, the Congress, and the governments of the states, functioning together as parts of a larger constitutional system. The courts operate in the midst of this system and must deal with some of the most explosive political issues it generates. The judges always have strong-minded and strong-willed opponents, elected by the people of the nation or of the states. In the nature of things, they expect recurrent outbursts of jealousy and resentment, charges of usurpation or worse, when their decisions trench on the authority or the will of powerful men and powerful groups. Nominally, the courts exist on sufferance. The President must appoint the judges, and the Senators confirm them. Their funds are appropriated by Congress, and their jurisdiction, with few exceptions, is defined by statute and not by the Constitution itself. The courts have felt themselves to be weak in relation to the immense forces arrayed around them. They are taught to believe they should be "lions under the throne," in Coke's phrase. Caution and prudence have been their watchwords.

Yet reality hardly warrants such fears. The courts exist

in fact by virtue of the idea they embody. Men everywhere are loyal to the hope of law, after centuries of experience both with law and with its alternatives; and Americans, after one hundred and seventy years, are content, for all their grumbling, with the Supreme Court as a factor in the American constitutional process. The courts have withstood every political attack on them in our history, and have emerged today the victor in all modern contests over their authority. Sometimes they lost a feather or two in the fight; occasionally they have wisely avoided joining battle. Strengthened by the rigors of the struggle, the Court has as much true political power today, in its own realms, as has ever been the case in its history.

What are those realms, and how are they defined? The survival power of the Supreme Court as a political institution has depended not only on the insight and courage of its greatest members, but also on the limitations of its role in the process of constitutional decision. The Court has eschewed direct participation in the work of other branches of government. It has ruled that it lacks the power to issue advisory opinions to the President or to Congress on the constitutionality of pending legislation or executive action. With occasional exceptions, its members have remained aloof from politics and refused to serve on public commissions or committees. It has confined its function to the duties it has found expressed in the third article of the Constitution, the exercise of "the judicial power of the United States," which is declared to "extend to all cases, in law and equity, arising under this Constitution, the laws of the United States, and treaties made, or which shall be made, under their authority." The catalogue goes on to include cases affecting ambassadors; all cases of admiralty and maritime jurisdiction; controversies involving the United States or the states; controversies between citizens of different states, and between a state or its citizens and foreign states, citizens, and subjects. The Court's jurisdiction is to be original only where states or ambassadors are parties; otherwise it is to be appellate jurisdiction, under regulations made by Congress. The trial of crimes, except in cases of impeachment, shall be by jury.

The words used were deeply familiar when they were written. "Cases in law and equity," "appellate jurisdiction," "controversies," "trial by jury"—this was language drawn from the long life of the common law, as well known to the men of 1789 as the shape of their barns and villages.

The peculiar constitutional feature of the American system of judicial review inheres in this interpretation of Article III. The courts are to act only as courts, in the common law way, deciding cases at law, in equity, or in admiralty, and conducting criminal trials with juries. A considerable volume of judicial decisions delineates the boundaries of this idea: the courts have refused to pass on controversies in which the parties had no personal interest, or those deemed purely "political," or those no longer alive. But what was the judge to do in the course of a genuine case, in genuine controversy, when one party relied on a statute and the other on a provision of the Constitution which, he said, denied the legislature the capacity to pass the statute under which his adversary claimed the right to prevail? The Constitution provides in Article VI that "this Constitution, and the laws of the United States which shall be made in pursuance thereof; and all treaties made, or which shall be made, under the authority of the United States, shall be the supreme law of the land; and the judges in every state shall be bound thereby, any thing in the Constitution or laws of any state to the contrary notwithstanding." Learned men have written learned books to determine whether this sentence, so explicit with regard to state judges, constitutions, and statutes, also gave the Supreme Court the power to declare unconstitutional acts of the President and of the Congress, its two formidable colleagues in the work of American government. These problems have recently been brilliantly canvassed in *The People and the Court,* by Charles L. Black, Jr. (New York, 1960), and they are considered at some length in Part II of this book. The debate over the legitimacy of judicial review, long-lived as it has proved to be, is settled by history.

## III

If we take the existence and propriety of judicial lawmaking as established, both in general and in the field of constitutional law, how should the function of the Supreme Court be defined? What directions should it be pursuing? By what criteria are we to judge its work?

If the Court is viewed in the perspective of constitutional structure, its habits of etiquette take on political meaning. It should respect the constitutional position of Congress, the Presidency, and the states. The judges should give weight, and a great deal of weight, to decisions reached by men who draw their authority from the electoral process. They should take this approach, whether or not it is called a "presumption of validity," not out of a sense of inferiority because they, the judges, have been appointed rather than elected; and not out of a sense of fear because the President and the Congress may crush the courts; but because courtesy is due to such decisions in the nature of the constitutional system. The Court's powers to interpret the Constitution are supreme in a vital but restricted sphere. They should only be invoked when the occasion warrants such final action.

But these familiar considerations of judgment and "self-restraint" hardly constitute a theory of judicial action. As a working guide, they have limited utility. They tell us when it may be wise for the Court not to act. But they tell us next to nothing about when the Court should act or what it should do when it does. The powers of the Court are a vital and altogether legitimate part of the American Constitution. They should be used positively and affirmatively to help improve the public law of a free society capable of fulfilling the democratic dream of its Constitution in the turbulent second half of the twentieth century. The Court should be the proponent and protector of the values which are the premises, goals, needs, and ambitions of our culture, as they have been expressed in its living constitution. The inescapable ethical ideas which determine how the men of any time think and react give ultimate shape to the decisions of the Supreme Court, as they do to the decisions of the judges of other courts. The Justices should discharge their duties with a sense of strategy and purpose, illuminated by their understanding of the Constitution as the charter of a nation intended to enjoy liberty.

The Supreme Court can substantially influence both the structure and the atmosphere of American life. Within the limits of its jurisdiction, it is concerned with the way power is distributed in our society—with the status of the military; the relative importance of the states, the regions, and the nation in a federal system; with the position of the individual as a member of the community, in his capacity as a voter, a defendant in criminal trials, a witness before Congressional committees, a trade union member, a businessman, a farmer, an inventor, or a bankrupt. It can help or hinder in some, but not all or even the most important of the economic activities of society. Thus it can interpret the laws that establish policies for the conduct of the relations between labor and management, the organization of markets, the procedures of taxation, and the scope of patents. But it can do little or nothing to control the development and exercise of fiscal policy, foreign policy, or banking policy. It can construe many important statutes, sometimes imaginatively, and it can occasionally declare them void. It cannot write them in the first place.

The controversies about the Court reviewed in this volume are of two sorts: some deal with the sources of the Court's powers and ideas, and others with their application in different fields. Taken together, these papers do not constitute a concrete program of action for the Court in all the principal areas where it is competent to make decisions. But they do illustrate, and this is particularly true of the essays in Part III, the kinds of issues involved in the Court's "sovereign prerogative of choice" when it decides some of its more difficult cases involving constitutional conflicts. The problems dealt with in Part III—the wartime evacuation from the West Coast of Japanese aliens and American citizens of Japanese descent, the Smith Act prosecutions of Communist leaders, and the allocation of authority to regulate economic affairs between the nation and the states— will serve, at any rate, to bring out some of the policy elections the Court cannot avoid when it construes the Constitution. In the first of these instances, for example, we can watch the Court facing policies adopted by the President and the Congress during a desperate war, in the belief that such policies were needed to help win the war. But the means chosen by Congress and the executive to prosecute the war posed a series of grave questions about the protection of the individual against arbitrary state action—protection of his right to live and move about under the equal protection of the law, to enjoy the privileges and immunities of other citizens, to be protected against imprisonment or exile without trial, or after a kind of legislative trial explicitly prohibited by the Constitution as a bill of attainder. These cases also raised questions about the inferential and partial suspension of the writ of habeas corpus, and about the circumstances under which the Court should decide or decline to decide constitutional questions. The other situations canvassed in Part III are quite as complex, and quite as controversial. Chapter 9, briefly treating thorny problems of federalism in the field of business regulation, is included here to recall that such issues are as important to the fundamental purposes of the Constitution as those of civil liberty.

Simple formulas are of little help, either to judge or to student, in evaluating how well the Court is doing its work. The judge necessarily deals with cases touched by large problems of policy and of politics. In most cases, the prior law is hardly unambiguous. The judge wishes to be faithful to the constitutional tradition: but what is its command?

The constitutional problems thrown up to the Supreme Court by the life of American society go beyond our easy and comforting habits of classification. These are not issues that can be resolved by invoking a rule of "strict" or of "broad" construction, by abjuring or welcoming "judicial lawmaking," by deciding to follow a "liberal" or a "conservative" course. Some lawmaking is implicit in the judicial function. And the work of the Supreme Court in constitutional cases, for all the pressure of their moment, is no more than a special instance of the judge's normal work. A canon of "strict" or "broad" construction is meaningless as a principle of decision for many, perhaps for most cases necessarily raising constitutional issues. And the common distinctions between "liberal" and "conservative" Justices, so dear to many who write about the Court, are perhaps the least useful of all.

These treasured words have great evocative power, given our history and our lifelong preferences. And they have real meaning, although they are often abused. There are of course definable differences between liberals and conservatives—differences of temperament and zeal; differences in the intensity of their desire for social advance, in attitudes toward novelty and change, action and inaction, freedom, order, and authority. Some are well brought out in the typically paradoxical passage from Justice Holmes which faces the title page—his detachment, coupled with his sense of purpose; his irony, yet his earnestness, too. Holmes knew that most hopes, however generous, are disappointed in the end. But he had his fighting faiths, and his sympathies quickened for the reformer (though not for the zealot) despite his comfortable acquiescence in the past. Here, as in much of his writing and his work, there is an uneasy balance between worldly cynicism and the sense of crusade.

If we look at some of the characteristic problems of the Court in terms of "liberal" and "conservative" labels, what are the results?

Consider federalism, for example. Where should liberals and conservatives, true to their faiths, stand on the battlefield of constitutional history, in the abiding contest over the national commerce power as a limitation on the regulatory authority of the states? Which group should rally to the standard of Hamilton, Marshall, Wilson, and Franklin Roosevelt, who upheld the national power? And which should join Jefferson, Taney, Eisenhower, and Senator Thurmond, in their defense of states' rights? Is it liberal or conservative to read the Constitution as favoring a single national economy, unrestrained by trade barriers erected under state law? Is it liberal or conservative to uphold experiments by the states with novel forms of action in the field of business regulation or welfare, even though they affect the commerce of the nation?

Should judges avoid the conflict between statute and

Constitution or seek to control it? Many have thundered against the power of appointed judges to overrule elected legislatures and executives as undemocratic. Which is the proper liberal side, and which the proper conservative, in that debate? That of Senators Norris and Borah, of Theodore Roosevelt, of Senator Ellender in these days? They all proclaimed the freedom of legislators to make laws and the wickedness of judges who said them nay. Or the position of Marshall, Brandeis, McReynolds, and Warren, who exercised this august power with conviction?

How does the liberal-conservative dichotomy help with regard to the powers of congressional committees? For those who remember Teapot Dome, or the midget in Mr. Morgan's lap, the answer is not hard. The liberal view surely favors a broad power of enquiry into any questions that concern the common good. Yet today it is apparent that those who would most strongly favor the powers of committees in cases of that kind are among the most positive in believing that there are some things about which no committee can enquire—often the same things about which Jay Cooke refused to testify on the ground that they were his "private" affairs, back in the 1870s, when his frauds had precipitated a financial crash into which Congress made enquiry.

And what of the civil liberties announced as law by the Constitution, its Bill of Rights, and the post-Civil War amendments? Is there a valid distinction in our constitutional heritage between liberals and conservatives on this vital subject? Chief Justice Hughes, Elihu Root, Henry L. Stimson, and John Lord O'Brian, men validly classified as conservatives for many purposes, were quite as staunch in their defense of civil rights as others we normally regard as liberals.

It is a disservice to insist that every question of constitutional development has a liberal or a conservative answer. The ultimate issues, for judges and for students of their work, are of a different order. The judges abide in a stream of constitutional history. Within that flow of thought, which of the possible alternatives best meets the needs of the times? Which better serves the ends of justice, the main goal of law? Which will contribute more to the development of society as the embodiment and exemplification of the vision of those who framed the Constitution and shaped its growth between 1789 and our own time?

# PART I

*Sources of Judge-Made Law*

# 1

# American Legal Realism and the Sense of the Profession

THE ARGUMENT of this essay can be summed up in four simple propositions:

First, we are all ultimately the creatures of our philosophies. We dance in patterns determined by our pasts, to tunes we hardly know we know. Our acts are governed by an anthology of principles, myths, illusions, and memories which jostle together in our heads and in our hearts. Sometimes, at rare moments in the history of civilization, if good philosophers ever actually did become kings, the dominant working rules of a culture might be dignified as rational and consistent systems of ideas. Normally, they represent a far more human mixture of the sensible and the absurd. From time to time, as we have bitter reason to know, the springs of action have been demonic creeds of hatred and conquest, based on driving beliefs about the supremacy of race, or faith, or class, or nation. Whatever their philosophical quality, however comfortable or uncomfortable they make us or others, we are possessed by our ideas. They determine

Delivered as the John R. Coen Lecture at the University of Colorado on April 7, 1961, and published in 34 *Rocky Mountain Law Review* 123–49 (1962).

how we see and respond to the circumstances of our lives. And, through our responses, the notions in our minds in their turn help to shape the world in which we have our being.

The second step in my argument is that the influence of ideas on events is especially marked in the realm of law, which can never cease its striving for rule by "principle." American law and American lawyers today are products of a tradition of thought and experience which embraces several incompatible premises. This fact exposes our law, and the society which seeks to govern itself through law, to the tension of unresolved conflict. Anxieties about the nature of law, and about the propriety of the way in which our legal institutions are functioning—and, most notably in recent years, anxiety about the propriety of the modes of action of the Supreme Court of the United States—have exacerbated the tension which is inevitable in the normal operations of any living system of law. For legal institutions must always perform three functions which cause strain under the best of circumstances: They must endlessly adjust the formal, stated rules of law to the pace of social and moral change. They must seek to raise the level of social behavior, and of the law in practice, up to that of the accepted standards of law. And thirdly, the law fails in its most important function unless all its agencies strive, through their own approved procedures, and according to their accepted rules, to bring the standards of the law closer to those of the ideal for law cherished by those with authority to speak for our culture in stating its law.[1]

The third proposition I shall seek to defend is that the prevailing American philosophy of law—the largely unstated code by which in fact we live, as lawyers and as citi-

1. This proposition is discussed in Rostow, *Planning for Freedom* 363–64 (1959). See also infra, pp. 20–21, 140–42, 166–68.

zens—prescribes a standard of high social responsibility for lawyers as judges, advocates, counsellors, legislators, and law professors. That standard is implicit in the view, which I believe is now rightly dominant in our culture, that law is not, in Blackstone's phrase, " 'a rule of civil conduct, prescribed by the supreme power in a state, commanding what is right and prohibiting what is wrong,' "[2] but rather a system of social order, an accepted procedure for making certain social decisions. Inescapably, the procedure of law must utilize general propositions and sets of propositions, the so-called "rules of law." Pound has described this "scientific element" in the law functionally as "a reasoned body of principles for the administration of justice . . . a means toward the end of law, which is the administration of justice. . . . Law is not scientific for the sake of science. Being scientific as a means toward an end, it must be judged by the results it achieves, not by the niceties of its internal structure; it must be valued by the extent to which it meets its end, not by the beauty of its logical processes or the strictness with which its rules proceed from the dogmas it takes for its foundation."[3]

And finally—my fourth proposition—I shall try to apply this conclusion to some concrete and ordinary problems to illustrate the kinds of responsibilities I believe we have as American lawyers. I shall concentrate on two of the many kinds of dilemmas which arise when we seek to evaluate the performance of our legal institutions in the light of these standards: the work of the Supreme Court of the United States and that of the organized bar. The contention of the fourth section will be that the Supreme Court of the United States has been meeting its responsibilities at a high level of accomplishment, on the average, making due allowance for

2. 1 Blackstone, *Commentaries* \*44.
3. Pound, "Mechanical Jurisprudence," 8 *Colum. L. Rev.* 605 (1908).

the ebb and flow of the common law process of adjudication and for the shortcomings of men even when they are Justices, but that the rest of the profession of law is not now rising to the challenge of its public responsibilities very well—certainly not well enough—and that in certain areas our performance is lamentably poor.

## II

I shall not linger long on the first theme of my argument —that our lives are dominated, for better or for worse, by ideas as well as by economic interests, technologies, and the impersonal tides of social change. A generation which has suffered the consequences of Hitler and is only beginning to confront Marxism as a fighting faith can hardly doubt the role of ideas in history. I do not mean to suggest that the steam engine and its successors did not revolutionize the context of our lives, nor that history can be interpreted without reference to science, economics, human stupidity, or the art and accident of war. Nor do I wish to propose, recalling Professor Sir Isaiah Berlin's brilliant metaphor, that the hedgehogs are right in seeing the world as a unitary vision and the foxes are wrong in sensing the separateness and contradictions of social happenings.[4] What I do mean is that in the end, as Heine once said, the "proud men of action . . . are nothing but unconscious instruments of the men of thought." Holmes put it very well, celebrating Marshall's anniversary:

> To one who lives in what may seem to him a solitude of thought, this day . . . marks the fact that all thought is social, is on its way to action; that, to borrow the expression of a French writer, every idea tends to become

4. Berlin, *The Hedgehog and the Fox* (1953).

first a catechism and then a code; and that according to its worth his unhelped meditation may one day mount a throne, and without armies, or even with them, may shoot across the world the electric despotism of unresisted power. It is all a symbol, if you like, but so is the flag. The flag is but a bit of bunting to one who insists on prose.[5]

The thesis is often challenged, and it is hardly beyond debate. But I find it difficult to deny, especially in the United States, where the germinal ideas of the Declaration of Independence and of the Constitution have played such a central role in framing our destinies. The thought should be especially vivid in our minds now, as we commemorate the Civil War our fathers fought to vindicate the abstract and even mystical thought that the union of the American people was indissoluble by the states.

### III

The power of men's loyalty to their ideas is nowhere so visible as in the law. Whether we view law through Blackstone's eyes or through Pound's, as readers of Austin or of Thurman Arnold, certain intractable features of the landscape are clear. We can think of law in terms of many competing and complementary definitions: as a code of rules laid down by a sovereign, a process of social decision, a prediction of when the public force will be invoked, a pattern of approved social behavior, more or less effectively acknowleged by courts and legislatures—the number of such formulas is almost infinite. Whatever the starting point or the end product of our analysis, we cannot ignore the fact that the law is featured by rules, articulated and re-articu-

---

5. Holmes, *Collected Legal Papers* 270–71 (1920).

lated in more or less abstract form, and that these rules play a part in the outcome of cases and other legal controversies. The art of generalization, we know, has an indispensable role in the legal process and is an indispensable feature of law as an institution of order. This generalizing aspect of law derives from the basic moral principle, acknowledged by every legal system we know anything about, that similar cases should be decided alike. The principle of equality before the law is easy to recite, and infinitely difficult to apply. It lies behind the weight given to precedent in legal systems and gives force to the yearning for certainty and predictability in law which each generation has expressed, in vain, since the beginnings of recorded time.

In the generation of lawyers and judges who prevailed in England and America about a hundred years ago, the rationalizing, system-building component of law became oppressive. Deference to precedent became not one wise principle among many in the growth of law, but a rigid and restrictive absolute, which is still considered to be at least the nominal rule of decision in England.[6] The men of that day, intoxicated by the notion of law as a science freed at last of its religious past, began to think of it as a self-contained body of rational precepts. They treated its rules not as tentative hypotheses, advanced to explain shifting bodies of social behavior, but as fixed propositions, laws of nature and of "reason" in some magical sense, sustained by autonomous authority and capable of surviving unchanged for indefinite periods of time. The so-called rules of law, which subsumed and organized groups and patterns of decisions, were invoked without reference to the purposes they had been called into being to serve, and without considering whether those ends were still appropriate. Orations at bar

6. Cross, *Precedent in English Law* (1961); Wasserstrom, *The Judicial Decision* (1961).

association meetings, and at the funerals of departed legal worthies, invoked the grandeur of "eternal principles" of law. The legal texts of the time, and the teaching in law schools, followed the same pattern. Whole areas of the law were reduced to the symmetry and consistency of logical order, with all their features clear and clearly derived from two or three general propositions deemed self-evident. Thus the dream was revived of law as a code of rules, and no more, so that with a little effort we could achieve its re-statement in books that would not fill a single shelf. Then judgment could be found, not made, and society could at long last enjoy a stable, certain, and perfectly predictable legal order.[7]

I sometimes wonder whether the lawyers of the day really believed in the "mechanical jurisprudence" they professed, and against which Roscoe Pound's early articles inveighed with such vehemence. After all, we live by a philosophy of law even when we have no legal philosophers to tell us what it is, or when they describe it inaccurately. The centuries-old habits of the common law survived the straitjacket of what Karl N. Llewellyn has recently called the Formal Style of thought about law. Professor Llewellyn described the phenomenon, which is still too much with us, in these terms:

> The Formal Style is of peculiar interest to us because it set the picture against which all modern thinking has played—call it as of the last eighty or ninety years, "the orthodox ideology." That picture is clean and clear; the rules of law are to decide the cases; policy is for the legislature, not for the courts, and so is change even in pure common law. Opinions run in deductive form

7. See C.H.S. Fifoot, *Judge and Jurist in the Reign of Victoria* (1959), for a witty and ironic account of the process and its denouement.

with an air or expression of single-line inevitability. "Principle" is a generalization producing order which can and should be used to prune away those "anomalous" cases or rules which do not fit, such cases or rules having no function except, in places where the supposed "principle" does not work well, to accomplish sense—but sense is no official concern of a formal-style court.[8]

No doubt the Formal Style of the age, and, perhaps more important still, the mediocrity and intense conservatism of many of the judges, had their consequences in the realm of affairs. Many cases were decided mechanically. The common law process of creative change, through which the law meets and molds the flow of social experience, was slowed up. The law became too static, too resistant to pressure from without, cut off from the sources of its vitality in the stuff of life.

The reaction of opinion was sharp and explosive, and it has continued in various forms to our own time. The need for the struggle remains, for the old orthodox idea of law as a fixed body of received rules, divorced from policy, has a tenacious hold on the minds of men. The battle cry of the counterattack was Holmes' famous opening page of *The Common Law,* published in 1881, and still the rallying point, and point of beginning, for most phases of the struggle to recover and re-establish effective methods for pursuing the reform of law and social reform through law.

The object of this book is to present a general view of the Common Law. To accomplish the task, other tools are needed besides logic. It is something to show

8. Llewellyn, *The Common Law Tradition—Deciding Appeals* 38 (1960).

that the consistency of a system requires a particular result, but it is not all. The life of the law has not been logic: it has been experience. The felt necessities of the time, the prevalent moral and political theories, intuitions of public policy, avowed or unconscious, even the prejudices which judges share with their fellow-men, have had a good deal more to do than the syllogism in determining the rules by which men should be governed. The law embodies the story of a nation's development through many centuries, and it cannot be dealt with as if it contained only the axioms and corollaries of a book of mathematics. In order to know what it is, we must know what it has been, and what it tends to become. We must alternately consult history and existing theories of legislation. But the most difficult labor will be to understand the combination of the two into new products at every stage. The substance of the law at any given time pretty nearly corresponds, so far as it goes, with what is then understood to be convenient; but its form and machinery, and the degree to which it is able to work out desired results, depend very much upon its past.

In Massachusetts to-day, while, on the one hand, there are a great many rules which are quite sufficiently accounted for by their manifest good sense, on the other, there are some which can only be understood by reference to the infancy of procedure among the German tribes, or to the social condition of Rome under the Decemvirs.[9]

These views and their reception measured deep movements in American and European thought. Great man though Holmes was, he did not strike off these passages, and

9. Holmes, *The Common Law* 1–2 (1881).

others of like tenor, wholly through private revelation. The view he took represented in large part a collision between the static notions of law which prevailed among lawyers at the time and the revolutionary development of historical studies. By 1880, the German, French, and English writers about history, sociology, and philology, after more than a century of cumulative effort, were beginning to transform our consciousness of the past and of the nature of the social process. Holmes' thought owed much as well to philosophy and to the impact on philosophy of science. William James and Peirce, both important philosophers of science and its methods, were his friends. The founders of American pragmatism shared with Holmes and other young Bostonians the delights of the Metaphysical Club, a philosophical society founded in 1870 or thereabouts to discuss "none but the tallest and broadest questions."[10] The development of science, and the ideas of Darwin and Huxley, were in the forefront of their thought. And, above all, by natural descent in the literature of law, Holmes and his fellow lawyers in the group were under the spell of Bentham and the other Utilitarians, but especially of Bentham, that extraordinary figure, far in advance of his time, whose writings have not yet begun to exhaust their capacity to stir men to action.

Holmes' *Common Law,* and his other scholarly papers, proved to be genuinely fruitful and productive. They have contributed to all the streams of thought and debate that have so strongly colored the intellectual universe in which the modern American lawyer is formed. For sixty years or thereabouts, following the publication of his book and his early articles, American law has been enlivened and illuminated by a Homeric series of debates addressed to the themes he had sounded.

10. Frank, "A Conflict with Oblivion: Some Observations on the Founders of Legal Pragmatism." 9 *Rutgers L. Rev.* 425, 427 (1954).

The protagonists were a singularly colorful and often eccentric group of highly individual individualists. And their debate was lively, vigorous, and usually very combative indeed. As Felix Cohen wrote, "In the lists of jurisprudence, the champion of a new theory is generally expected to prove the virtue of the lady for whom he fights by splitting the skulls of those who champion other ladies."[11] If you run over their articles and book reviews in the bound volumes of the old law journals, you can still catch an authentic whiff of cordite. The contributors to the debate were, and some of them still are, a formidable lot, and I hope the next generation can produce their equals. The lists included Hohfeld and Walter Wheeler Cook, Bentley, Pound, Jerome Frank, Kocourek, Underhill Moore, Oliphant, Dickinson, Llewellyn, Thurman Arnold, Radin, Yntema, both Cohens, Hutcheson, Goodhart, Arthur Corbin, McDougal and Lasswell, Fuller and Kantorowicz. Many words have been used to describe the attitudes toward law which were expressed and applied in the course of this debate: pragmatism and positivism; functionalism and institutionalism; realism and idealism; jurisprudence sociological, operational, gastronomic, non-Euclidean, transcendental; the jurisprudence of values, of skepticism, and of cynicism. On the whole, none of the labels is of much use in describing either the terms of the debate or the prevailing state of thought which is its outcome.

I started by stressing a difference of view on the place of legal rules in the legal process as the beginning of the modern American battle over the function and nature of law. The significance and propriety of these rules has remained a central issue in almost all phases of the discussion. The debate was part of a more generalized reconsideration of the

---

11. F. S. Cohen, *The Legal Conscience* 77 (1960).

respective roles of reason and nature in the process of learning, and in the creation of organized bodies of knowledge. In the legal literature, as in the literature about the philosophy of science, the words "rule" and "reason," "fact" and "principle," were used in a bewildering variety of denotations, which added to the excitement, if not to the coherence of the argument.

There was a general atmosphere of skepticism, often of mistrust, as the reformers approached the citadel of the rules of law. They agreed, by and large, on two positions: first, that under legal customs all would accept, many, perhaps most of the cases which reached appellate courts could only be decided in one way; and second, that in many instances the judge had a significant range of choice in deciding the case: choice in finding the facts, which Judge Frank stressed, or choice among rules and in their interpretation. As Cardozo put it in his classic Storrs Lecture at Yale:

> My analysis of the judicial process comes then to this, and little more: logic, and history, and custom, and utility, and the accepted standards of right conduct, are the forces which singly or in combination shape the progress of the law. Which of these forces shall dominate in any case, must depend largely upon the comparative importance or value of the social interests that will be thereby promoted or impaired. One of the most fundamental social interests is that law shall be uniform and impartial. There must be nothing in its action that savors of prejudice or favor or even arbitrary whim or fitfulness. Therefore in the main there shall be adherence to precedent. There shall be symmetrical development, consistently with history or custom when history or custom has been the motive force, or the chief one, in giving shape to existing rules, and with

logic or philosophy when the motive power has been theirs. But symmetrical development may be bought at too high a price. Uniformity ceases to be a good when it becomes uniformity of oppression. The social interest served by symmetry or certainty must then be balanced against the social interest served by equity and fairness or other elements of social welfare. These may enjoin upon the judge the duty of drawing the line at another angle, of staking the path along new courses, of marking a new point of departure from which others who come after him will set out upon their journey.

If you ask how he is to know when one interest outweighs another, I can only answer that he must get his knowledge just as the legislator gets it, from experience and study and reflection; in brief, from life itself. Here, indeed, is the point of contact between the legislator's work and his. The choice of methods, the appraisement of values, must in the end be guided by like considerations for the one as for the other. Each indeed is legislating within the limits of his competence. No doubt the limits for the judge are narrower. He legislates only between gaps. He fills the open spaces in the law. How far he may go without traveling beyond the walls of the interstices cannot be staked out for him upon a chart.[12]

In short, the judge is inevitably concerned with policy, since law is "a means to social ends, and not an end in itself."[13] He makes law, and does not merely find it.

Many of the writers who participated in the discussions

---

12. Cardozo, *The Nature of the Judicial Process* 112–14 (1921).
13. Llewellyn, "Some Realism about Realism—Responding to Dean Pound," 44 *Harv. L. Rev.* 1222, 1236 (1931).

concentrated on the artificial and unreal character of many legal rules. They were preoccupied with demonstrating that existing rules were meaningless, or circular, or self-contradictory, like the concept of "implied malice" which drew Holmes' scorn.[14] Some then went on, seeking to formulate new rules which would more accurately describe the law in action. Law, Sabine said, is "what it does,"[15] not what the judges say they are doing, or why. Others sought to investigate the effects of the existing law, as in court administration, bankruptcy, or divorce, or the relation between doctrines of law and patterns of custom or usage.

Many of the realists were heatedly accused of nihilism or worse, and charged with denying the generalizing element of law altogether. They were alleged to believe that decisions were based on unstated interests or value preferences, and that the reasons given for decisions were in fact afterthoughts, cynical rationalizations, representing the judge not as a conscientious lawyer, working within the permissible limits of his discretion, but as a willful autocrat. By and large (though with several exceptional and occasional aberrations) the charge was not justified: the realist literature agreed with Pekelis' striking remark, amending one of Holmes' most famous quips, that "concrete cases cannot be decided by general propositions—nor without them."[16] The realists—or most of them—were not trying to deny the inevitability of rules in a system of law that sought at any given time to decide like cases alike. What they were trying to achieve was an awareness of the relationship between

14. Holmes, "Privilege, Malice and Intent," 8 *Harv. L. Rev.* 1 (1894); Holmes, *Collected Legal Papers* 117 (1920).

15. Sabine, "The Pragmatic Approach to Politics," 24 *Am. Pol. Sci. Rev.* 865, 878 (1930). This view, essentially Gray's, was effectively criticized by Cardozo, op. cit. supra note 12, at 125–30.

16. Pekelis, *Law and Social Action: Selected Essays* 20 (1950).

rules and policy, viewing law as an instrument for social action in a society constantly in flux, "and in flux typically faster than the law, so that the probability is always given that any portion of law needs reexamination to determine how far it fits the society it purports to serve."[17]

When all the rules were re-examined and reformulated, when everyone understood and accepted the tentative nature of rules and their relation to the customs and morals of society, what then? Should modern lawyers, worthy to be welcomed as brothers into the fellowship of "Realism," "Liberalism," and "Enlightenment" devote their attention to the law as it was at their moment of study or to the law as it ought to be? In the early stages of the campaign, the rebels were anxious to concentrate—temporarily, in Llewellyn's phrase—on the law that was, and to set aside for the future the problem of the law that ought to be.[18] It was difficult enough, they thought, to show that the law recited in appellate decisions had lost contact with the mores of the community and the law in action. The first job was to clear away the circular syllogisms and the meaningless concepts; to dispose of rules which had not other reason to support them than that so it had been in the time of an ancient Henry; and to annul, test, reformulate, and review all legal rules in the light of their factual background and effect.[19]

But was this the whole task of law and of legal scholarship? Was there no more to the lawyer's job than to see to it that the law corresponds to the felt needs of the community and maintains adequate means for knowing such needs, through its use of analytic procedures and of methods and data drawn from economics, political theory, psychology, and sociology? Is the only end to be served that the law

17. Llewellyn, supra note 13, at 1236.
18. Id. at 1223, 1236, 1254.
19. Id. at 1240.

discover itself accurately, realistically, to make it the mirror of custom, rather than an instrument of higher values?[20]

One of the most significant criticisms of the realist movement stressed this thought—that the realists denied the problem of judging the goodness or badness of law, beyond the single issue of the correspondence between the law in the books and the law in action: that is, between positive law and custom. Had not Holmes, following Bentham, laughed at the very idea of natural law and favored the "separation" of law and morals?[21] Had he not said that justice was not his business as a judge, but only playing the game according to its rules? And did he not remark that "the prophecies of what the courts will do in fact, and nothing more pretentious, are what I mean by the law"?[22]

There is a paradox in this charge against the modern movement in American thought about law, for the legal realists were among our most devoted and effective reformers, both of law and of society. Professor McDougal commented on the charge in these terms:

> The American legal realism which Professor Fuller attacks is . . . a bogus American legal realism. John Austin, Kelsen, and others, from abroad and at home, may have done their bit to "separate the inseparable," but most of the men whose names appear upon Professor Llewellyn's famous list of American legal realists are innocent men. So also are most of their followers. They do not deny that the law-in-fact (rules and behavior) embodies somebody's ethical notions (how absurd it would be to deny it!); on the contrary, they are the

20. See note 1 supra.

21. See Holmes, *Collected Legal Papers* 310 (1920); Biddle, *Justice Holmes, Natural Law, and the Supreme Court* (1961).

22. Holmes, *Collected Legal Papers* 173 (1920).

people who have been most insistent that it has too often embodied an ossified ethics, inherited from previous centuries and opposed to the basic human needs of our time. More clearly than any of their critics, the realists have appreciated that legal rules are but the normative declarations of particular individuals, conditioned by their own peculiar cultural milieu, and not truths revealed from on high. Most of their writing has in fact been for the avowed purpose of freeing people from the emotional compulsion of antiquated legal doctrine and so enabling them better to pursue their hearts' desires. Not bothering to explain how judges can legislate, it is they who have insisted that judges do and must legislate, that is, make a policy decision, in every case. The major tenet of the "functional approach," which they have so vigorously espoused, is that law is *instrumental* only, a means to an end, and is to be appraised only in the light of the ends it achieves. Any divorce they may at times have urged between *is* and *ought* has been underscored always as *temporary,* solely for the purpose of preventing their preferences from obscuring a clear understanding of the ways and means for securing such preferences. Directly contrary to Professor Fuller's charges, they have sought to distinguish between the *is* and the *ought*, not for the purpose of ignoring or dismissing the *ought*, but for the purpose of making a future *is* into an *ought* for its time.[23]

On the whole, Professor McDougal is right in his judgment, although there is a great deal on both sides of the

23. McDougal, "Fuller v. The American Legal Realists: An Intervention," 50 *Yale L. J.* 827, 834–35 (1941).

debate about "the law that is" and "the law that ought to be" which is purely formal, inconclusive, and irrelevant.[24] There is more to modern American jurisprudence than the cheerful clatter of breaking idols, as we can see in the debate that is raging about the work of the Supreme Court.

Holmes had put his definition of law into the future tense. It was never enough, he said, to discover what the law really was at a given moment. What would it become tomorrow? What forces would influence the law to change, and what fruit would come of the process of change? To answer that question, Holmes urged with equal vigor, the lawyer had to understand and consider the ideas playing on the formation of law—the pressures for social change in many areas, from banking and bankruptcy to labor law and the law of torts. He had to master all the sciences of society, from anthropology to statistics. And he had to know the judges, their prejudices and predilections, their zeal to participate in the growth of the law, or to resist it. After all, Holmes spoke of law not only as a prediction of what the judges would in fact decide, but also as the "witness and external deposit of our moral life," and of its history as "the history of the moral development of the race."[25]

During the past twenty years or so, the stress in the American literature about law has been on this part of the equation—the quest for standards and values in the process of guiding the evolution of "the law that is" into the law we think it ought to become. The formulation and acceptance of ends, these writers know, helps to fix the line of growth of the law. Of those who have contributed this feature to the

24. Insightfully reviewed in Jenkins, "The Matchmaker, or Toward a Synthesis of Legal Idealism and Positivism," 12 *J. Legal Ed.* 1 (1959); also treated in "The Enforcement of Morals," infra, p. 45.

25. Holmes, *Collected Legal Papers* 170 (1920).

body of our thought about law, I might mention particularly Felix Cohen, F.S.C. Northrop, Messrs. Lasswell and McDougal, Henry Hart, Friedrich Kessler, Jerome Hall, Lon Fuller, and Edmond Cahn. Their work has helped to correct and offset the relative neglect of the problem of values which characterized the more positivistic outlook of the earlier legal realists.[26]

The emerging awareness of these three themes in their relations to each other constitutes a new synthesis of ideas about law, which tends to dominate the universe of American law today. (1) That synthesis accepts, and nowadays accepts without protest, the use of generalization, as a limited but essential part of the process of making legal decisions. (2) It stresses the links between the actual law and what Ehrlich and Northrop, following Montesquieu, call the living law of society, the mass of its customs and usages, animated by the existing spirit of its laws, the norm for law toward which it seeks to move in its day-to-day processes of lawmaking. This phase of the problem requires the lawyer and judge to go far beyond the traditional data of the law books, and to investigate the functioning of society and the minds of men. And (3) it recognizes the necessity to acknowledge and to seek to define the standards of aspiration in the minds of judges and other lawmakers which govern the development both of society itself and of its spirit of law. Some identify this third element in the legal process, a culture's ideal for the future of its law, as "natural law," a phrase of many ambiguities, and seek to study it objectively, with all the apparatus of modern scholarship.

26. This theme in the American literature corresponds to a worldwide revival of interest in the problem of standards for law, stimulated by the problem of law under circumstances of fascist and communist dictatorship. See Radcliffe, *The Law and Its Compass* (1960).

## IV

This set of working rules about the nature and social function of law has certain corollaries for the profession of law. If a lawyer or a judge or a law professor understands law to be no more than a beautifully articulated set of formal rules, derived from Blackstone and the dictionary, then he can be a good and conscientious lawyer by putting the right words in the right order and turning the crank of logic to get the right result. The lawyer's duty has quite another connotation if he believes law to be the instrument through which a changing society seeks to express and fulfill its aspirations for justice. If the lawyer lives by a limited and old-fashioned version of legal positivism, he professes to leave "policy" changes, and their impact on law, entirely to others—to the legislatures or the economists or the political process. A judge of this persuasion is suffused with a glow of satisfaction if he recites the received words in the received order and obtains a result which seems to conform to the letter he has learned. If the result is contrary to what he thinks society regards as right, just, and desirable, he may glow with extra pleasure, for to many devotees of law in this sense, nothing so demonstrates the rigor and value of the law as a harsh result.

If, however, the lawyer, judge, legislator, or law teacher has absorbed the concept of law I have been trying to describe, he knows that he cannot escape so easily. He must live with uncomfortable thoughts. He sees every social conflict, every case, no matter how small, as an inseparable part of a larger whole. For him, each settlement, each decision, each opinion derives its validity and its legitimacy from his conscientious effort to make certain that it represents not only law, but good law. The lawyer, the legislator, the judge, and the law professor have different functions, different degrees of discretion, different zones of choice. But they confront the same standard of duty and responsibility. The modern lawyer can find no workable boundary between law and policy, for he acknowledges law to be policy expressed in certain forms. His motto is Brandeis' remark, "No question is ever settled until it is settled right." For him, the sense of the profession, the sense which justifies it and makes it worthy of his dreams, is precisely that it is and must be the appointed agency of our society's sense of justice.

If we look at the work of our profession, and at its influence on society and on the law, in the light of the standard whose development and acceptance I have been discussing, to what conclusion are we led?

First, what of the Supreme Court, our highest institution of law, which has been criticized recently as it has been criticized throughout its history, as a partisan and arbitrary body, recklessly writing its own prejudices into the law? If I am right in my summary of the prevailing American view of law, and if that view correctly states what our society expects of its law, most of these criticisms stand revealed to be untenable and mistaken.

I have discussed on other occasions some of the popular criticisms of the Court—that its powers of judicial review are undemocratic; that it is behaving as a legislative and not a judicial body in its interpretations of the Constitution; that it is going too far and too rapidly in its development of our law of civil rights; and that it is violating the Constitution by interfering with the constitutional prerogatives of the state governments. I shall not undertake here to repeat what I have said in those papers to defend the main lines of the Court's work and to answer its critics in detail.[27]

27. See chapters 3–5.

I might, however, briefly discuss the most significant recent attack on the Court, Professor Wechsler's Holmes Lecture at the Harvard Law School.[28] In that influential speech, Professor Wechsler advanced the view that in its recent work, and notably in some of its most important recent decisions, the Court has breached basic standards of judicial propriety and wandered into the forbidden realm of decision by fiat. He implied that his approach could be resisted only by those "who, vouching no philosophy to warranty, frankly or covertly make the test of virtue in interpretation whether its result in the immediate decision seems to hinder or advance the interests or the values they support."[29] The nub of Professor Wechsler's argument, distinguishing political from judicial decisions, appears, I think, in this passage from his lecture:

> All I have said, you may reply, is something no one will deny, that principles are largely instrumental as they are employed in politics, instrumental in relation to results that a controlling sentiment demands at any given time. Politicians recognize this fact of life and are obliged to trim and shape their speech and votes accordingly, unless perchance they are prepared to step aside; and the example that John Quincy Adams set somehow is rarely followed.
>
> That is, indeed, all I have said but I now add that whether you are tolerant, perhaps more tolerant than I, of the *ad hoc* in politics, with principle reduced to a manipulative tool, are you not also ready to agree

28. Wechsler, "Toward Neutral Principles of Constitutional Law," 73 *Harv. L. Rev.* 1 (1959), reprinted in Wechsler, *Principles, Politics, and Fundamental Law* 3–48 (1961) [hereinafter cited as Wechsler, with page references to the book]. Herbert Wechsler is Harlan Fiske Stone Professor of Constitutional Law at the Columbia Law School.

29. Wechsler 17.

that something else is called for from the courts? I put it to you that the main constituent of the judicial process is precisely that it must be genuinely principled, resting with respect to every step that is involved in reaching judgment on analysis and reasons quite transcending the immediate result that is achieved. To be sure, the courts decide, or should decide, only the case they have before them. But must they not decide on grounds of adequate neutrality and generality, tested not only by the instant application but by others that the principles imply? Is it not the very essence of judicial method to insist upon attending to such other cases, preferably those involving an opposing interest, in evaluating any principle avowed?[30]

Some have found in the words and tenor of the lecture contradictions and obscurities, particularly with regard to the weight the Court should give in doubtful cases to the presumption of constitutionality, and to the contrary views of the legislators or executive officers whose decisions are being reviewed by the Court.[31] I do not deny that these ambiguities exist in the text, nor that they raise difficult problems. Moreover, I find that the concepts of "reason," "principle," "generality," and "neutrality" on which Professor Wechsler's argument depends are employed in several ways and apparently derive from different definitions. They seem to apply an original philosophic system, which

30. Wechsler 21. See F. S. Cohen, *Ethical Systems and Legal Ideals* 34–40 (1959).

31. See Miller and Howell, "The Myth of Neutrality in Constitutional Adjudication," 27 *U. Chi. L. Rev.* 661 (1960); Mueller and Schwartz, "The Principle of Neutral Principles," 7 *U.C.L.A.L. Rev.* 571 (1960). See also the powerful article of Judge Clark and Mr. Trubek on the same themes, Clark and Trubek, "The Creative Role of the Judge: Restraint and Freedom in the Common Law Tradition," 71 *Yale L.J.* 255 (1961).

Professor Wechsler has not yet published, for analyzing the judicial process. Perhaps fair criticism of the premise and thesis of his Holmes Lecture should wait on the appearance of Professor Wechsler's jurisprudential views, for the lecture is clearly part of a much larger whole. It was also, however, an act of current significance in the formation of thought. We must do our best, therefore, as is so often the case, to try to reconstruct the mastodon from the few bones and teeth which happen to be on hand. The task is somewhat simplified by the availability of an approved gloss. Professor Wechsler has agreed with the reading given his lecture by Professor Henkin in a recent paper, and I shall start at least by examining that interpretation of his words.[32]

To Professor Henkin, Professor Wechsler's text implies no more than the commonplace with which I began this analysis: that generalized rules are essential to the legal process in order to protect society against judicial partiality and to assure that like cases be decided alike. As Professor Henkin says felicitously, in trying to restate Professor Wechsler's argument as "a call for principle," "one might do worse for the beginning of a definition than to suggest that judicial doctrine and principle are those reasons for reaching a result which can be stated in a judicial opinion."[33] If this is indeed an adequate reading of the lecture, Professor Wechsler's charge, backed by the high and deserved authority of his reputation, is a most serious one— that the Supreme Court is not behaving like a court at all, but is deciding similar cases differently, depending on whether favored or disfavored parties or interests are before

32. Henkin, "Some Reflections on Current Constitutional Controversy," 109 *U. Pa. L. Rev.* 637, 652–62 (1961). Louis Henkin is Professor of Law at the University of Pennsylvania Law School.

33. Id. at 655.

the Court—parties or interests favored or disfavored, let us be clear, not because their positions should be considered different in fact and in law, but simply because the judges happen to be partisans of one and not the other. The charge, in short, is that the judges are applying personal and idiosyncratic standards of policy in shaping the development of the law, and not their understanding of what the community's standards, stated in the Constitution or the statutes, have become. In a recent article, Dean Griswold of the Harvard Law School, while not committing himself to Professor Wechsler's view, has carefully indicated that he regards the question as an open one:

> If decisions are reached on the basis of "absolute convictions" rather than through the painful intellectual effort of judgment in the light of the law, then the judicial process is not in its finest flower. . . . Though it is clear that judges do "make law," and have to do so, it remains the fact that this is, at its best, an understanding process, not an emotional one, a self-effacing process, not a means of vindicating "absolute convictions." It is a process requiring great intellectual power, an open and inquiring and resourceful mind, and often courage, especially intellectual courage, and the power to rise above oneself. Even more than intellectual acumen, it requires intellectual detachment and disinterestedness, rare qualities approached only through constant awareness of their elusiveness, and constant striving to attain them. If one regarded himself as having a special mission to fulfill, or if he were quite largely the prisoner of his absolute convictions, he would not meet the highest standards of judicial performance. When decisions are too much result-oriented, the law and the public are not well served. . . .

> Our judges carry a heavy burden. They make a su-
> preme contribution in our society. They are entitled
> to our thoughtful and respectful consideration as they
> carry out their difficult task of disinterested exposition
> and development of the law of the land.[34]

To me, Professor Wechsler's lecture—though not Dean
Griswold's comment on the issues raised in it—represents
a repudiation of all we have learned about law since Holmes
published his *Common Law* in 1881, and Roscoe Pound
followed during the first decade of this century with his
path-breaking pleas for a result-oriented, sociological jurisprudence, rather than a mechanical one. It would raise the
element of rules, of precedent, of what he calls "principle"
or "reason" in the judicial process to a position of absolute
primacy which all we know about law denies.

In this regard, Professor Wechsler goes well beyond Professor Henkin's reassuring interpretation of his lecture. For
Professor Wechsler, unlike Professor Henkin, would require opinions of a defined kind and quality in every case,
or have the Court abstain from action—presumably leaving
in effect lower court opinions or actions of other branches
of the government which might have even less legal justification. And Professor Wechsler's criteria for the goodness
of an opinion are more categorical than those suggested by
Professor Henkin.

For this reason, as best I can read his text, I conclude
that Professor Wechsler's argument is an attack on the integrity of the Supreme Court. For him, a decision has "any
legal quality," which I interpret to mean "legitimacy," only
if it is "entirely principled," that is, only if it "rests on reasons with respect to all the issues in the case, reasons that in

34. Griswold, "Foreword: Of Time and Attitudes—Professor Hart and
Judge Arnold," 74 *Harv. L. Rev.* 81, 93–94 (1960).

their generality and their neutrality transcend any immediate result that is involved."[35] The quality of "legal quality" (or legitimacy) seems to be sharply different in Professor Wechsler's system from simple error, taken for granted
as a normal and inevitable feature of the legitimate judicial
process.[36] And it emerges as a curiously shifting and elusive
entity, to be recognized intuitively, and then only by some.
According to Professor Wechsler's rule, a judicial decision
must be branded illegitimate, and condemned to limbo, if
two conditions are satisfied: (1) if the Court fails to give a
satisfactorily reasoned explanation of its result in terms of
neutral principles; and (2) if the Court could not have given
such an explanation, that is, if no one outside the Court
succeeds, presumably within a reasonable interval of limitation, in advancing suitable reasons of principle to account
for the Court's decision. But how can we tell that "no one"
has given or can possibly give an account of the decision
which meets the standard? The judges, presumably, have
tried, although they would hardly agree with Professor
Wechsler's verdict of failure.

Professor Wechsler illustrates and applies his test in his
discussion of three recent cases, which represent some of
the Court's most important modern work.[37] These cases, he

35. Wechsler 27. See also Wechsler 21–23.

36. I may be wrong in reading Professor Wechsler's text as so sharply distinguishing "legal quality" from the commonplace of error or of poor
opinion-writing. Despite his patient and generous efforts, in conversation
and in letters, however, I find it impossible to read the lecture otherwise, for
(quite apart from the language he uses) the tenor and sequence of his argument seems to attach far more drastic consequences to decisions and opinions lacking "any legal quality" than to those merely in error (see, e.g., his
comment at pp. 35–36 that while Mr. Justice Holmes' "clear and present
danger" test failed as analysis, one must respect it as an attempt to develop
a principled delineation of the problem).

37. Smith v. Allwright, 321 U.S. 649 (1944); Shelley v. Kraemer, 334 U.S. 1
(1948); Brown v. Board of Education, 347 U.S. 483 (1954).

says, "have the best chance of making an enduring contribution to the quality of our society of any that I know in recent years."[38] But in these cases Professor Wechsler believes that the Court did not advance "clear" reasons of principle to defend its decisions;[39] and, despite earnest effort, he has failed to adduce satisfactory rationalizations for the decisions himself.[40] Therefore, in his view, the choices of other branches of the government should have been allowed to survive,[41] since the presumption of constitutionality was not overcome. The results he applauds should have been achieved by political and not by judicial means. The decisions were not merely erroneous, but lacked legal quality. They represent *ad hoc* and unprincipled decision-making, and the Supreme Court as an unprincipled power organ.

We are left with the cold but correct proposition that we should obey an erroneous construction of the law—even one lacking legal quality—until it is changed, by reason of our general duty to obey the law in a Rechtsstaat.[42]

I do not have the same difficulties Professor Wechsler has in fitting these cases, hard as they are, into perspectives of constitutional development. Many of the Socratic questions

38. Wechsler 37.

39. Wechsler 34. The requirement that the courts "impose a choice of values on the other branches or a state, based upon the Constitution, only when they are persuaded, on an adequate and principled analysis, that the choice is clear," is one of the most dangerous standards for judicial action in the lecture. Clear to whom? The dissenting Justices? It does no service to judges whose most routine tasks imply difficult analyses of complex factual situations, the evaluation of converging and competing interests and values, and the ordering of all the other forces which affect the growth of the Constitution, to tell them that they cannot act unless all becomes "clear." See "The Democratic Character of Judicial Review," infra pp. 176–80; C. L. Black, Jr., *The People and the Court* 13 (1960).

40. Wechsler 47.

41. Wechsler 27.

42. Wechsler 47. See Radcliffe, *The Law and Its Compass* 82 (1960).

he poses by way of criticism seem easy to answer, or to leave for a future court, in accordance with the habits of the common law. For example, the impact of Court-enforced racial covenants on land use, affecting the social and political lives of whole communities, strikes me as readily distinguishable from purely private utilizations of property and hardly alien to traditional "public policy" limits on one's freedom to use or dispose of his own. But others have dealt with Professor Wechsler's treatment of these cases.[43] I shall address myself here to his premise: even if we were to conclude, as he does, that the opinions in question are inadequate or unsatisfactory, does it follow *for that reason* that the decisions were not only erroneous, but that they lacked "legal quality," and that the act of making them was a usurpation of power?

For me, Professor Wechsler's view is much too narrowly based. Even the task of reaching the conclusion that a court's decision is erroneous calls for a far deeper and wider appraisal of the policies it represents, and of their alternatives, than a verbal analysis of the opinion as a piece of literature or rhetoric. And it takes much more, in the light of what we know of the historical limits of the judicial power, to conclude that an erroneous decision, or a decision defended by an inadequate opinion, is *ultra vires*.

Speaking of the generalizing, propositional element in law, Pound wrote—and I repeat what I quoted earlier—that law is "a reasoned body of principles for the administration of justice . . . a means toward an end, and it must be judged by the results it achieves . . . , not by the beauty of its logical processes or the strictness with which its rules

43. See, e.g., Pollak, "Racial Discrimination and Judicial Integrity: A Reply to Professor Wechsler," 108 *U. Pa. L. Rev.* 1 (1959); C. L. Black, Jr., "The Lawfulness of the Segregation Decisions," 69 *Yale L.J.* 421 (1960). See Henkin, op. cit. supra note 32, at 635, 661–62.

proceed from the dogmas it takes for its foundation."[44] Of course we should all prefer the courts to write clear, coherent, and persuasive opinions, strictly disciplined by what Dean Griswold rightly calls the "tightly guided process" of the judicial tradition. Of course we want our judges to be impartial, detached, and mindful of the limits of their discretion, as well as conscientious in discharging the burden and responsibility which that discretion imposes upon them. In this connection I often think with admiration and respect of the fact that Mr. Justice Brandeis, for all his convictions about the "curse of bigness," never wrote an opinion in the government's favor in an antitrust case.

But, if we know anything at all about law, we know that the goal which Professor Wechsler makes his only test for judicial propriety is impossible to achieve; that it never has been achieved by any common law court, nor by any other court; and that it never can be achieved, in the nature of the judicial process. It is the essence of our system of law that we require our judges to do their best to make their decisions in conformity with the rules of judicial action, with great deference to the past and a strict sense of the boundaries of their power. And, for reasons which go deep into our history, we require them in most cases, but not in all, to write opinions conforming to standards which tradition has established for that exacting task.

Any lawyer who has worked through a line of cases about easements or trusts or bills and notes or any other legal subject knows that no court has ever achieved perfection in its reasoning in its first, or indeed in its twentieth opinion on the same subject. Law professors make their modest livings in large part by dissecting judicial opinions and helping their students to see how imperfectly most of them satisfy

44. Pound, supra note 3.

Professor Wechsler's rule and other, even more important standards for the evaluation of judicial action. In the nature of law as a continuing process, constantly meeting the shocks of social change, and of changes in people's ideas of justice, this characteristic of law must be true, even for our greatest and most insightful judges. They grapple with a new problem, deal with it over and over again, as its dimensions change. They settle one case and find themselves tormented by its unanticipated progeny. They back and fill, zig and zag, groping through the mist for a line of thought which will in the end satisfy their standards of craft and their vision of the policy of the community they must try to interpret. The opinions written at the end of such a cycle rarely resemble those composed at the beginning. Exceptions emerge, and new formulations of what once looked like clear principle. If we take advantage of hindsight, we can see in any line of cases and statutes a pattern of growth and of response to changing conditions and changing ideas. There are cases that lead nowhere, stunted branches and healthy ones. Often the judges who participated in the process could not have described the tree that was growing. Yet the felt necessities of society have their impact, and the law emerges, gnarled, asymmetrical, but very much alive—the product of a forest, not of a nursery garden nor of the gardener's art.

Sometimes, of course, the structure and content of a court's opinion can be explained by the debates of the judges who must vote on it. One is an enthusiast for one principle, others for another. The human process of persuasion within an appellate court accounts, as we know, for many anomalies and worse in the final published version of a court's views.

Beyond these normal problems of intellectualizing the judicial process—problems of insight, scholarship, and policy—there are special pressures which are strongly felt by the Supreme Court of the United States. Exercising high political powers, the Court must have a high sense of strategy and tactics. Its influence on our public life depends in large part on the Court's skill in advocacy and its sensitivity to the powerful forces which from time to time, in different combinations, must resist its will. When the Court decides to accept or reject cases, to decide them on this ground or that, to issue warning dicta which are then not made the basis for decision, it is necessarily performing a function far more complex than Professor Wechsler's call for candor in meeting *every* issue in *every* case on the basis of neutral principles of adequate generality. If the Court had in fact lived by Professor Wechsler's rule, it would have disappeared long ago from the stage of American life. The great Chief Justice, John Marshall, is the classic exemplar and exponent of political prudence in the employment of the Court's powers. Wisely judging the strength of the conflicting forces whose conjuncture influenced the growth of the law, carefully husbanding the Court's strength for the crucial issues, shrewdly choosing among alternative possible premises for its opinions, he still had the energy, vision, and courage to make the written Constitution into the constitution-in-fact for a nation. His opinions were a powerful educational force in the dialogues of the community, his decisions the walls, foundations, and boundary lines of an heroic architectural plan. But few of them can be described as full and direct answers to every problem presented by the cases before the Court.[45]

For the last thirty years, the Supreme Court has been dealing with a rising tide of new demands and new prob-

45. The prudential factors in the choice of cases, and of grounds for decision, are realistically canvassed in Bickel, "Foreword: The Passive Virtues," 75 *Harv. L. Rev.* 40, 42–51 (1961).

lems. Our society has lived through a grinding depression, two wars, and the difficult and novel strains of the Cold War. It has maintained a large military establishment in times of nominal peace. And, most important of all, it has been called upon to make good the promises we made to our Negro citizens almost a hundred years ago, at a time when the place of the Negro in our society has been revolutionized and the problem of race relations has taken on momentous contours in the setting of world politics.

The Court has been struggling with the judicial problems cast up by these events. No student of its work could agree with all its decisions, nor with all the opinions written to explain them. Certainly I do not. I have criticized both the results and the opinions in many of its cases. But I should deny that the present Supreme Court is doing the expository, opinion-writing part of its job any worse, or any better, than most of its predecessors. By my lights, many of its opinions, and of its decisions too, are quite human and erratic variations on certain themes. But behind the variations, it is not hard to see the long-term trends. These long lines of constitutional development, I believe, are entirely in the spirit of our constitutional tradition. They represent the honorable attempt of honorable judges, sensitive to their calling, to do their duty as judges, not as legislators or as rulers by fiat. I stress that the work of the Court is work in process, and that the positions it takes today will not necessarily be those it takes tomorrow. So it was in the time of Marshall and Taney and Hughes. And thus it must always be, as long as we elect to make the judicial process of Anglo-American tradition one of our chief means of self-government.

The opinions of Marshall, and of every other strong judge who has sat on the Court, have been criticized in exactly the terms Professor Wechsler uses. Generations of writers about law, and of law teachers, have dissected the erratic reasoning of *Marbury v. Madison* and discovered that the statutory construction on which *Gibbons v. Ogden* rests is artificial and strained. So be it. It is too bad. It would be much better if our judges could consistently write convincing opinions, which earned an "A" by Professor Wechsler's rule; it would be better still if they reached the results of "good law" in all cases, whether through peccable or impeccable judicial opinions. But no human beings, not even law professors, could possibly bring such instantaneous order to the swirling freshets the judges must confront every day of their lives. As Fifoot wrote recently, reviewing the development of certain judicial doctrines and of theories about them in nineteenth-century England: "Faced with the fragments of life, the current law of any place and time can but approximate to a principle or indicate a tendency."[46] We must accept the fact that under the best of circumstances judges will often write opinions which fail to convince many, or all, or the best lawyers of their time, or of later times. Their decisions may nonetheless turn out to have been right or wrong, with the benefit of hindsight—in error or in creative anticipation of a principle theretofore unsensed. In the nature of the judicial process, Professor Wechsler's rule puts unwarranted and misleading stress on one phase of the judicial craft—a vital phase, but decidedly not the whole of it nor even its most important feature.

Having said this, I should go one step further. I should be the last to deny the importance of the analytic process in the workings of law. But there is an inescapable Bergsonian element of intuition in the judges' work—in their ordering of "facts," in their choice of premises, in their reformulation of the postulates we call "rules" or "principles," in their

46. Fifoot, op. cit. supra note 7, at 56.

sense of the policy or policies which animate the trend or change it. These are the secret roots, as Holmes said long ago, "from which the law draws all the juices of life." They may be, as he said "the unconscious result of instinctive preferences and inarticulate convictions,"[47] but in the end they must rule. This is not to say that the law is "a mass of unrelated decisions" or "a product of judicial bellyaches."[48] The force of law as a system and tradition is and should be great in defining the scope of judicial discretion. The judicial process and the academic study of law alike become mature and responsible when both judges and academic students of the law acknowledge the legitimate interplay of these factors in the act of decision and seek to deal with them as functionally, and as directly, as the state of our knowledge permits.

If Professor Wechsler uses the words "principle," "general principle," and "reason" to mean the reasoning of judicial opinions which convince some, or all, or only one good lawyer, in what sense can it be said that this requirement carries with it a requirement of "neutrality" as well?[49] Neutrality, perhaps, in the spirit of Anatole France's remark that in the eyes of the law the rich and the poor are under an equal duty not to sleep beneath the bridges of Paris. Neutrality, of course, in the sense that judgment should not be biased by fear, or bribes, or, most important of all, by the lively political expectation of votes or favors to come. If

47. Holmes, *The Common Law* 35–36 (1881). This central feature of the judicial process is briefly summed up in Corbin, "The Judicial Process Revisited: An Introduction," 71 *Yale L.J.* 195, 199–201 (1961), and discussed more fully in Clark and Trubek, supra note 33 at 257–76. See also H. W. Jones, "Law and Morality in the Perspective of Legal Realism," 61 *Colum. L. Rev.* 799 (1961).

48. F. S. Cohen, *The Legal Conscience* 70 (1960).

49. Professor Wechsler concedes the ambiguity of the word, but defends the choice of an enigmatic word for an enigmatic subject. Wechsler xiii.

this is all "neutrality" means, then it is hard to see what all the fuss is about. Professor Wechsler's notion of neutrality must go further.

Could it mean that Marshall's major premise in approaching any constitutional question—that the Constitution he was interpreting was the blueprint for a nation, not for a confederation of sovereign states—was not a permissibly "neutral" principle? Professor Wechsler does not clearly indicate whether strongly held views of this order about constitutional principles qualify as "neutral," save in his passing comment on the "preferred position" controversy.[50]

There is another possibility. Does Wechslerian "neutrality" mean that in construing the Constitution the Justices should never declare statutes or administrative action invalid, unless their action satisfies a standard which cannot be met? Is it the doctrine of judicial self-restraint carried to the point of complete passivity? Would it deny all visible autonomous discretion to judges who have been entrusted by history with the duty to interpret and apply the Constitution as law, in the setting of law suits? Does it mean that in their essential task of discrimination—that is, of deciding when situations should be treated differently by the law— the judges should disregard inequalities of bargaining position, or in voting power; that the protection of individuals and minorities against transitory majorities ceases to be the dominant theme of the Bill of Rights; that in reconciling the competing claims of different parts of the Constitution, the Court not be required or allowed to decide, to recall the theme of a recent Coen lecture, whether in a given instance, and in the absence of statutory guidance, the constitutional interest in a fair trial outweighs in constitutional importance the constitutional interest in a free press? It is

50. Wechsler 35. See, however, Henkin, op. cit. supra note 32, at 658–60.

difficult, at least it is difficult for me, to determine how Professor Wechsler would answer these questions. But doubts of this order as to his meaning remain after many readings of his lecture.[51]

Criticisms like those we have been considering do not detract from the greatness of the work Marshall did. Nor should they be considered to detract from the achievements of our Court today. "The life of the law has not been logic: it has been experience." That is the hard lesson Professor Wechsler has forgotten. His test does justice to neither aspect of the process of law. On the side of experience, Wechsler would deny the propriety of judgment, which Cardozo made his central theme; and his view of "logic" represents an inadequate and rudimentary notion of the philosophy and methods of systematic thought.

If we turn for a moment from the Supreme Court to other institutions of the legal profession, and seek to look at them in the light of the standard I have sought to state, what findings are indicated? One could examine the work of lawyers and of law professors. But I shall comment here on only a few aspects of the work of the organized legal profession.

The national, regional, and local bar associations, the American Law Institute, and the American Bar Foundation are developing rapidly. In the main, they are no longer merely social clubs, or trade unions, concerned with fighting off competition from the accountants, trust companies, and insurance agents. They have sponsored important research

51. Professor Wechsler does not, of course, favor a static Constitution, bound to constructions prevalent in the 18th century. He welcomes the process of adaptation and growth in the interpretation of constitutional provisions, as long as that process is controlled by the criteria he advances. Wechsler 22–26, 32–36.

reports, like those of the Association of the Bar of the City of New York and the studies of the American Law Institute. They have engaged in a variety of desirable programs for the advanced professional training of lawyers. And they have participated in some efforts at law reform, most notably those in the field of procedure and judicial administration, and in efforts to raise the standards of judicial appointment.

While much useful work has been done, and many promising initiatives are being undertaken, I think the disinterested observer must conclude that as yet the legal profession has not begun to fulfill its obligation to society as an effective force for the vindication and improvement of law.

Let me mention a few items of unfinished business as examples of the kinds of issues we must face as lawyers if we can hope to justify ourselves to society. Our arrangements for providing legal aid to the poor, both in civil and criminal cases, are in most communities lamentably inadequate. The present state of legal aid programs is a standing reproach to the legal profession. In most states, the quality of judges is only fair. The practice of electing judges, or of appointing them for limited terms, survives in most of the states, a serious barrier to the possibility of truly impartial justice. In many, many communities, the judicial "fix" is reported to be commonplace—a disgrace we have tolerated far too long. In the field of procedure, despite the progress made under the federal rules and their analogues in many states, we still find indefensible delays in courts, cases shuttling back and forth between courts, and masses of decisions on purely procedural points which deny the very premise of procedural reform. Our police practice, and our procedure in criminal cases, are being slowly improved, thanks to the vigilant oversight of the Supreme Court in this field. But the process of reform still depends far too much on the accident of litigation, rather than on the affirmative efforts of bar associations, legislatures, and judicial councils to bring existing practice up to the standards announced by the Court. Far too little is being done to improve and reform substantive law. The enactment of new corporation laws and codes of correction, and the progress of the Commissioners of Uniform State Laws, highlight as exceptions the slow movement in this area and the weakness of national efforts for improvement.

Beyond issues of this order, typical and general as they are, there looms a far more serious and fundamental criticism of the performance of our bar and of our law schools.

At the present time we are witnessing and enduring a sinister challenge to the authority of law in our society. In many parts of the South, governors and legislatures openly defy the courts of the United States and seek by one subterfuge after another to prevent the orderly enforcement of the Fourteenth Amendment. These efforts are supported by private groups, operating both publicly and in secret. They employ boycotts, intimidation, and open violence to prevent Negroes from enforcing their legal rights and to weaken and disperse those within the decent and law-abiding majority who are trying to uphold the purposes of the law.

Thus far, to my knowledge, the organized bar, save for a few notable exceptions like that of the Houston Bar Association, has stood silent, and walked by on the other side. It helped to repel the dangerous attacks on the jurisdiction of the Supreme Court mounted several years ago by Senator Jenner of Indiana and others. But it has done nothing more affirmative to assist the courts and the nation in dealing with our crisis of legality. When explosions of mob violence occurred in New Orleans last fall, as they had occurred earlier in Little Rock, I do not recall seeing photographs of leading lawyers, or bar association presidents, standing with the few children, parents, and ministers who braved the threats and insults of the mob. Nor do I recall public statements from the leaders of our profession, since the time of Senator Pepper's appeal in 1956, urging public support for the law and willing compliance with its obvious purpose.

With lonely splendor, the federal judges in the South have been doing their duty under circumstances of appalling difficulty. The law of the nation, which no majority would overturn, conflicts with the prevailing customs of a region of the nation. This fact presents a difficult, but by no means an unknown problem in the experience of law. The federal judges in the South have proved themselves worthy of the finest traditions of our legal system. Many of them, I assume, might not have voted with the Supreme Court had they been its members when the segregation cases came up for decision. That possibility makes their conduct now doubly noble. Their courage and devotion in upholding the law, in the face of rancorous and bitter hostility in their own communities, has written a proud page in our legal history.

These judges deserve more than our praise from safe and distant places. We, the bar, and we, the American public, have left them too long alone in the line of battle. As Governor Collins of Florida has repeatedly urged, public opinion should be effectively mobilized and brought to bear if we are to remain a community of law. The profession of law has a plain duty to lead in the effort to recreate a climate of legality in our society. I hope that President Kennedy will soon do what only a President can do in galvanizing American opinion. And I wonder whether it would be useful for congressional committees to investigate some of the really gross activities which the White Citizens' Councils and their allies are carrying on throughout the South. I make the suggestion as one who believes in preserving broad powers of investigation for the Congress, as the Grand Inquest of the

American people. At the same time, I have been and I am critical of many features of the record. Many of the investigating committees which have sought to expose Nazi and Communist activities during the last twenty-five years have done questionable jobs, with extremely high costs in intimidation. But I am reluctant to believe it is beyond the will and wisdom of our law to devise fair procedures for legitimate enquiries into alleged patterns of coercive behavior which fall outside even the most latitudinarian concept of legitimate political activity. In this perspective, I submit that if any activities deserve to be called "subversive" and "un-American," those carried on by the White Citizens' Councils and kindred groups surely qualify. What could be more alien to our constitutional tradition than the work of organized bodies which seek to thwart the writ of the courts; to drive from their jobs and homes people whose only offense is to believe in the law; to close the public schools and destroy the basis of modern democratic society?

The challenge to social order implicit in this situation is more than the negative one of ending active resistance to the law. The formal law of equality has been growing steadily in the United States for two generations, case by case, statute by statute, executive order by executive order. It has been nourished by the social advance of the Negro in our society, and it has helped to make that advance possible. We know that in many areas the law-in-fact—the living law—does not yet match the precepts announced by the Supreme Court as the law of the Fourteenth Amendment. The problem is a national one, not a regional one. In some parts of the North there are virtual boycotts by banks or real estate agents which prevent Negroes and members of other minorities from buying homes of their choice. Such boycotts are almost certainly illegal under the Sherman Act or under state laws against restraints of trade. The problem of assuring effective equality in voting, or indeed assuring the vote at all, is one in which practice is far behind the law, as the valuable work of the Civil Rights Commission has demonstrated. The same conclusion can be drawn, as we all know, in the field of employment opportunity, where, among many other barriers to equality, we still confront the phenomenon of "lily-white" trade unions.

The task of the profession in this area should be to lead, not merely to insist that the trickle of final decisions by the Supreme Court be obeyed. There is work to be done in every community, North and South, before we can begin to claim we are living up to our own standards. The task is urgent. Violence breeds violence. The Negro citizen has shown commendable patience, tolerance, and faith in his quiet and disciplined demeanor in the South. But the rule of turning the other cheek is a hard one. It may not endure indefinitely if we fail to make the performance of our law match its professions.

In the end, however, the reasons which make action on this front a necessity are different. They are reasons of conscience, not of prudence. These things should be done not because they are politic, but because they are right.

# 2

# *The Enforcement of Morals*

IT MIGHT BE USEFUL to review, from an American point of vantage, the controversy occasioned by Lord Justice Devlin's Maccabaean lecture.[1] For the Justice's brilliant and original paper has been heatedly attacked as "illiberal." In the popular sport of classifying all positions on all subjects as either liberal or conservative—and the sport is quite as popular in the United States as it is in other countries— there is an intriguing difference between the rules of the game as it is conventionally played on the opposite sides of

1. *The Enforcement of Morals,* the Maccabaean Lecture in Jurisprudence of the British Academy, 1959 (Oxford University Press, 1959); Prof. H.L.A. Hart, "Immorality and Treason," *The Listener* 162–63 (July 30, 1959); Richard Wollheim, "Crime, Sin and Mr. Justice Devlin," *Encounter* 34–40 (November 1959). I shall refer hereafter to these three documents as Devlin, Hart, and Wollheim.

This paper evolved in response to the stimulus of invitations to talk under the auspices of undergraduate societies and Faculties of Law at several British universities during the academic year 1959–60, and was given as a lecture at King's College, London, on March 14, 1960. I am grateful to my hosts on those agreeable occasions for their kindly pressure to prepare the successive drafts of the paper, and for their helpful criticisms of it, particularly those of the members of the Political Society, King's College, Cambridge, and of Prof. Hart and his other guests at a most stimulating lunch at University College, Oxford.

First published in [1960] *Cambridge Law Journal* 174.

the Atlantic. In Great Britain, the suggestion that law has a moral content seems to raise theocratic ghosts in many quarters, perhaps in most; and clearly, theocracy is "conservative." In the United States, however, it is just the other way around. Every American schoolboy—or at least every American law student—considers Austinian positivism, and the strict separation of law and morals, to be certain hallmarks of a position labeled "conservative," "rigidly technical," "reactionary," or worse. And the view of law as an instrument for carrying out the moral purposes of its own tradition, and those of the society it rules, is a familiar touchstone of orthodox "liberalism."

Since the debate occasioned by Sir Patrick's lecture, like all such controversies, has become somewhat confused, I shall attempt to summarize his argument before taking up the criticisms which have been addressed to it.

I

Sir Patrick Devlin's lecture plucked extremely sensitive nerves. His point of departure was the Wolfenden Report on Homosexual Offences and Prostitution, in itself a subject to stir deep feeling. As a judge, he scrupulously refrained from taking a position on the recommendations of the Wolfenden Report, beyond some guarded words of sympathy for its point of view and of praise for its value as a carefully reasoned and dispassionate study of its theme.[2] His lecture was addressed to the jurisprudential premise of the Report —the proposition that it is not the business of the law to take positions on matters of morals, or to intervene in the private lives of citizens, save insofar as it may be necessary "to preserve public order and decency, to protect the citizen from what is offensive or injurious, and to provide sufficient

2. Devlin at 2, 18, 19, 20, 21.

safeguards against exploitation and corruption of others, particularly those who are specially vulnerable because they are young, weak in body or mind, inexperienced, or in a state of special physical, official or economic dependence."[3]

The distinction between crime and sin implied by this passage in the Wolfenden Report has strong support. Those who accept it would define sin as an offense against the moral law, crime as an offense against rules enacted to protect public order, to prevent injury to others, or to safeguard the young, the insane, women, animals, or others who may be considered special wards of the law in a society of free and responsible men. For this purpose, there are three possible meanings of the term "moral law." It may denote the moral code of a religion. Or it may refer to a body of ideas we can identify as the accepted moral code of a community at any stage of its development—its prevailing mores, in effect. Finally, the term "moral law" may mean the moral decisions of each individual, spun out of his own conscience, or the view of morality taken by a selected group of philosophers. If these are the only three possible definitions of the words "moral law," the relevant one in this context is the second—the moral law as the embodiment of the moral ideas of a given community at a given time. In our secular Western societies, we have given up attempting to base law directly on religious principle, as we have given up requiring religion to be observed. Many would put great stress, as I should, on the moral responsibility of the individual and on the contribution which philosophers of morality may make to thought and to life. But it would be anarchy to claim that society could tolerate the "right" of an individual to act entirely in accordance with his own ideas of right and wrong, or even those of Socrates or Spinoza.

3. Id. at 4.

Can sin in this sense—as a violation of society's moral code—be distinguished from crime? Those who hold the principle expressed in the Wolfenden Report would say that a given act—murder, for example—may happen to be both a crime and a sin. That fact represents no more than coincidence, or what Professor Hart has called an "intersection" of crime and morals.[4] In the case of murder, such theorists of law would claim, the positive law and the moral law happen to cover the same area, but in pursuit of different objectives.

Lord Justice Devlin attacked this view with arguments of experience and arguments of logic. As a matter of history, he said, English law has never admitted so sharp a separation between law and morals, and as a judge he would find the duty of passing sentence almost intolerably difficult if it did.[5] In crimes of violence, he points out, the consent of the victim is not a defense. Nor may the victim end the prosecution after the event by forgiving his aggressor. The offense may have been committed most discreetly, without disturbing public order. If protecting the individual from unjustified injury inflicted by others were the only public interest at stake, his approval would remove any possible basis for public action. But it does not. A man incurably ill, or one afflicted with an overpowering sense of guilt, may beg to be killed. If a doctor or a friend yields to the plea, the act is murder nevertheless—not because it involves a breach of public order, but because it violates a moral principle

4. H.L.A. Hart, "Positivism and the Separation of Law and Morals," 71 *Harv. L. Rev.* 593, 598–99 (1958).

5. Devlin at 6: "As a judge who administers the criminal law and who has often to pass sentence in a criminal court, I should feel handicapped in my task if I thought that I was addressing an audience which had no sense of sin or which thought of crime as something quite different. Ought one, for example, in passing sentence upon a female abortionist to treat her simply as if she were an unlicensed midwife?"

about which society believes and feels strongly enough to insist upon its vindication, the principle which Dr. Glanville Williams has recently called the sanctity of life.

Having disproved the juristic theory of the Wolfenden Report, at least as an explanation of English law, Sir Patrick turned to the problem of defining the relationship between the positive and the moral law. Is it, he asks, a good theoretical relation or a practical working alliance, or a bit of both? He sets out on his inquiry by asking himself three questions:

1. Has society the right to pass judgment at all on matters of morals? Ought there, in other words, to be a public morality, or are morals always a matter for private judgment?
2. If society has the right to pass judgment, has it also the right to use the weapon of the law to enforce it?
3. If so, ought it to use that weapon in all cases or only in some; and if only in some, on what principles should it distinguish?[6]

A society possesses a public morality, Sir Patrick says, simply because it is a society. "What makes a society of any sort is community of ideas, not only political ideas but also ideas about the way its members should behave and govern their lives; these latter ideas are its morals.[7] . . . without shared ideas on politics, morals and ethics no society can exist. . . .For society is not something that is kept together physically; it is held by the invisible bonds of common thought."[8] A common morality is part of the "bondage" of society in this sense, and part of the price one pays for having society. No society can avoid having convictions and passing judgments on questions of morality deemed to con-

6. Id. at 9.
7. Id. at 10.
8. Id. at 11–12.

cern society as a whole. A collective judgment on an issue of public morality is something more than a majority opinion, or even a unanimous opinion, that a man is doing wrong in what society considers to be his private affairs. There must first be a collective judgment that the matter affects the basic norms of the community's common life.

How can one tell what this common morality is? The metaphor Sir Patrick uses to explain his definition of the common morality is one of the most controversial features of his lecture. It is an illustration entirely natural to a common law judge, and peculiarly irritating to an academic philosopher. The collective moral judgment of a society, Lord Justice Devlin said, is in the final analysis symbolized, and expressed, by the actions of the men in the jury box: twelve "right-minded" men, twelve men-on-the-street, or the Clapham omnibus, drawn at random and held to represent the moral views of the community at large. The standard of British law, he says, does not require the counting of heads in any direct or mechanical sense; it depends on opinions presumed to be held by a mythical but extremely useful creature known as "the reasonable man."

> For my purpose I should like to call him the man in the jury-box, for the moral judgment of society must be something about which any twelve men or women drawn at random might after discussion be expected to be unanimous. This was the standard the judges applied in the days before Parliament was as active as it is now and when they laid down rules of public policy. They did not think of themselves as making law but simply as stating principles which every right-minded person would accept as valid. It is what Pollock called "practical morality," which is based not on theological or philosophical foundations but "in the mass of con-

tinuous experience half-consciously or unconsciously accumulated and embodied in the morality of common sense." He called it also "a certain way of thinking on questions of morality which we expect to find in a reasonable civilised man or a reasonable Englishman, taken at random."[9, 10]

At this point, Sir Patrick's exposition may be rather misleading, at least to a popular audience. While the jury is surely one medium through which the common morality of jury-using societies is expressed, the jury does not function alone. The judge charges the jury, comments on the evidence, and greatly influences the way in which the issues are presented to it for decision. Part of the respect with which judges are viewed derives from their role as appointed and independent spokesmen for the law of the community and for its moral sense as embodied in its law. The jury does not always follow the judge in his view of the purpose of some part of the law. But it listens. Secondly, for all the vividness of Sir Patrick's definition, it is incomplete. Parliaments, borough councils, royal commissions, local and national bodies of many kinds, writers, teachers, leaders of thought, all function also as spokesmen of the common morality, as the jury does, distilling, expressing, applying and helping to shape the society's moral code. The twelve men in the jury box have the last word, or almost the last word, as to whether a man goes to prison or to the gallows. But they are exposed in advance to many conditioning voices, some of decisive influence.

Confronting his second interrogatory, Sir Patrick concludes that the state has the right to punish violations of the code of public morality through the criminal law for

9. *Essays in Jurisprudence and Ethics* 278 and 353 (judge's note) (1882).
10. Devlin at 16.

reasons implicit in the definition itself: if, as he says, "a recognised morality is as necessary to society as, say, a recognised government, then society may use the law to preserve morality in the same way as it uses it to safeguard anything else that is essential to its existence."[11]

But this general proposition, as Sir Patrick is the first to assert, does not in itself settle particular cases. All crime may be sin, in the Justice's analysis, but he does not believe that all sin should be made criminal. The two spheres are indissolubly linked, but they are not and should not be co-extensive.

In deciding how far the law should go in enforcing the common morality, Sir Patrick says, lawmakers must strike a balance, as they must in every other aspect of the conflict between liberty and order. The state cannot be completely shut out on questions of morality. But the individual can hardly "be expected to surrender to the judgment of society the whole conduct of his life."[12] The state's interest in enforcing a given rule of behavior accepted by the community as right must be weighed by the lawmakers against a series of principles, which I should say are as much a part of the society's "common morality," in Sir Patrick's definition of the phrase, as its views about marriage, sexual behavior, or violence. As Sir Patrick states them, the principles which ought to guide the modern British (or American) lawmaker in determining the limits of the law in this sphere are rules of experience and propriety in the use of social force—principles of peculiar centrality for a society which aspires to freedom. If the outcome of such a balancing cannot result in exact definitions, it hardly follows that it can yield no definitions at all.

Lord Justice Devlin suggests that these rules govern mod-

11. Id. at 13.
12. Id. at 16.

ern democratic lawmakers as principles upon which "most people would agree."[13] They have the same status and force in lawmaking, he suggests, as do the principles of judicial precedents in the common law process of deciding cases in court.[14] Put in an order somewhat different from Sir Patrick's, his restatement of the prevailing law in this regard is as follows: The state should preserve and protect as large an area of privacy and of freedom for the individual as possible, especially in matters of morals and of conscience. This rule is not and should not be confined only to thought and speech; it extends to action also, as in the case of conscientious objection to military service and the disapproval of wire-tapping both in detection and in the formation of law. The law is and should be concerned with the minimum and not the maximum. The penalties of the law can be enforced, but the law cannot compel a man to be or to become upright. Its machinery is not very efficient. The law should not be burdened with tasks it cannot perform, or cannot perform without becoming a Leviathan.

These considerations lead to several related principles of considerable moment in his argument. "Nothing should be punished by the law that does not lie beyond the limits of tolerance. It is not nearly enough to say that a majority dislike a practice; there must be a real feeling of reprobation," indeed of "disgust," "deeply felt and not manufactured,"[15] "honest and dispassionate."[16] The presence of such intense feelings, believed by "the reasonable man" to be shared by all "right-thinking" men, is a necessary but not a sufficient condition for legal action in the sphere of

13. Id. at 17. Sir Patrick's exposition of the principles controlling the law-making process in this area appear at pp. 17–23 of his lecture.

14. Id. at 17.

15. Ibid.

16. Id. at 23.

morals. Legal intervention is not justified only because there is a strong and pervasive feeling that the conduct in question is extremely threatening and extremely reprehensible to basic rules of community life. If the law should rest simply on "disgust," Sir Patrick says, "it would be wrong."[17] The fact that there is so much immorality which has never been brought within the law shows that the toleration of a good deal of immorality does not necessarily unravel the fabric of society:

> before a society can put a practice beyond the limits of tolerance there must be a deliberate judgment that the practice is injurious to society. There is, for example, a general abhorrence of homosexuality. We should ask ourselves in the first instance whether looking at it calmly and dispassionately, we regard it as a vice so abominable that its mere presence is an offence. If that is the genuine feeling of the society in which we live, I do not see how society can be denied the right to eradicate it. Our feeling may not be so intense as that. We may feel about it that, if confined, it is tolerable, but that if it spread it might be gravely injurious; it is in this way that most societies look upon fornication, seeing it as a natural weakness which must be kept within bounds, but which cannot be rooted out. It becomes then a question of balance, the danger to society in one scale and the extent of the restriction in the other. On this sort of point the value of an investigation by such a body as the Wolfenden Committee and of its conclusions is manifest.[18]

There is a further principle to be given great weight in decisions on such questions. The lawmaker should be acute-

17. Id. at 17.
18. Id. at 18.

ly aware that limits of tolerance shift and that even intense public feelings change. Yet the law itself is often difficult to amend, especially where reform may seem to imply the lawmakers' approval of conduct regarded by the public as immoral. The law should therefore be slow to act.

> By the next generation the swell of indignation may have abated and the law be left without the strong backing which it needs. But it is then difficult to alter the law without giving the impression that moral judgment is being weakened. This is now one of the factors that is strongly militating against any alteration to the law on homosexuality.[19]

Where the lawmakers are satisfied that the preceding conditions have been met, they should consider an additional question before determining to make breaches of the moral law criminal: do the instruments of the criminal law offer appropriate ways for dealing with particular deviations from the code of morality? The tools of the law are "fines, imprisonment, or lesser forms of supervision (such as Borstal and probation) and—not to be ignored—the degradation that often follows upon the publication of the crime. Are any of these suited to the job of dealing with sexual immorality? The fact that there is so much immorality which has never been brought within the law shows that there can be no general rule. It is a matter for decision in each case; but in the case of homosexuality the Wolfenden Report rightly has regard to the views of those who are experienced in dealing with this sort of crime and to those of the clergy who are the natural guardians of public morals."[20]

For these reasons, then, in Sir Patrick's exposition, the course of wisdom in lawmaking should be to place as few

19. Id. at 19.
20. Id. at 21.

moral prohibitions as possible within the criminal law. The enforcement of the criminal law plays a part in the development of the common morality, but other forces are of equal or of greater importance: the influence of thought and religion and of careful studies; and social experience with the tides of feeling and with the limited reach of law.

Thus Sir Patrick's answer to his third question would establish severe limits on the ways in which society should exercise the inherent powers he says it possesses, in accordance with the answers he offers to his first two questions. He concludes that the extent to which the state should undertake to act against sin is, in his vocabulary, essentially a practical question, not to be settled by clear and simple lines of logic. I should prefer to phrase the matter differently. The lawmakers' conclusion in each instance, I should say, is a logical one, but it is the logical function of several variables, not of one. The boundary line, therefore, is fixed by judgments as to the relative strength of the several variables at different times and under different circumstances.

As I read "The Enforcement of Morals," these are the main points of the author's argument. I have put to one side three themes, not crucial to his position, which have, I think, colored the reception of his lecture.

The first is a forthright and affirmative view of the primary place of the Christian religion in the inner life of both the moral and the positive law of England.[21] That Christian morals are the basis of the criminal law, the Lord Justice says, is an historical fact which both free-thinker and non-Christian can accept, without offense to his convictions. In this secular age, most of the literature of legal philosophy ignores the problem which Sir Patrick puts with such eloquence and insight. The reasoning of his lecture stands

21. Id. at 23–25.

without benefit of this passage as an exercise in sociological jurisprudence. While his assertion frames a question to be considered with the utmost seriousness by historians of law and by students of legal philosophy, it raises issues of difficulty reaching far beyond the scope of his paper.

The second element in Sir Patrick's lecture which I regard as extrinsic to its essential logic is of another order. At several points, he seems to say rather gloomily, a relaxation of moral standards is the primrose path to social decay. "It may be that history is a tale of contraction and expansion and that all developed societies are on their way to dissolution. I must not speak of things I do not know; and anyway as a practical matter no society is willing to make provision for its own decay."[22] The trouble with this cry, the perennial reproach of the older to the younger generation, is that it is as impossible to document today as it was in the time of Isaiah or Oswald Spengler. It is hard to conclude, reading Fielding and Smollett, or the life of Melbourne, or the diaries of Boswell, or looking at the pictures of Hogarth, that we really are worse behaved than our ancestors. I rather doubt it, and in any event Sir Patrick Devlin is very young to accept such views. Perhaps they reflect the impact on a sensitive man of years at the assizes. If that is the case, his recent promotion to the less sordid docket of the Court of Appeal should work a cure.

The third embellishment to the logical sequence of Sir Patrick's lecture is his use of the analogy of treason. If, he says, an accepted code of morals is as essential to the life of a community as its political ideas and its political system, enforcement of the public morality is as proper as the legal prohibitions against treason, sedition, and disloyalty. "Society cannot ignore the morality of the individual any more

22. Id. at 19. See also pp. 11–12, 14–15, 22.

57

than it can his loyalty; it flourishes on both, and without either it dies."[23] The inherent right of a state to defend itself against destruction is unchallengeable. Certainly no American, descended both from Jefferson and from Lincoln, can deny either the privilege of revolution or the duty of the state to resist it. The problem of preserving the common morality of a society is generically related to that of protecting the state and society against forcible overthrow, but in many ways it is different.[24] While Sir Patrick's analogy is pertinent, his treatment of it, within the limits of a lecture on another topic, is necessarily incomplete. At what point do ideas and political acts, otherwise normal and innocent, become crimes against the safety of the state? What criteria can Millian societies use with propriety to fix the frontiers between protected intellectual and political freedom and prohibited sedition? Are such criteria, and the processes of applying them, comparable to those which Sir Patrick develops for determining when immoral behavior should be made criminal? The appropriate limits of legal action against "disloyalty" and "sedition," under circumstances presenting varying degrees of external danger, are matters which American law has had to face in considerable detail especially since 1917. The problem is one of great delicacy and difficulty, and the solutions we have reached, while far from final, are often disturbing, and sometimes wrong.[25] On the whole, Sir Patrick's case would be clearer if

23. Id. at 23. See also pp. 11, 14–15. I have discussed the legal problems raised by laws regarding loyalty in "Needed: A Rational Security Program," infra, p. 267.

24. I am indebted to Prof. Helen Silving for the observation that in psychoanalytic terms sex crime and treason are related.

25. My views on several aspects of these problems are developed in "The Japanese American Cases—A Disaster," p. 193; "The Democratic Character of Judicial Review," p. 147; "Needed: A Rational Security Program," p. 267; "The Supreme Court and the People's Will," p. 114; "The Court and Its Critics," p. 83.

his analogy to treason were put aside, or developed in greater detail. The two problems are akin, but by no means commensurate, since they involve the application of similar rules to quite different areas of social experience. There is, for example, no general sense of public outrage at the thought of Karl Marx sitting quietly in the Reading Room of the British Museum and writing a book which helped to detonate the universe. On the contrary, the code of public morality would regard his conduct, whatever its ultimate consequences, as highly respectable and worthy of protection on deeply cherished principles of personal freedom.

By way of shorthand comment, one can say little beyond the commonplace: that in both areas the wise rule is for the law to do as little as possible. Extensive legal action, either in the political sphere or in that of morals, has in the past usually led to abuses which threatened one of the great ends of any legal system, what Montesquieu called the "tranquillity of mind" of the individual, drawn from a legal order so constituted that no man need be afraid of another. Even when qualified by Sir Patrick's latitudinarian principles—privacy, tolerance, rationality in lawmaking, a strong sense of the minimalist character and limits of the law, etc.—his analogy grates in the ears. It brings bleak echoes to the mind of any student of British and American legal history, the memory of battles which did much to shape our modern constitutions. Adjusting the criminal law to the shifting boundaries of privacy is hard enough, without invoking the shades of Wilkes and Junius, Erskine and Tom Paine.

II

Professor Hart's critique of "The Enforcement of Morals" starts with the claim that Sir Patrick's argument repudiates the liberal position stated in the Wolfenden Report and classically put by Mill: "The only purpose for which power can be rightfully exercised over any member of a civilised community against his will is to prevent harm to others."[26] On the next page, however, Professor Hart concedes that Mill's thesis may well be too simple. "There are multiple criteria," he writes, "not a single criterion, determining when human liberty may be restricted. Perhaps this is what Sir Patrick means by a curious distinction which he often stresses between theoretical and practical limits. But with all its simplicies the liberal point of view is a better guide than Sir Patrick to clear thought on the proper relation of morality to the criminal law; for it stresses what he obscures—namely, the points at which thought is needed before we turn popular morality into criminal law."[27] He then continues with a paragraph which I read as a volte-face, amending Mill's approach beyond recognition and accepting the major premises of Sir Patrick's argument, and the whole of its substance, as I have summarized it here, save for minor nuances of style, taste, and emphasis.

> No doubt we would all agree that a consensus of moral opinion on certain matters is essential if society is to be worth living in. Laws against murder, theft and much else would be of little use if they were not supported by a widely diffused conviction that what these laws forbid is also immoral. So much is obvious. But it does not follow that everything to which the moral vetoes of accepted morality attach is of equal importance to society; nor is there the slightest reason for thinking of morality as a seamless web: one which will fall to

26. Hart at 162. H.L.A. Hart is Professor of Jurisprudence at Oxford University.
27. Id. at 163.

pieces carrying society with it, unless all its emphatic vetoes are enforced by law.[28]

The burden of this aspect of Professor Hart's criticism of Sir Patrick Devlin seems to be that the Judge fails sufficiently to stress the importance of thought, reason, and study, as compared with strong popular feeling, among the forces that should guide lawmaking. On reviewing Sir Patrick's treatment of the principles which, in his striking metaphor, govern the making of British legislation in the same way that the principles of past decisions influence the judicial process, I do not find this a fair criticism.[29] But even in Professor Hart's terms, I find his strictures unacceptable. I conclude that they fall into a trap against which he has often and cogently warned others: of failing to distinguish the "law that is" from the "law that ought to be."

Some years ago, Professor Hart gave a Holmes Lecture at the Harvard Law School, defending the early "positivists" and their separation of law and morals.[30] Bentham and Austin, he pointed out, were trying to free men's minds of the incubus of Blackstone in defining law, and in thinking about it. They were fighting the last stages of the battle to secularize the state—to liberate legal thought from the view that positive law was not really law if it was contrary to natural law, in some sense of that elusive term; and that because a rule was morally right it was by that token a legal rule. Hence they stressed the distinction between the law that is—the actual pattern of prevailing decision—and the

---

28. Ibid.

29. See pp. 53–56, supra.

30. "Positivism and the Separation of Law and Morals," 71 *Harv. L. Rev.* 593 (1958), answered by Prof. Lon L. Fuller, "Positivism and Fidelity to Law —A Reply to Professor Hart," 71 *Harv. L. Rev.* 630 (1958). Mr. Fuller is Professor of Law at the Harvard Law School.

law that ought to be, according to criteria of natural law or standards of justice which individuals or groups sought to persuade society and its lawmakers to accept. My approach to Professor Hart's Holmes Lecture is somewhat different from Professor Fuller's. I have no difficulty with the distinction between the "law that is" and the "law that ought to be." It seems to me useful and helpful in ordering thought about law. But throughout his Holmes Lecture, Professor Hart equates this pair of phrases with another which he seems to regard as synonymous—the separation of law and morals.[31] I cannot understand why Professor Hart treats these two dichotomies as identical and inter-

31. Throughout his lecture paragraphs start with the "is-ought" distinction and then the language shifts, referring to the subject matter of the paragraph as the distinction between law and morals. See Hart, op. cit., supra, note 30, at pp. 597 (second full paragraph); 600–01 (first three paragraphs of Section II); p. 615 ("The third criticism of the separation of law and morals," which starts Part IV, is to be compared with "I now turn to a distinctively American criticism of the separation of the law that is from the law that ought to be," the opening words of Part III, on p. 606); p. 624 ("the Utilitarian or 'positivist' insistence that law and morality are distinct," referring to the theme of Part V, dealing with "the confusion of what is and what ought to be law," p. 621). Prof. Hart has told me that he did not intend to treat these distinctions, "is-ought" and "law-morals," as exact synonyms or equivalents, and perhaps the root of my misinterpretation of his text lies in the possibility that he would offer a more limited definition than I should of the moral element in law. See pp. 612–13, where he warns of the danger of "thinking in a too simple-minded fashion about the word 'ought.' This is not because there is no distinction to be made between law as it is and ought to be. Far from it. It is because the distinction should be between what is and what from many different points of view ought to be. The word 'ought' merely reflects the presence of some standard of criticism; one of these standards is a moral standard but not all standards are moral." This comment, however, would not justify his usage of these two sets of words, even when fully developed. It would identify morals as one of the possible components of the legal "ought," along with prudence, safety, habit, etc. But it would continue to exclude morals from the law that is. If I have misread Prof. Hart's purpose, I regret it. My only defense is that at least for one reader his text is ambiguous.

changeable, nor, in so far as I can follow him, do I understand why he considers it important to do so.

In Professor Hart's view, every legal system which has
merited the citizen's moral obligation of obedience has met
certain minimal "moral standards," and contained certain
fundamental elements derived from and related to the as-
sumption that it aims at the goal of justice.[32] Indeed, Professor Hart is willing to claim that such fundamental rules of
a moral character are a "natural" necessity in law, at least
in any legal order we have hitherto known or can now
imagine. Secondly, in addition to this minimal but indispensable moral element in law and its administration, there
is another link between law and morality, even in the perspective of Professor Hart's strict "separation" of law and
morals: at many points positive rules of law contain or mirror moral principles. Historically the law has been influenced by moral opinion, which it has in turn helped to
shape.[33] Beyond these two aspects of the relationship of law
and morals, there is a more basic issue. Every rule of "the
law that is" at any time contains a moral core, a core of
"purpose," related to its core of denotation. It is animated
by a conception of policy, a decision made at some point
in time that the rule in question represents a just way to
approach a given problem. The effective purpose of the
rule may be that of the original legislators or judges who
formulated it, or that of the later parliaments and judges
who successively applied it, interpreted it, and gave it coherence, direction, and momentum. Looking at the statute
involved as a whole, or at the whole body of judicial precedents we may be considering, in the full setting of their
history, enforcement, and effect, we can see a line of policy,
an articulation of the social ends the rule is supposed to

32. Id. at 621–24.
33. Id. at 598–99.

serve. As the rule or practice develops through time, we may sometimes say that the process of its growth is simply an elaboration of ideas and purposes which were there all the time, hidden seeds of later flowers; at other times we may regard the change in the character, scope, and impact of the rule as too great to permit so comforting a bow to precedent. In the latter case, we habitually say, the law has changed in a more fundamental sense: the older "ought" has become the new "is." The moral ideas—by which I mean the totality of the law's ideas as to just public policy—of the more remote and the more recent past have come together with those of the present, through the chemistry of our lawmaking procedures, and have evolved a new rule. In this way, in Holmes' phrase, the law becomes the "witness and external deposit of our moral life," its history "the history of the moral development of the race."[34]

One can use different forms of language to describe this process. On the whole, I should prefer, with Professor Hart, to say that each stage of the way involves lawmaking, though not arbitrary or discontinuous lawmaking, but lawmaking nonetheless, according to the prevailing rules of judicial and legislative practice. Whether we employ one formula or another to identify the path of legal change, most English and American lawyers, I suspect, would now agree, as pupils of Austin, Holmes, and Maitland, on the essential nature of what happens.

Against this background, what is Professor Hart's charge against Sir Patrick Devlin?

Sir Patrick posed a question about "the law that is" in relation to the existing code of public morality—that of de-

---

34. I believe and hope that the preceding paragraph corresponds to Prof. Hart's analysis, especially at pp. 627-29 of his Holmes Lecture, although it does not use the terminology he would prefer. Holmes' remark appears in "The Path of the Law," 10 *Harv. L. Rev.* 457, 459 (1897).

termining whether the existing positive law appropriately corresponds to the existing state of public morals. Professor Hart reproaches him for not sufficiently emphasizing that the given state of public morality may represent irrational and unjustified prejudices, embalmed in the customs and outlook of the people. The law that is at any time, Sir Patrick says, has a moral base. The law may be good or bad law, according to moral criteria other than those of the common morality embodied in it. Or it may have become bad law in another sense, by failing to keep up with changes in the common morality itself—changes in the view society now takes of privacy, the permissible limits of freedom, the consequences of enforcement as compared with those of non-enforcement, etc. The essence of his position in this connection, I think, is that the criminal law should express, and must express, some of the strong positions of a society's common public morality. It can appropriately change only when the community's lawmakers are persuaded that the common morality has changed—that the practice being condemned, like witchcraft, does not exist, or, like heresy, should be taken from the sphere of public morals and transferred to that of private affairs.

While I take it that Professor Hart accepts Sir Patrick's thesis, in this limited sense, he addresses to it an objection which he considers basic:

> We are not, I suppose, likely, in England, to take again to the burning of old women for witchcraft or to punishing people for associating with those of a different race or colour, or to punishing people again for adultery. Yet if these things were viewed with intolerance, indignation, and disgust, as the second of them still is in some countries, it seems that on Sir Patrick's principles no rational criticism could be opposed to

the claim that they should be punished by law. We could only pray, in his words, that the limits of tolerance might shift.

It is impossible to see what curious logic has led Sir Patrick to this result. For him a practice is immoral if the thought of it makes the man on the Clapham omnibus sick. So be it. Still, why should we not summon all the resources of our reason, sympathetic understanding, as well as critical intelligence, and insist that before general feeling is turned into criminal law it is submitted to scrutiny of a different kind from Sir Patrick's? Surely, the legislator should ask whether the general morality is based on ignorance, superstition, or misunderstanding; whether there is a false conception that those who practise what it condemns are in other ways dangerous or hostile to society; and whether the misery to many parties, the blackmail and the other evil consequences of criminal punishment, especially for sexual offences, are well understood. It is surely extraordinary that among the things which Sir Patrick says are to be considered before we legislate against immorality these appear nowhere; not even as "practical considerations," let alone "theoretical limits." To any theory which, like this one, asserts that the criminal law may be used on the vague ground that the preservation of morality is essential to society and yet omits to stress the need for critical scrutiny, our reply should be: "Morality, what crimes may be committed in thy name!"[35]

But Sir Patrick did not fail to urge the necessity for independent, dispassionate and far-ranging study and judgment by lawmakers as one of the binding rules of British lawmak-

35. Hart at 163.

ing, even when the lawmakers confront popular feelings worked up to "a concert pitch" of moral indignation.[36]

Professor Hart, however, reads the Judge's text as repudiating what he calls a "rationalist morality"—to me a most puzzling and obscure phrase, in this context. Does it imply that our lawmaking is or should be controlled by independent and autonomous Gods of Pure Reason, installed somewhere in our political systems and endowed with the power to determine such questions for society, free of the prejudices to which lesser men are subject? This is hardly a plausible reading of Professor Hart's text, nor a likely position for a liberal democrat to take. If, however, Professor Hart means that it "would be wrong" for lawmakers to act on the basis of disgust alone;[37] that they should make a separate and independent judgment that a practice is injurious to society as well as odious;[38] that they should consider the implications of the half-dozen qualifying principles whose exposition requires almost one-third of Sir Patrick's lecture, then I fail to understand how his position differs from that of the Justice.

In this connection, Professor Hart criticizes Sir Patrick for failing explicitly to include among his accepted rules of lawmaking a requirement that the lawmakers weigh up and compare the human misery caused by the immoral behavior and that incident to its punishment. Sir Patrick does enjoin lawmakers to consider whether the tools of law, including the degradation of publicity, are in fact suitable means for dealing with a particular moral breach, and, with reference to homosexuality, he commends the Wolfenden Report for regarding seriously the views of experienced persons on this point. If Professor Hart means only that the punishment

36. See pp. 54–56, supra.
37. Devlin at 17.
38. Id. at 18.

should fit the crime and the criminal, and that the law should avoid excessive or vindictive punishments, I should suppose that the thought could fairly be read into Sir Patrick's general views on criminal law, as expressed in his lecture. If Professor Hart means more than that—if, that is, the misery of punishment (and the risks of blackmail) constitute a special factor to be taken into account more for one class of offenders than another—then I fail to follow his reasoning.

Yet, in the passage quoted on p. 65, Professor Hart concludes that Sir Patrick Devlin's theory would give inadequate scope to "reason" in resisting the demand of aroused prejudice for a legal condemnation of what the community regards as sin. Under Sir Patrick's view, Professor Hart says, we could only pray that the limits of tolerance might shift.

From Professor Hart, this is a most unexpected point. For Professor Hart has urged elsewhere that even Nazi law was law, to be treated as such until it was changed,[39] and he has been a vigorous leader in teaching lawyers that man can do much more than pray when he is confronted by bad law. What man should not do, however, in Professor Hart's view, which I fully share, is to fall back on Blackstone and pretend that the bad law is not there, or is not law.

Perhaps one may test Professor Hart's thesis in another and less explosive context than the law of the Wolfenden Report: that of polygamy. In some of the Mormon areas of the United States, polygamy has been, and still is, a practical problem for the law. There have been occasional prosecutions and convictions, even in recent years. Should we ask whether the preference of the common morality in the United States for monogamy, enforced by the criminal law, is based on "ignorance, superstition or misunderstanding"?

39. Hart, op. cit., supra note 30, at 615–21.

Does it derive from "a false conception" that those who practice polygamy "are in other ways dangerous or hostile to society"?[40] Should we inquire whether polygamy is tolerable if confined, but "gravely injurious" if allowed to spread?[41] Should we condemn ordinary bigamy, contracted for pleasure, but except polygamy based on sincere religious belief? Suppose we engage in all these acts of critical scrutiny and rational investigation which to my mind both the Professor and the Judge enjoin. Should we not then conclude that monogamy is so fundamental a theme in the existing common morality of the United States that the condemnation of polygamy as a crime is justified, even though in the end the repugnance to it rests on "feeling" and not on "reason"? The Supreme Court of the United States has upheld such laws, in the teeth of the constitutional provision that "Congress shall make no law respecting an establishment of religion, or prohibiting the free exercise thereof." And the federal law is still enforced, although the old territories of Utah and Arizona have long since become states, and the normal jurisdiction over crime and marriage has passed from Congress to the state governments.[42]

I cannot conclude that Professor Hart's analysis of this problem would differ from that of Sir Patrick Devlin, even in form.

Professor Hart's paper also criticizes Sir Patrick's comparison of laws protecting the common morality and those protecting the state against treason, sedition, and disloyalty. His criticism is placed on grounds quite different from those suggested earlier.[43] Professor Hart seems to urge that the in-

40. Hart at 163.
41. Devlin at 18.
42. Reynolds v. United States, 98 U.S. 145 (1878). See also Musser v. Utah, 333 U.S. 95 (1948) (state prosecution for advocacy of polygamy as a conspiracy to commit acts injurious to public morals).
43. See pp. 57–59, supra.

herent governmental power of self-defense is greater than
its power in the realm of morals. I should not go so far.
Linking the two problems, Professor Hart urges, is "gro-
tesque" and "absurd" unless it can be clearly shown that
offending against a given item in the code of common
morality is likely to jeopardize the whole structure. "Private
subversive activity is, of course, a contradiction in terms because 'subversion' means overthrowing government, which
is a public thing . . . [we may] say that though there could
not logically be a sphere of private treason there is a sphere
of private morality and immorality,"[44] or, to use Sir Patrick's terminology, a sphere of "private behaviour in matters of morals."[45] The issue is not to be disposed of so simply. The racial theories of Houston Chamberlain, the constitutional theories of John C. Calhoun, the social theories
of Karl Marx, the theology of Martin Luther, to cite a few
random instances, were all used as tools of revolutionary
action; yet all were produced, published, and initially discussed under circumstances which we should today regard
as those of protected private (and public) behavior in matters of thought, speech, and politics. So, too, the intellectual
and political movement of modern socialism in Western
countries, though it often professed to use revolutionary
terms and even to advocate revolutionary means, in fact
helped, with other forces, to produce through peaceful procedures of persuasion and democratic action not the overthrow of ordered government but a long series of changes
both in the forms of government and in the content of prevailing ideas of social justice. When words, books, meetings,
speeches, marches, petitions, and political acts become a
threat to the existence of the state is a question of fact.

44. Hart at 163.
45. Devlin at 10.

When the law should interfere depends upon an appraisal of the danger to government in relation to other values which our culture also prizes. Laws against disciplined fascist or communist groups, for example, or even those against the advocacy of fascist or communist programs, raise one set of issues in times of relative peace and stability, quite another in times of war or civil disturbance. Despite the inevitable brevity of his treatment, Sir Patrick's statement that it is impossible to set "rigid bounds to the part which the law may play"[46] in the suppression either of vice or of treason is closer to the reality of the problem than Professor Hart's "logical" distinction between the privacy of morality and the public character of all subversion.

## III

Mr. Wollheim's critique of Sir Patrick Devlin's lecture is paradoxical and inconsistent. Sir Patrick's essay contains "little reasoning," Mr. Wollheim says, "that is at once valid and acceptable."[47] Its conception of society as a community of ideas, which I should have thought was a commonplace of sociology and anthropology, is an old notion, he claims, whose modern forms are communism and Catholicism; and it has been the pride of the civilized parts of Europe to oppose to it the liberal theory of politics, which declares that the identity and the continuity of a society resides not in the common possession of a single morality, but in the mutual toleration of different moralities.[48] At one point we are told that Sir Patrick views toleration and his other principles of lawmaking as part of the common morality, drawn from the

46. Devlin at 15.
47. Wollheim, p. 40. Mr. Wollheim teaches philosophy at the University of London.
48. Id. at 38.

same sources as the community's opinions on matters of sexual behavior and violence.[49] At another Mr. Wollheim says that this reconciliation of Devlinism and what he calls "liberalism" will not work, because "toleration cannot be seen as a morality conformity to which issues in uniform behaviour."[50] But to Mr. Wollheim the problem of Sir Patrick's lecture does not exist unless there is "behaviour of a uniform kind over a fairly large area of human activity."[51] A society can be marked by universal toleration, Mr. Wollheim says, and yet display no common pattern of behavior: for what is tolerated may in each case be different. Devlin's insistence that it is in the nature of a society to possess a community of moral ideas is therefore incompatible with liberalism; and those who find liberalism acceptable must reject the concept of society on which the whole of Devlin's argument rests.

This extraordinary sequence can be derived from Mr. Wollheim's definition of liberalism, quoted above. For him, the question of uniformity of behavior is not evidently of importance, although he discusses it at length. The point of his argument, it would seem, is that in the perspective of liberal political theory the moral code must be permissive, and not enforced. A liberal society, in his sense of the term, could be entirely conformist, as long as its patterns of behavior derived from free choice, and not the coercion of a community insisting on deference to its

49. Id. at 36.

50. Id. at 39.

51. Id. at 38. Surely this point, if I understand it, is illusory verbal play. The most liberal of liberal societies betrays some uniformities of behavior it regards as right: i.e., to abstain from murder or polygamy. The question is, how much uniformity exists? And how much should be enforced by law? Does Mr. Wollheim mean that a monogamous society must allow Mormons or Mohammedans to practice polygamy, in the name of mutual toleration of different moralities, or lose its title to liberalism?

shared fundamental ideas about the organization and conduct of society.

It is apparent that Mr. Wollheim uses the word liberalism
in a most private sense, although he identifies his argument
with the feelings and loyalties normally clustering around
liberalism as a movement in modern thought. His definition would equate "liberalism" with anarchy, and deny all
known societies the title of "liberal," for even those commonly regarded as most liberal have betrayed *some* depar-
tures from the rule of moral permissiveness, in regard to
their toleration of unpunished violence, their rules of family structure, their acquiescence in private or public property, etc.

But even if one were to accept Sir Patrick's idea of society
as a "moral entity," Mr. Wollheim continues, his conception of the moral base of society is "totally irrationalist,"
and excludes "what it has been the triumph of civilisation
to establish: the taming of the conscience by reason."[52]

Mr. Wollheim concludes his article with a paragraph I
find ambiguous.

> Of course the ultimate position may be correct: in the
> history of ideas as many bad arguments have been pro-
> duced for true conclusions as for false ones.
>
> But there may well be those who, reading *The En-
> forcement of Morals,* are led not merely to reject it
> but to reject in advance any argument of a similar kind.
> They may feel that any attempt to draw a line between
> sin and crime that makes reference to notions like the
> moral community or society's unqualified right to self-
> preservation is doomed to be unacceptable, and equal-
> ly that any discussion of the subject that fails to men-

52. Id. at 39.

tion human fallibility and the self-development of the individual and his faculties must be miserably incomplete. To those who feel like this I would lend a sympathetic ear. But I must, regretfully, point out that nothing I have set down here, none of the limited and local argument I have used against Devlin, can increase, to any measurable degree, the authority of what they say.[53]

Read in one perspective, Mr. Wollheim's conclusion may be no more than a warning that what he regards as Devlin's failure to define the relation between crime and morals in terms of notions like the moral community and society's right to self-preservation is hardly proof that others may not in the end succeed. Read in the context of his article, however, with its various concessions and admissions, and its apparent reliance on a narrow definition of liberalism, his final sentences come close to abandoning all that has come before, including the version of liberalism he has espoused; for he approaches the view that an entirely permissive morality is untenable and that the relation of crime and morals must in the end be described and defined in terms of notions like the moral community and society's right to self-preservation, that is, in terms of the notions with which Sir Patrick has built his argument. Only an anarchist, Mr. Wollheim says, could deny the inherent right of society to protect itself against destruction, but that right is "acceptable only when 'self-preservation' is understood in a far narrower sense than that in which it figures in Devlin's argument."[54]

In part, Mr. Wollheim's argument rests on a rather care-

53. Id. at 40.
54. Ibid.

less and airy reading of Sir Patrick's text.[55] For the rest, what he seems to be expressing is the fear that Sir Patrick would weigh the elements of judgment differently from the way in which he would do so, in deciding when legal intervention to enforce morals is permissible. Since Sir Patrick is painfully the judge in refusing to indicate how the interplay of principle should be determined in a given situation by the lawmakers, I can see no justification for Mr. Wollheim's alarm, as a matter of reasoning from Sir Patrick's text. The alarm seems rather to proceed from an emotional reaction to some of the language Sir Patrick uses, and to the embellishments mentioned on pp. 56–59 as extrinsic to his theme.

Mr. Wollheim makes another point, charging Sir Patrick with inconsistency.

> For we are told at one point (in answer to the second question) that society has an unlimited right to enforce morality and then we are told later on (in answer to the third question) that there are certain conditions—conditions, it is true, capable only of very vague formulation—under which society ought not to enforce morality. But if "right" here is used to mean "right," and "ought" here is used to mean "ought," how can the argument taken as a whole avoid the charge of self-contradiction?[56]

Part of Mr. Wollheim's difficulty here is that both he and Sir Patrick sin against the pure canon of Hohfeldian termi-

---

55. The principles of lawmaking, discussed supra at pp. 52–56, for example, are barely mentioned in Mr. Wollheim's article, save as "vague and imprecise" ideas. Nor can I see any justification, in the light of those principles, for arguing that Sir Patrick's concept of society's right of self-preservation would apply as rigorously to amelioration as to corruption, and should thus be invoked against all change. See Wollheim at 40.

56. Wollheim at 36–37.

nology. But very few theorists of law, and even fewer judges, customarily use Hohfeld's analysis of the familiar legal terms right, duty, privilege, power, and their correlatives and opposites. The sin is so common, save among the faithful at Yale, that we had better ignore it as charitably as possible. The correct Hohfeldian way of putting Sir Patrick's thesis, I should think, would be to say that the state has the "power" to protect its public morality through the law; that the citizen has no "immunity" against such action; that the state, however, is under the "duty" in exercising its "power" to enforce and respect certain equally real "rights" and "privileges" of its citizens, in accordance with the principles governing British lawmaking to which he addressed so considerable a part of his lecture; and that in some instances the state may have a "disability," or perhaps may not have the "privilege" to qualify these rights and privileges of the citizen even in the name of self-defense.[57]

The point of verbal usage aside, however, I find that Mr. Wollheim's attack fails, in the terms in which he puts it. I cannot read Sir Patrick's lecture, as Mr. Wollheim apparently does, to assert that society's "right," or, as I should prefer, its "power," to enforce morality is "unlimited," or that Sir Patrick adheres to a theory of distinctions which prefers one criterion of distinction to many. Sir Patrick does say that society's "right" to defend itself is "theoretically" unlimited save by the application in various circumstances of "elastic" and "practical" principles of personal freedom, toleration, and privacy, by awareness of the limitations and dangers of law enforcement, by a strict rule that the law ought to interfere with the individual's moral freedom only in extreme

57. Wesley N. Hohfeld, "Some Fundamental Legal Conceptions as Applied in Judicial Reasoning," 23 *Yale L. J.* 16 (1913), reprinted in *Fundamental Legal Conceptions and other Essays by Wesley Newcomb Hohfeld* (Cook ed. 1923). Prof. Hart is of course an enthusiastic contemporary Hohfeldian.

cases, etc. Taking Sir Patrick's vocabulary in its setting, and reading his lecture as a whole, it seems quite unjustified to stress his distinction between "theoretical" and "practical" limits as proof that he regards his principles governing lawmakers as weak, insignificant, and subordinate factors in the legal process. At intervals in his article, indeed, Mr. Wollheim concedes as much. For at times he concludes, as I do, that in Sir Patrick's analysis the principles which control the enforcement of morals by law are also part of the common morality, derived from aspects of experience and aspiration as profound as those which determine a society's attitude toward property, sex, and violence.

## IV

I should conclude, therefore, that both Professor Hart and Mr. Wollheim wind up in the grip of Sir Patrick's essential argument: that any society possesses a common morality, which it is empowered to enforce according to the modalities of its own legal system. Both of the Judge's critics seem to fear that his views would justify democratic authoritarianism, encouraging the majority to enlarge the area of public morality and narrow the area of private affairs. I can find nothing in Sir Patrick's argument to support this threat. The balance between order and freedom, as he presents it, is still a balance, depending upon the weight given by detached and "reasonable" lawmakers to a series of principles of equal dignity. Because Sir Patrick puts Point Three of his argument third is hardly a reason for inferring that he regards it as less important than Points One and Two.

In perspective, Sir Patrick is far from a Hobbesian. His stress on the principles which limit the power of the state to act in the enforcement of morals puts him rather in the main line of English liberal political theory, which extends from Hooker and Locke to Mill and beyond, a tradition which regards the utmost possible liberty for the individual as the first goal of political action, without denying the existence of the state or its right to exist.

I have deferred to the conclusion a theme which runs through both these critiques of Sir Patrick Devlin's lecture: that he bows to an irrational or subjective view of the common morality and does not insist that "reason" should triumph at all costs over the emotional feelings of man. It is a strange criticism to hear made in this post-Freudian age, which has been forced, as man has rarely been required to do before in his history, to acknowledge the power of the irrational in human affairs. It is a strange criticism to meet in an intellectual universe which has long had the advantage of a literature which includes Montesquieu and Sir Henry Maine, Max Weber, Durkheim, Ehrlich, Spencer, and Buckle. And it is a strange criticism to confront in England, where the risk of majoritarian tyranny is minimized by custom and the temper of the people, not by a written constitution and a Supreme Court. Sir Patrick does not yield to his critics in his stress on the need for calm and dispassionate deliberation as a binding rule which lawmakers are obliged to respect, nor does he ignore the ways in which popular prejudices and popular views of moral problems change with time. To me, he seems clearly right in stating as a fact that the common morality of a society at any time is a blend of custom and conviction, of reason and feeling, of experience and prejudice. A page of history, to recall Holmes' famous quip, may not be worth a volume of logic; but in the life of the law, especially in a common law country, the customs, the common views, and the habitual patterns of the people's behavior properly count for much.

The stress on custom as a source of law, so characteristic

of our legal order, hardly implies that reason has no place in law or that law is no more than a passive register of social history. The law changes, as the society changes its notions of what it wants to achieve through law; and in that process it has been the pride of law to lead as often as it has followed. The distinction between the "rational" and the "irrational" in the process of forming moral opinion—and indeed, in reaching other conclusions as well—is probably impossible to establish with any rigor. But nothing in Sir Patrick's lecture would weaken the primary importance of detached and dispassionate scholarship, conducted at the highest level of reasonableness we can attain, in the work of social reform and the reform of law.

Perhaps the point is easier to accept if we view the problem of enforcing morals not in the perspective of criminal law, which deals with prohibited conduct, but in that of more affirmative action to accomplish moral purposes through law. Men often say that one cannot legislate morality. I should say that we legislate hardly anything else. All movements of law reform seek to carry out certain social judgments as to what is fair and just in the conduct of society. What is an old-age pension scheme but an enforcement of morality? Does not the income tax, for all its encrusted technicality, embody a moral judgment about the fairness of allocating the costs of society in accordance with ability to pay? What other meaning can be given to legislation about education and trade unions, betting, public housing, and a host of other problems?

To accept the proposition that law is founded on a collective code of common morality does not weaken the individual's responsibility for reaching moral judgments and his obligation to help see them fulfilled. That view of law does not diminish the burden of freedom for man, nor permit him to retreat into blind, subjective deference to the code of his tribe. There is nothing in Sir Patrick Devlin's formulation, or in sociological jurisprudence generally, to prevent "the law that is" from evolving into the law we think it ought to become, or to make the serious student of ethics yield without a struggle to the prejudices of the man on the Clapham omnibus.

# PART II

*The Nature and Legitimacy of*
*Judicial Review*

# 3

# *The Court and Its Critics*

THE PEOPLE ARE the ultimate guardians of the Constitution, not the judges alone, or the other public officials
who take their oath to defend it. I am certain that the people
are loyal to the system of government which has served us
well since 1789. They want to live under its protection, and
seek through the arrangements of law to fulfill its promise.
But the people cannot do their part in the constitutional
process unless they understand it. It is therefore a matter of
the utmost importance that the people know about the
Constitution and its history, and about the way in which it
has been interpreted and applied, decade after decade, as
the basic law of a vast, complex, and dynamic society.

In the climate of a democracy, I hope it will never be
enough for those whom we have chosen to govern us to say:
"Obey us, for we are the law. Hold your peace, and do what
you are told to do by a policeman, a judge, or a legislature."
We are a law-abiding people. We know that order is one of
the necessary conditions for freedom under law. We obey
the authorities about as faithfully as most other people. But
we want to know—we have the right to know—why the law
we must obey is what it is. We want to be satisfied that the
law we must obey is right, or is on the way to becoming

Public lecture given under the auspices of the Houston Bar Association
at Houston, Texas, in 1959, and published in 4 *South Texas Law Journal*
160 (1959).

right. For us, law is more than a command, although it is of course also a command. Law is an appeal, too, an appeal to our sense of justice and to the ultimate and continuing values of our constitutional tradition. Above all, the law is a creation for which we are finally responsible, as citizens and electors. No matter how firmly the task of interpreting the law is delegated in the first instance to courts and legislatures, there is no escape in a democracy from the citizen's burden of saying the last word. Too often in recent years we have tended to slight that responsibility and leave the tasks of law to our judges alone.

The tradition of community responsibility is the basis for the common law. And the common law is the matrix of our constitutional law, providing its atmosphere, its modes of action, and the creative vigor with which it defines the role of judges.

The very phrase "common law," or customary law, bespeaks the sovereignty in lawmaking of the people, not the king or his judges. In one sense, the common law is no more than a library of judicial decisions and opinions and the methods by which they are written. Through these opinions, judges seek to perceive, to express, and to enforce the customs and aspirations of the communities they serve. They do this in the course of settling disputes among people, and between people and the state. It is their duty to adjudicate such disputes in ways which reflect and further the community's common sense of justice.

But the judges lead the community's sense of justice as they follow it. They represent a stubborn legal tradition, and have never hesitated to assert its values and its ideas of fairness, both in procedure and in result. And part of the ancient, common custom of the community, the first source of the law, is that in its turn the community treats the considered opinions of learned judges with great respect, and hesitates to reverse them. Loyal as our people have been to the judges, however, they have often differed with them, and altered the law in consequence. Thus they add statutes or other legislative acts to the content of the common law, guiding the work of the judges and controlling it.

This vast and slowly moving body of precedents, statutes, and customs, shot through with the law's own distinct heritage of techniques and purposes, provides society with its organizing principle. That scheme or structure of powers and rights, of duties and privileges, defines and orders the relation of man to man, and of man to the government. It is intended both to change and to remain constant: to change, as new social needs and forces emerge and have their impact on the common customs of the community; to remain constant, in the sense that the community adheres to its ideal of law, which in itself grows and develops as it is tested and applied in situation after situation. For us, the ideal of law and of its aspirations is best summed up in the parts of the Constitution dealing with civil, personal, religious, and political rights.

Perhaps the most dramatic illustration of the thought that the law rests on the shared values of the community and its culture is our judges' habits in writing opinions. In this regard, the Anglo-American law is quite different from that of the Continental countries, where the law is more directly Roman in its forms. In England, in the United States, and in the countries of the British Commonwealth, the judges write long, personal opinions—essays on the law—good or bad as the case may be, but highly individual and often illuminating. They dissent quite freely from majority judgments. Their opinions frequently provide a revealing view of the process by which the law grows, in its common law way, from case to case. In France and Italy, the courts' opinions are usually brief, arid, and without much argument.

Normally, they present the results of cases as the inevitable, logical consequences of provisions in the statutes, concealing or minimizing the element of personal choice which is an inescapable part of the course of judgment.

Law students and lawyers sometimes come to feel, as they slowly drown in the sea of judicial verbiage, that the writing of opinions is a custom developed for their special torture. But there is more to it than that. Opinion-writing is a peculiar and powerful aspect of our legal system, reflecting something beyond even Jefferson's "decent respect to the opinions of mankind."

You will find the habit codified in many state constitutions or statutes requiring the judges to write opinions explaining their decisions in every case. Occasionally, indeed, judges are required to file written opinions before the state treasurer can pay their salaries.

Sometimes the rule is thought to have a prudential value: lazy or stupid judges may be shamed by the requirement into doing their work more faithfully. Indeed, Jefferson himself, as President, affronted by the overpowering influence of Marshall, urged that the Justices of the Supreme Court be required to write individual opinions in each case, as was the general practice in England. The mind of a lawyer totters at the thought of the extra libraries of books we should have had to house and to read had Jefferson's thought prevailed. But it is easy to understand Jefferson's fury. What he harshly called Marshall's habit of "caucusing opinions in secret," and delivering them "as if unanimous, with the silent acquiescence of lazy or timid judges," enraged him. How could we impeach judges, wrote Jefferson, "if a crafty Chief Judge sophisticates the law to his own mind," and smothers the evidence on which an impeachment might be based?[1] Every judge should write his own

1. 2 Warren, *The Supreme Court in United States History* 113–14 (1922).

opinion, Jefferson urged, to "prove by his reasoning that he has read the papers, that he has considered the case, that in the application of the law to it, he uses his own judgment independently and unbiased by party views and personal favor or disfavor."[2]

We can sympathize with the great President in his frustration. No more striking instance of our genius for checks and balances can be imagined than the Jefferson era, with its Federalist Supreme Court. It was galling for Jefferson, at the height of his influence, to confront the serene and magisterial power of Marshall, who spoke like an oracle and shaped the confederation to his broad concept of a strong national government superimposed upon a system of strong states. Jefferson's irritation as President induced him, at least in the passions of the moment, to alter the favorable opinions of the Court's role in judicial review he had expressed earlier, and led him into the naïveté of suggesting that those with whom he differed must have been corrupt. It was foolish to imagine that a multiplication of opinions could have protected the Court against the authority of Marshall's mind and person. Marshall was one of the great architects of the nation, delineating in broad strokes the view of its powers which has survived in the main to this day. John Randolph of Roanoke said of one of his opinions, "All wrong, all wrong, but no man in the United States can tell why or wherein."[3]

But however misguided Jefferson was in his faith in written opinions, there are several other aspects of the custom I should like to mention. The written opinion is of course a technical document, settling a law suit. It is designed to explain to the litigants why their rights were de-

2. Id. at 114.
3. Cardozo, *Law and Literature* 11 (1931).

termined as they were, and to guide lawyers in their practice as to the relationship between the future of a particular
branch of law and its past. The courts' opinions are the
heart and soul of the common law method of legal growth.
The law gropes its way forward, sometimes slowly, sometimes in great leaps, as the judges seek to accommodate the
changeless ultimates of the legal heritage to the changing
circumstances of historical motion.

Beyond that function, the opinion is a piece of rhetoric
and of literature, intended to educate and persuade. In
the clearest possible way, it represents the conception of
the judges speaking directly to the people, as participants
in an endless public conversation on the nature and purposes of law in all its applications. It recognizes the special
responsibility of judges, appointed for a time as delegates
of the people, charged with the duty of doing justice to the
men before them, as spokesmen for the people of their
common or customary conception of law.

Justice Cardozo once said, "I am told at times by friends
that a judicial opinion has no business to be literature. The
idol must be ugly, or he may be taken for a common man.
The deliverance that is accepted without demur or hesitation must have a certain high austerity which frowns at
winning graces."[4] The Judge then devoted the balance of
one of his most appealing lectures to denying this thesis.
He showed that literary power in the writing of opinions
was of the utmost importance to the law. The judge, he said,
is seeking to adapt law to justice. "He is expounding a science, or a body of truth which he seeks to assimilate to a
science, but in the process of exposition he is practising an
art."[5]

It can do us nothing but good to acknowledge the fact

4. Id. at 1.
5. Id. at 40.

that conscientious judges, however cautious, inevitably make law, case by case, and do not merely find it in the skies or in the books. They make law as judges, not as legislators. As judges in the common law mold, they fit the past to the present and the future, drawing on their insights and their knowledge of public affairs to separate the essential from the nonessential, the ultimate from superficial, in the interpretation of statutes and precedents, and the accommodation of clashes between the Constitution and inferior levels of law. In a free society, we do not want, or at least we should not want to worship idols or symbols, ugly or beautiful. We have long since grown past the notion that because judges wear robes or wigs there are statues or demigods on the bench. Judges are men, speaking as men, conscientious men, by and large, devoted to their duty and discharging it to the best of their ability.

Thus, finally, the reasoned judicial opinion bespeaks a concept of political responsibility in the process of lawmaking and judicial administration. In a society of free men, a court's views of the law have to be accepted, rejected, or modified by the sober second thought of their successors and of the community. The judges must write down their reasons for a decision because they are partners with us, the citizenry, in an agreed procedure for reaching responsible decisions. The written opinion is therefore not the last, but the first stage of the debate. In this perspective, the judges are advocates before a greater tribunal which in its turn must settle these issues by its own deliberative procedures—election, or constitutional amendment, or a vote of its representative organs. We do not live under a system of judicial supremacy, as Dean Ribble of the University of Virginia Law School has pointed out elsewhere.[6] In our

6. Ribble, "Judicial Review and the Maintenance of the Federal System," in *Chief Justice John Marshall, a Reappraisal* 61 (W. M. Jones ed. 1956).

universe, the people are supreme, but only when they act through their slow and considered procedures of political decision.

These observations apply to any branch of the law, and not especially to the circumstances which have made for most of the controversy about the Supreme Court of the United States throughout our history. Why, you may well ask, did I start off with such a backward approach to the problems which particularly concern us here? The answer I should give is that while the burning issues of constitutional passion in our lives have often concerned urgent political problems, they all arise of necessity in the context of law suits, to be settled by the methods, according to the rules, of our common law legal pattern, step by empirical step, advancing and retreating, fitting, molding, shaping the law to custom and custom to the immemorial values of the law.

The makers of the Constitution rejected Jefferson's proposal, based on practice in some of the colonies, to have the judges rule on the constitutionality of legislation in advance of its enactment. This plan would have made the Court in fact what it has often been wrongly charged with being: a third chamber of the legislature. Equally, they rejected Edmund Randolph's plan, which would have allowed Congress to veto all state laws passed in contravention of the Constitution. Instead, they adopted the system we have, through which the judicial power they knew and understood—the judicial power of common law courts—was placed in the Supreme Court and such lower courts as Congress might from time to time authorize. The federal courts therefore pass on constitutional questions only in the course of actual cases in litigation before them, and, in the main, only when such cases cannot be settled on any lesser ground. This is a limitation which puts many vital constitutional problems almost beyond reach of judicial settlement, as purely political questions. And it means that many more are considered long after the event, with the benefit of experience and in the light of a concrete factual setting. The rule has been narrowly interpreted, to deny the possibility in the federal system even of advisory opinions, such as are available in many states. It is a rule of strict separation of powers, confining the immense powers of judicial review to the framework of common law routine.

Nor is the problem of responsibility different in kind or in degree in constitutional cases and in those concerned with less exalted branches of law. The people have the same responsibility for the law of property or of bankruptcy that they have for the Bill of Rights. These areas of law, too, arouse strong feelings and cries of judicial usurpation. In these areas, as in all others, the judicial opinion is a plea as well as an order; an argument, not merely a command.

If, then, the common law model for judicial action in constitutional cases is so familiar to us, and so deeply rooted in our entire history as a people, why have we had recurring periods of vehement debate about the decisions of the Supreme Court, and indeed about its right to declare statutes and acts of the executive unconstitutional? The simple answer, I suppose, is that we have a good deal of controversy about the Court because our constitutional system has delegated to it extremely difficult, important, and inherently controversial questions, upon which it must pass in the first instance when they are inescapably presented for adjudication in law suits.

The Constitution of the United States is not a compact of separate sovereign states, but an act of the people. Its very first words are "We the people of the United States"—not "We the legislatures or governments of the several states." It was, and is, the promulgation of a constituent assembly and of special ratifying conventions, not of state legislatures and of governors. It was not even adopted by the amendatory procedures of the Articles of Confederation. It is not a treaty, but a new creative act, a charter emanating directly from the sovereign people. By that Constitution, lines of power are sketched in—delegations are made to the Congress and to the President, to the Supreme Court and to such inferior courts as Congress may establish, and powers not delegated to the organs of national government are reserved to the states or to the people themselves. Through this instrument, as 170 years of history attest, the people look to the courts, and especially to the Supreme Court of the United States, to enforce boundaries of power derived by them from the Constitution, against Congress and the President, governors and state legislatures, generals and erring judges, great trade unions, corporations, or other private groups seeking to exercise governmental power. Every federal system has faced the same problem, that of enforcing limitations on delegated authority. Many of them have adopted our solution—Australia, Canada, Western Germany, and the new European Economic Community, most notably.

The Supreme Court has always been required to pass on another class of questions as well—that of protecting the constitutional rights of the individual against both the state and the power of a transient majority. From the earliest days of the Republic, those closest to our political life have feared our capacity for political passion, and sought forms of protection for the isolated individual, and the minority without political power, against "the despotism of the many." Our Constitution, James Russell Lowell once said, is an obstacle to the "whim, but not to the will of the people."[7]

---

7. 3 Warren, *The Supreme Court in United States History* 473 (1922).

## The Court and Its Critics

Much popular and even professional misunderstanding of the work of the Supreme Court derives from the fact that in carrying out these functions the Court must sometimes declare acts of state or national government unconstitutional. In the settling of a particular law suit, it may be required to evaluate what has been done in the light of the language, history, and apparent purposes of a constitutional provision. Such decisions are almost always the starting point for the charge, frequently heard in our history, that the judges are meddling in politics and substituting their views of policy for those of the elected organs of government. In its simplest form, the thesis was answered in the *Federalist* papers, by de Tocqueville in his great book on American democracy, and by lesser writers at intervals since. But the issue survives.

In deciding a constitutional case, the Court must deal with the policy of a constitutional provision. It must decide whether the act of the legislature or of the executive called into question before it is authorized by the Constitution, which has higher authority as an act of the people. The political content of the judge's work is therefore to interpret and enforce the broad intention of the Constitution. That task is rarely easy, since few provisions of the Constitution are beyond ambiguity. And it often has a political character. Judges and others have held differing views as to the purpose of particular articles of the Constitution. As Chief Justice Hughes once said, there is no reason to expect more unanimity on difficult problems of law than in the higher reaches of physics, philosophy, or theology. For our purposes, however, the point is clear: there is a political element in constitutional interpretation, requiring a judge to be thoroughly steeped in the history and public life of the country. This is the reason why so many of our finest Justices, like Marshall, Taney, and Hughes, came to the Court from active political life. But this political element in constitutional interpretation does not turn, and certainly should not turn, merely on personal or partisan or idiosyncratic views of politics, but on the differences serious men might well have in seeking to understand and apply the spirit and language of a Constitution intended to last for centuries.

Let me recall a famous example. After the Civil War, Congress and several states passed test oath laws, which would have barred many callings to men who could not swear that they had not participated in the rebellion. Such laws would have deepened the wounds of war and delayed the healing process of union. They would have denied the nation several Justices of the Supreme Court, Attorneys General, and other distinguished public servants. The Supreme Court declared such laws unconstitutional as bills of attainder and ex post facto laws, "substituting" their judgment, in the popular phrase, for that of elected legislatures, and interfering with legislative control over membership in the bar and other licensed callings. The cases turned on the meaning the judges found in the idea behind the constitutional prohibition against ex post facto laws, that is, of retroactive punishment, and in the prohibition of bills of attainder—an ancient form of legislative punishment, of which impeachment is perhaps the only significant survival. Bills of attainder had been used notoriously in political cases, and were entirely forbidden by the Constitution, both to the nation and to the states. While *Ex parte Garland* required some creative and imaginative law on the part of the Supreme Court, there being no prior cases of much similarity, I can assure you that when it was made the decision was popular in this part of the nation.[8]

8. 4 Wall. 333 (U.S., 1866). The dissent of four Justices castigated the Court for weakening the protection of the nation against disloyalty and in-

All this is familiar, yet difficult to accept: it is often said, and deeply resisted. Legislators and governors, Congressmen and Presidents, are proud and powerful men. They find it hard, as Jefferson did, as both Presidents Roosevelt did, as Lincoln and Jackson did, to bow before decisions of the Supreme Court when that Court denies them powers they passionately believe were conferred upon them by election. If they are reminded that the Supreme Court is the umpire of the federal system, they answer that it is changing the rules, usurping the function of the players, and refusing to call fouls.

## II

Against this general background, I propose now to take up some of the recent criticisms which have been leveled against the Supreme Court.

I shall put to one side those few voices, less often heard with each passing day, which still valiantly repeat the arguments of Calhoun—that the Constitution is a treaty among sovereign states, and therefore that the states, or rather their legislatures, are to be the final judges of their own powers and those of the national government. These echoes of nullification and of interposition, which were once as popular in Hartford, Connecticut, as in Charleston, South Carolina, are denied by the massive weight of our experience as a united people. As the distinguished Vice President and former Senator from Texas, Lyndon Johnson, said in the Senate, in a speech of great power and feeling, "We are

terfering with the power of Congress and of the states to fix proper qualifications for the practice of professions. This decision, and its companion cases, were violently attacked in the North. Impeachment was the mildest relief mentioned in speeches and newspapers of the time.

all sons of Appomattox." He might well have added that we are all also sons of Lexington and Concord, of Midway and Iwo Jima, and of the Constitutional Convention at Philadelphia. The arguments of nullification are yielding, I am happy to observe, to the silent power of our history.

But critics who fully accept the main principles of the Constitution have also spoken out, and spoken out strongly, against the trend of recent decisions. The respected Chief Justice of Texas joined thirty-five other state supreme court chief justices last summer, at the annual meeting of the Conference of Chief Justices, in a protest against what they deemed a dangerous development in Supreme Court adjudication.

They resolved as follows:

> 2. That in the field of federal-state relationships the division of powers between those granted to the national government and those reserved to the state governments should be tested solely by the provisions of the Constitution of the United States and the Amendments thereto.
>
> 3. That this Conference believes that our system of federalism, under which control of matters primarily of national concern is committed to our national government and control of matters primarily of local concern is reserved to the several states, is sound and should be more diligently preserved.
>
> 4. That this Conference, while recognizing that the application of constitutional rules to changed conditions must be sufficiently flexible as to make such rules adaptable to altered conditions, believes that a fundamental purpose of having a written constitution is to promote the certainty and stability of the provisions of law set forth in such a constitution.

5. That this Conference hereby respectfully urges that the Supreme Court of the United States, in exercising the great powers confided to it for the determination of questions as to the allocation and extent of national and state powers, respectively, and as to the validity under the federal Constitution of the exercise of powers reserved to the states, exercise one of the greatest of all judicial powers—the power of judicial self-restraint—by recognizing and giving effect to the difference between that which, on the one hand, the Constitution may prescribe or permit, and that which, on the other, a majority of the Supreme Court, as from time to time constituted, may deem desirable or undesirable, to the end that our system of federalism may continue to function with and through the preservation of local self-government.[9]

These resolutions rested on a report of the Conference's Committee on Federal-State Relationships as affected by Judicial Decisions, of which Chief Judge Brune of Maryland was chairman. This report—I shall refer to it hereafter as the Brune Report for convenience—was approved by the resolution of the Conference. The Committee had commissioned five lengthy research memoranda by members of the law faculty of the University of Chicago. While these papers were not available in time to have been discussed before the Conference last summer, as had been planned, the judges passed a resolution of appreciation to the authors, attesting that their research papers were "of inestimable value to the Committee in the preparation of its own report."[10] This is curious, since the Chicago pro-

9. The Report is conveniently reprinted in the *Harvard Law Record* of Oct. 23, 1958.

10. 8 University of Chicago, *The Law School Record, Special Supplement* 2 (1958).

fessors' monographs do not in any way support the conclusions of the Brune Report.

While there have been other important criticisms of the Court recently, the Brune Report recapitulates most of the ideas which have been expressed in the course of the current debate about the Court. By reason of the eminence and sobriety of its authors, I think their carefully considered report is a convenient focal point for the balance of my remarks.

The Brune Report, like many collective papers, shows the trace of several pens. That it is not altogether consistent makes it a more human and revealing document, not necessarily a weaker one.

The Brune Report is concerned with the effect of recent Supreme Court decisions, viewed against the background of acts of Congress and of federal administrative agencies, on the distribution of power between the national government and the government of the several states. It recognizes the necessity for entrusting part of the power to pass on these questions to the Supreme Court of the United States. It fully accepts the necessity for men to obey the law, and to respect it, until it is properly changed.

Here one of the first ambiguities of the Brune Report emerges, at least for me. It is not clear to this reader whether the judges are urging important changes in the law governing important classes of situations, or only criticizing the Supreme Court for moving in the right general direction, but too fast. The Report recognizes that the common law judicial process necessarily involves an element of policy-making—that is, of judicial legislation—on the part of judges who must choose between alternative rules in deciding a case or frame a new one, if no suitable rule exists or can be adapted for the purpose. If they are criticizing the Court for moving too fast, they ignore the Court's limited control of its docket. Despite some modern leeway, it must decide most of the cases brought before it.

The Brune Report also recognizes that the distribution of powers in a federal system necessarily involves uncertainty, and that the Supreme Court has had different views on the scope of Congress' power over interstate commerce, and other issues basic to federalism, in the course of its history. Here a second ambiguity emerges. The Brune Report says the Court has gone too far in assuming a policy-making role, or at least has done so unnecessarily and without proper judicial restraint. While the authors of the Brune Report acknowledge the lawmaking element in our common law method of deciding constitutional cases, they also criticize the Court for acting "legislatively"—that is, for assuming primarily legislative rather than judicial powers in lawmaking. It is not clear to me whether they intend this charge. Their Report seems to say both that the Court has gone beyond the proper and acknowledged limits of judicial legislation in interpreting the Constitution, and, less severely, that the judges who signed the Report take a different view of some of the constitutional provisions. The Report concludes by deploring the pace of change in constitutional law, the Court's willingness to overrule precedents, and the multiplicity of dissenting and concurring opinions on the Court, thus bringing Jefferson's criticism of the Court to full circle.

The central question with which the Report is concerned is the distribution of power between state and nation. Its central concern is the future of the federal system. Its central fear is that we are witnessing the euthanasia of the states as effective and vital centers of political power in the United States. The Report recognizes that changing technology, the facts of economic life, and the impact of our international situation have greatly increased, and inevitably increased the importance of the national government in our public life. It rightly stresses the importance of dividing and dispersing power among the autonomous institutions of society if we are to remain a community capable of freedom. As Mr. Justice Brandeis once said, "The doctrine of the separation of powers was adopted by the Convention of 1787, not to promote efficiency but to preclude the exercise of arbitrary power. The purpose was not to avoid friction, but, by means of the inevitable friction incident to the distribution of the governmental powers among three departments, to save the people from autocracy."[11]

While I fully share the judges' loyalty to, and interest in, the preservation of the states as strong and vigorous governmental units, I cannot agree with them that either the nature of the times or the decisions of the Supreme Court in recent years have in fact weakened the states or greatly altered their relationship to the national government. We remain a nation of the One and of the Many. The One is strong, as it must be strong, in a turbulent, dangerous world. But the Many are strong too. You have only to look at any state budget to see the growth in authority of state governments, the number of functions now being performed, and on the whole better performed than ever before, to realize that they have shared with the national government in an expansion of duty which the people now expect from all government. Roads and education, hospitals and welfare plans, conservation and mental health, correction and law enforcement, redevelopment and industrial control—can anyone say that the state governments are withering on the vine in all these areas?

Ah yes, the critics say, but in all these areas the work of the states is subject to ultimate federal control. They are

11. Myers v. United States, 272 U.S. 52, 293 (1926) (dissenting opinion).

not really free, for they must answer to Congress for some things, and to the Supreme Court for others. They share power, and therefore they lose it.

Let us review the main areas the state court judges selected for comment in their Report on recent trends: they concern chiefly the impact of congressional action under the commerce clause, or other of its acknowledged powers, on the validity of state action in the same field; and on the steady evolution of the due process and equal protection clauses of the Fourteenth Amendment as criteria with which the states must comply in exercising their authority.

The Brune Report concludes that the Supreme Court has expanded national power, and correspondingly contracted the powers of the states, by assuming legislative authority and acting without judicial restraint. The Court might be charged with one sin or the other, but not with both. The criticisms of the Brune Report are not supported by the evidence. The Supreme Court has not by its own legislative act enlarged the powers of the nation and contracted those of the states. On the contrary, with great restraint it has allowed both the nation and the states increasing latitude both to regulate and to tax, and chosen for itself, at the cost of a great deal of hard work, a difficult policy of accommodating and conciliating the exercise of national and of state legislative powers, leaving as much authority as possible to the states. Similarly, in applying the Fourteenth Amendment to state licensing statutes, to the hiring and firing of state employees, and to state criminal proceedings, the Court has not restricted state power. It has only insisted, in Professor Freund's phrase, that under the Fourteenth Amendment the states should "turn square corners" in dealing with sensitive areas of human liberty, by following procedures consistent with due process of law.[12]

12. Freund, *The Supreme Court of the United States* 87 (1961).

## Judicial Review

The expansion of federal power, and the contraction of state power, can occur in two ways: either through congressional action, with the permission of the Supreme Court as interpreter of Congress' constitutional authority, or through Supreme Court denial of power to the states.

As we all know, since 1937 the Supreme Court has allowed Congress almost as complete freedom as Marshall did in exercising its powers over interstate commerce. Congressional action is the main source of expanding federal authority in government. Are the authors of the Brune Report reproaching the Supreme Court not for judicial self-restraint, but for a lack of self-restraint, in failing to curb Congress in its various legislative experiments in the field of business, protection against subversives, etc.? They cannot have it both ways. Congress, and not the Court, has moved to act in many areas of authority which have long been dormant and unused. Before this trend, the Court has been not only restrained, but almost passive.

When Congress has acted in a field—in the regulation of navigation, or grain warehouses, or sedition, or labor relations, to take a few examples—the Supreme Court has two choices: it can regard state legislation in the same field as completely suspended, in deference to national action, or it can seek to accommodate the two systems, holding state legislation ineffective only when it is *inconsistent* with the national law. Congress can always settle the matter by providing in the statute it passes for the supersession or retention of state law. It rarely does so.

This is one of the most delicate problems in federalism that the Court ever faces. It is almost entirely a problem of interpreting statutes, not the Constitution. And whatever the Court does in this field can always be cured by congressional action, if Congress is so disposed. In certain areas, such as bankruptcy legislation, the Supreme Court has almost invariably suspended state legislation considered to be in the same field as a national statute. In others, like the regulation of navigation, business, or labor, it has sought to preserve as much as possible of the competing legislation of the states.

In the field of labor regulation, the Brune Report tells us, the Supreme Court has produced some uncertainty and confusion, which is as much due to Congress' failure to clarify the law as it is to the Justices' opinions. While this is true, it is probably inevitable, and it is rather unkind of the Brune Report to criticize the Court for the result. The Supreme Court could have suspended state law in this field more broadly in order to effectuate the national labor relations policy of the Congress. Having chosen the course of deferring as much as possible to state law in the field, and giving it as much effect as possible, there was no way for the Court to avoid intricate and complex decisions, matching state and federal laws section by section.

As for state law in the field of sedition against the United States—the much discussed *Nelson* case—it should be noted that in that case the Supreme Court affirmed an excellent opinion by the Supreme Court of Pennsylvania and thus did not remove a power which Pennsylvania claimed in any way. In my opinion, the *Nelson* decision was correct. It is amply supported by prior authority: no cases were overruled to reach the result. And it clears the way for effective and efficient protection against sedition. It should serve the desirable purpose of keeping to a minimum the dangerous agitation of public opinion which always arises when the laws seem to make heresy, or unpopular opinion, a crime. We have greatly suffered in this regard in recent years.[13] I can see no reason why action to overthrow the government

13. Experience in this field is well reviewed in Brown, *Loyalty and Security* (1958).

of the United States need be considered a local crime as well as a national one.[14]

In the area of federal-state relations, as the Brune Report concedes, there have been many extensions of state power in recent years. The Supreme Court has been just as generous to the states as to the nation in finding constitutional authority for many forms of regulatory action and taxation. The famous case of *Erie v. Tompkins* in 1938 struck down a century of error, in the courts' phrase, and said that in cases in the federal courts based on diversity of citizenship, there was no federal common law, but that the federal judges must apply the appropriate state law, as construed by the state court judges.[15] In the field of taxation, the state's power to tax interstate and international business has been greatly extended over strong dissents by Justice Frankfurter, whom the state judges regard as the justice most sympathetic to their cause.[16] And in the area of obtaining jurisdiction over out-of-state parties, again the state judges recognize that the Supreme Court has enlarged their powers, not reduced them.

Thus in this area—the consequence of federal legislation to state power, or the various emanations of the commerce clause—the several charges of the Brune Report are not tenable, as the Report itself seems to acknowledge. The Court has exercised painful self-restraint, by and large, in accepting the legislative views of both national and state legislatures. Unless the Brune Report is criticizing the Hughes Court of 1937, its charges fall. The contemporary Supreme Court has been most solicitous of state authority.

14. Compare the careful analysis of Cramton, "Supercession and Subversion," 8 University of Chicago, *Law School Record, Supp.* 24 (1958).

15. Erie R. Co. v. Tompkins, 304 U.S. 64 (1938).

16. Youngstown Sheet & Tube Company v. Bowers, 79 S. Ct. 383 (1959); Northwestern States Portland Cement Co. v. Minnesota, 79 S. Ct. 357 (1959).

The commerce clause of the Constitution, which has gone through several cycles of interpretation in the history of the Court, has never been restored to the stark majesty of Marshall's opinions, which would deny the Court any power to review congressional exercise of the commerce power, as it would never review the exercise of Congress' power to declare war.[17] Congress has great authority over the national economy, as it should. But the states regulate large segments of it too. My own feeling is that in this area the Court often gives the states too much power, not too little. Sometimes it sacrifices the substance to the shadow of federalism, and permits many state-erected protective trade barriers—arrangements which it was one of the great aims of the Constitution to sweep away. Judicial restraint here exposes us to the risk of a Balkanized and over-regulated economy, not a great free continental market.

The other group of cases the Brune Report considers are those arising under the Fourteenth Amendment, where the Court interprets the Amendment as requiring state authorities to meet certain standards of fairness and deliberateness in passing on admissions to the bar, licensing in general, and the administration of criminal justice.

I, for one, cannot understand how it can be seriously urged that the Court's interpretation of the Fourteenth Amendment constitutes an invasion of states' rights, an expansion of federal power, and a contraction of state power. All these cases decide, and say, is that the Constitution demands that the state procedure by which a public employee is hired or fired, or a license is given or denied to a lawyer, a doctor, or a real estate broker should be fair, providing for a notice of charges, an opportunity to be heard, a rational basis of decision, and an opportunity for review of the proceedings in the light of the standards of due process

17. Gibbons v. Ogden 22 U.S. [9 Wheat.] 1 (1824).

and equal protection of the law. Does this go beyond the great case of *Ex parte Garland,* which struck down test oaths after the Civil War? State licensing statutes have multiplied in recent years. No one denies the power of the state to protect itself against badly trained professional people or professional people of poor moral character. What the Court has said, and in my view rightly said, is that state action of this kind, on which a man's reputation and his right to make a living depends, must be conducted by the state in a fair and honorable way. I do not propose to discuss the intricacies of the basis for decision in the two cases which occasioned the outcry. It suffices to say here that in one of the cases, the New Mexico case, all the Justices agreed that there was no evidence in the record to support the state court's conclusion of the man's unfitness to practice law, and in the other, a California case, the California court itself made no statement of the reasons for its decision.[18] Some of the more alarming possibilities opened up by these cases have now been set at rest by later cases.[19] They stand for a sound, old, respectable position—that when the state acts, it must act fairly. It is noteworthy that the Brune Report does not deny this principle, which seems to me to be the essence of true federalism and in no way a threat to it.

In the second area of Fourteenth Amendment cases, that of state criminal law administration, we come to the field where I believe the Supreme Court has done some of its finest work in this century. Here again, the Brune Report differs with the Supreme Court on the outcome or opinions of particular cases, but seems to acknowledge the soundness of what the Supreme Court is in general trying to do.

18. Schware v. Board of Bar Examiners, 353 U.S. 232 (1957); Konigsberg v. State Bar, 353 U.S. 252 (1957).

19. Lerner v. Casey, 357 U.S. 468 (1958); Beilan v. Board of Education, 357 U.S. 399 (1958).

Fifty years ago, President Taft commented that the conduct of our ordinary state court criminal cases was a disgrace to a civilized nation. In the late twenties, the Wickersham Commission, appointed by President Hoover, studied criminal law administration and came to the same conclusion. The Supreme Court began at about that time to assert the view that a criminal conviction obtained in a proceeding marred by notable unfairness should be reversed because the trial itself did not meet the standards of due process of law. This line of cases began in 1932, with *Powell v. Alabama,* the case of the Scottsboro boys, where the Court's opinion was written by one of its most conservative justices, Mr. Justice Sutherland.[20] Since then, term by term, the Court has sought to assert its influence to raise the standards of local police work and of the administration of criminal justice in state courts. Would anyone deny that a conviction based on a confession obtained by third degree methods does not meet the standards of due process of law? That a defendant in a capital case should be represented by counsel? That a jury should be fairly chosen from a group truly representing the community?

It is important in this field to note what the Court has not done—it has not followed Justice Black's urging and imposed the whole federal Bill of Rights on the state courts.[21] It has rather pursued the deliberate line laid down by Justice Cardozo, in seeking to allow the states as much freedom and diversity as possible, as long as their procedures do not violate what the Court considers standards of propriety basic to the life of a civilized society.[22] That line allows the states much latitude. It necessarily requires a large volume of litigation and requires the lower federal

---

20. Powell v. Alabama, 287 U.S. 45 (1932).
21. Adamson v. California, 332 U.S. 46 (1947).
22. Palko v. Connecticut, 302 U.S. 319 (1937).

courts, in habeas corpus proceedings, to review the trials already held in state courts. It means a more confused and less certain body of law than would develop if the Court accepted its only alternative, Justice Black's position, and held the state courts to the rules which prevail in the federal courts. It leads to doubtful and paradoxical results, like the Court's double jeopardy decision—a case which sharply recapitulates the debate within the Court on these momentous problems.[23]

Here again, out of deference to state authority, the Supreme Court is following a course which involves it in a great deal of hard work and leads to a complex body of decisions, necessarily drawing fine lines. The Court has exercised great self-restraint in these cases, and has erred, if at all, on the side of accommodation to the habits of the states. Of course it is offensive to the vanity of state judges that federal district judges and the Supreme Court of the United States sit in judgment on their work. But that continuing oversight in the name of national standards is what we mean by checks and balances. The Court is dealing here with a problem of far-reaching importance, and a problem which is inescapably, and properly, in its province.

In all these cases, the Supreme Court is talking not about state *power,* but about the *procedures* through which power is exercised. These cases take no state powers away. All the Court is doing is to press the state courts and the state legislatures to improve their procedures for the administration of criminal justice, their procedures for licensing, and their procedures for hiring and firing state employees. I can discern no threat to the balance of power between the states and the nation in this slow, arduous, considerate, and creative process.

23. Bartkus v. Illinois, 359 U.S. 121 (1959).

So much, then, for the specific areas the Brune Report covers.

What of its more general charges—that the Court has indulged either in legislation and policy-making, or too much legislation and policy-making? That it has been too divided, and written too many opinions? That it has failed to exercise self-restraint?

When viewed against the background of our common law method for handling constitutional problems, these questions, too, answer themselves. The Court has not sought these cases. They have come before it, the product of troubled times. Many reflect the circumstances of the period through which we are living—the tensions of the Cold War, and the threat of Communism, which have led us, in dealing with novel and difficult problems, to adopt novel and difficult, and often dubious procedures for their solution. The multiplication of cases in some areas—the relation of civil to military authority, for example—derive from the circumstances of two recent wars and the necessity for maintaining large armed forces in a time of uneasy peace. In other areas—labor and criminal law, for example—the large number of cases is the consequence of the fact that the Court has deliberately chosen a course which permits maximum authority to the states. Many of the cases are hard to decide precisely because the Supreme Court has exercised self-restraint and is exceedingly deferential to state power.

So, likewise, with the divided and numerous opinions of the Court. Those opinions are often misunderstood. The area of agreement among the judges is far wider than the area of disagreement. Our Justices are not divided today, as they were in the time of Taft and Hughes, on great substantive issues of constitutional policy. They differ, of course, sometimes on relatively important problems. But usually their dissents are on the applications of agreed rules to particular facts, or on the procedure the Court should follow in enforcing them. In any event, as we have seen, the tradition of writing free, personal, and extensive opinions is an integral and important part of our common law tradition, and Jefferson, at least, thought many opinions were preferable to one.

I cannot see, either in the areas discussed in the Brune Report or elsewhere, any substance in the charge that the Court has gone beyond its own judicial function in handling the policy content of the cases before it. The Brune Report says, "we realize that in the course of American history the Supreme Court has frequently—one might indeed say customarily—exercised policy making powers going far beyond those involved say in making a selection among competing rules of law."[24] The reasons for this tradition are apparent. The primary duty of the Court is to forge the public law of a great nation—to expound a Constitution rooted in the past, bound to it by unbreakable ties of aspiration, but necessarily capable of adaptation to the changing needs of the present and the future. The abiding policies of the Constitution are the main subject matter of the Court's work. They call for a sense of history, and of the realities of our public affairs, what Judge Hutcheson of Texas once called the hunch of intuition about the inner life of American democracy.

So far I have been concerned with a defense of the Court's work, or rather an evaluation of the puzzling and inconsistent conclusions of the Brune Report. I do not wish to be misunderstood as defending every opinion or every decision the Supreme Court has made. It is dealing with a heavy docket of hard and difficult cases. Its disposition of those cases is often debatable. Judges still persist in reaching

24. Brune Committee Report, op. cit. supra note 9, at 4.

the right result for the wrong reasons, and often the wrong result, too, in the eyes of the critics. But the pattern of the Court's work is in the grain of its tradition. There is no substance in the charge that the modern Court has by its own legislative views enlarged the powers of the nation and contracted those of the states. Its contribution to federal-state relations, as distinguished from that of Congress, has been strongly marked, at the cost of much hard work for itself, by a desire to conciliate the friction of state and federal power, leaving as much power as possible to the states. In applying the Fourteenth Amendment to state criminal procedures, the Court has taken a strong and on the whole a most desirable line, in seeking to raise standards of local police action and state court criminal practice. This is work of which the nation should be proud.

The criticisms of the Brune Report, and like criticisms of the Court, are comparatively easy to answer at the level of logic. But their significance is deeper. Through these criticisms, honorable men are uttering a protest which they find it hard to reduce to logical form. It is not so much a protest against the Court as against the tide of social change reflected in the Court's opinions. The law reflects and seeks to control a flow of turbulent movement. It deals with forces of immense power—the desire through governmental action to govern the economy, to assure equality of legal rights for all, to carry out many of the neglected promises of our constitutional tradition. Confronting these insistent pressures, the Court might resist blindly, as it has done from time to time in its history. Or it could move, as it has, to tame and channel these forces as best it can within the framework of our constitutional system. I, for one, believe the course it has chosen is the right one. The alternatives, however appealing to our sense of nostalgia, would risk a complete break with the high values of our past.

## III

The Brune Report did not mention the school segregation cases, the most important of all the sources of present tension in our country about the role and policy of the Supreme Court. These cases, like the others which were mentioned, are the product of a long line of decisions, developing one by one in a common law way. In 1898, the Court decided that separate but equal train facilities met the requirements of the Fourteenth Amendment. Then it began to whittle away at the proposition, in a line of decisions going back at least to 1917. Zoning ordinances, cases about juries and voting lists, places of residence and the use of parks, common carriers, graduate schools, colleges, marked out the path. By 1954, no one who had followed the trend could have anticipated a different outcome when the question of public schools was inescapably presented to the Court. The changing social position of the Negro in American life; his experience during the war; the new light thrown on racial tensions by the ordeal of Hitler and the racism of the Communists; the claims of countries liberated by the war from colonial status—all these forces framed the problem of race relations as it confronts the nation today. But I believe the outcome would have been the same without these external elements.

All men are created equal, the Declaration of Independence says. De Tocqueville's great book on American life starts with the idea of equality, which he rightly considers the key to American democracy. The problem of race relations is a national problem, not a regional one. It is as real in New York or New Haven as it is in Chicago or Little Rock. It is a problem we must resolve as a nation, as we have always resolved our problems, after contemplation and debate, sometimes after suffering and conflict; but in the end by agreement, and not by force alone. These cases have brought trouble, but it is trouble we must face. Imagine, if you will, the trouble we should have faced had the decisions gone the other way.

Let me close by saying what I believe to be true: That every thoughtful observer of the problem recognizes, and recognizes sympathetically, the human difficulties these decisions involve, both for white citizens and for Negro citizens, in many parts of the country—here in the South, and on the South Side of Chicago too; in Harlem; and in the Negro ghettoes of many of our northern cities. We all know that many citizens, South and North alike, believe these decisions are wrong. Yet, as a practical matter, they cannot be reversed by constitutional amendment, by congressional action, or by prospective changes in the composition of the Court. They are the law, since no majority can be imagined to undo them.

The next stages of this debate will be a test of our maturity and of our capacity for self-government. It will be a debate. It is a debate. In that debate, we must reason with each other as brothers, those who believe as I do that the Court was right, and those who believe it was wrong. Out of that reasoning, a consensus will emerge. The debate cannot be left to the judges or even to the lawyers alone. Forums like this one are important steps in the process of decision.

I am certain that in the end the force of the ideal will prevail in this debate—the force, that is, of the body of principles represented by the Declaration of Independence and the Constitution. These principles have been the strongest power in American history, stronger than the power of money or envy, of fear or of hate. May it always be so.

# 4

# *The Supreme Court and the People's Will*

TOWARD THE END of the war, the German authorities ordered the Vichy government to build an aircraft factory in a cave near a small and remote French village. The French engineers assigned to the job were as painstaking, as meticulous—and as slow—as they dared be. They constructed elaborate ventilating systems, extensive dining rooms, and other arrangements for the welfare and safety of the working force. At length, when they could delay no longer, they began to make aircraft. Each stage of the project was of course known to the local leaders of the Resistance and reported fully by them to Allied headquarters in London. As the first machines were at last loaded on trucks and started toward their destinations, they were ambushed in a forest and destroyed. In reprisal, the German army commander ordered fifty villagers picked by lot and had them shot.

A few weeks later, in midsummer 1944, as the tide of war turned, the French underground forces of the neighborhood captured the German garrison. Strong voices urged

Lecture at a Forum on "The Supreme Court in the American Constitutional System," University of Notre Dame Law School, 1958; published in 33 *Notre Dame Lawyer* 573 (1958).

that at least fifty German soldiers be executed in turn. There were plausible arguments of international law for such a course: that the factory and its work violated the armistice agreement and that the shooting of the villagers breached the laws of war. But one of the leaders of the group was a retired colonel of the regular army. After a long night's debate, his view prevailed. The men of the Maquis, he said, were soldiers of France. And the French Army did not kill its prisoners.

This episode illustrates much of what I propose to say. It is an instance in which the authority of the law, in some recognizable sense, prevailed over the passionate will of an aroused majority. Democracy was revealed as a process more complex than the taking of a single vote. And the law was vindicated, as it must be finally vindicated in a society of consent, not merely as a command—for here the colonel had no power to command—but as an appeal to what every man knew, at the decisive level of his own consciousness, was his own culture's vision of the right.

In this situation, the normal social machinery of order had almost completely broken down. It was being re-established as quickly as the pride and habits of a people long accustomed to government could put it together. But on that heated summer night in the village square, which had witnessed so much over the centuries, under the statue of some marshal or poet or minister of France, the angry men of the Maquis yielded unwillingly to their own ideal of law. The spokesman for the law was a man whose opinion had some symbolic meaning for his audience by reason of his status. But a retired colonel in his hunting clothes hardly represented either the dignity of a court or the coercive power of the state.

The subject with which I am concerned is the function of the Supreme Court of the United States in our system of government. We are experiencing another in the long cycle of political attacks on the integrity of the Court—the most serious since the Court-packing proposals of 1937. I believe that these attacks represent a challenge to the very possibility of survival of our constitutional system as an institution for assuring the free government of free men.

In deciding constitutional cases the judges must not only interpret the law and find the law, but make law too, as surely as they make law when they decide cases of tort, contract, or corporations. In a passage often quoted, Holmes once said, "I recognize without hesitation that judges do and must legislate, but they can do so only interstitially; they are confined from molar to molecular motions."[1] And one recalls Jeremiah Smith's pungent remark, after he left the Supreme Court of New Hampshire for the Harvard Law faculty: "Do judges make law? Of course they do. Made some myself." There is no tangible meaning in the charge often advanced that the Supreme Court is not interpreting the Constitution but acting as a super-legislature when it changes its views and reverses old cases. The Court's opinions may be good or bad as constitutional law—good or bad, that is to say, as projections and applications of what the Court conceives to be the purposes and ends of the Constitution. But no valid distinction of kind can be drawn between the interpretive and the creative aspects of the judicial process in constitutional law or in any other branch of the law. This is not to say that the judges arrogate to themselves functions of the Congress or of the people in their creative reading of the Constitution. Such action on their part is an indistinguishable and inevitable part of their work as judges.

The topic I shall discuss is the propriety of this activity

1. Southern Pac. Co. v. Jensen, 244 U.S. 205, 221 (1917) (dissenting opinion).

in a community which regards itself as a democracy. How can a society of majority rule condone the exercise of such far-reaching power by judges who are appointed for life? Is it true, as many have said, that the role of the Supreme Court in construing the Constitution makes it an oligarchic or aristocratic excrescence on our Constitution, to be abolished if possible, or at the least restricted to the narrowest possible jurisdiction?

This issue has been a matter of debate throughout our national history, and it is being vehemently debated today. Anxiety on this score has colored the temper in which some of our best judges have approached their work. Many have found in this issue a paradox impossible to reconcile with their faith as democrats.

I do not propose here to review the earlier stages of the controversy, nor to take an apologetic or a defensive position about the Court's power—indeed, its duty—to declare statutes or acts of the executive unconstitutional, where such a declaration is necessary to the decision of a case properly before it.[2] Such a power appears to me to be implicit, at the very least, in the Constitution itself. I am quite content to read the supremacy clause as making the power explicit, both with regard to state statutes and to acts of Congress, which are declared to be the supreme law of the land only when made "in Pursuance" of the Constitution.[3] This

2. Other aspects of the subject are treated in *The Democratic Character of Judicial Review*, infra, p. 147.

3. U.S. Const., Art. VI, cl. 2. In Art. III, § 2, the judicial power is established as extending "to all Cases, in Law and Equity, arising under this Constitution, the Laws of the United States, and Treaties made, or which shall be made, under their authority." Hart and Wechsler go much further and consider the power to be clear beyond possibility of doubt, in terms both of the language and the legislative history of the document, *The Federal Courts and the Federal System* 14–19 (1953). The contrary view is most fully presented in Haines, *The Role of the Supreme Court in American Government and Politics, 1789–1935*, at 16–26, 227–45 (1944).

feature of the Court's authority was accepted by many contemporaries and asserted in the *Federalist* papers. It has been exercised by the Court from the beginning, as comparable power had been exercised by colonial courts. And it stands now, whatever the Founding Fathers may in fact have meant, as an integral feature of the living constitution, long since established as a working part of the democratic political life of the nation.

So notable a doubter as Judge Learned Hand has recently come around to the view that the Court's power is legitimate, even in cases under the Bill of Rights, although in his opinion the power exists only by judicial fiat. The judges properly engrafted the practice of judicial review upon the Constitution, he concludes, by applying the maxim that a document must be construed to assure the accomplishment of its clear purposes. The denial of the power, he contends, would have denied the constitutional experiment any chance of success. Without an arbiter to construe the Constitution, the system would have collapsed into endless conflicts over the boundaries of authority, otherwise incapable of resolution. And no branch of government other than the Court, Judge Hand says, could have taken on the task with anything like an equal expectation of preventing failure.[4]

There is no substance in the supposed paradox of having appointed judges interpret the written constitution of a democratic society.

Popular sovereignty is a more subtle idea than the phrase "majority rule" sometimes implies.

The Constitution of the United States is the juridical act of the American people, not that of their Congress. It was, and is, a commitment to what the Founders called the republican form of government. Manhood suffrage was not

4. Hand, *The Bill of Rights* 14–30 (1958).

universal in 1789 and equal manhood suffrage is not universal today. Equal manhood suffrage is, however, the ideal of the present stage of our constitutional theory as the ultimate source of sovereign authority in the American political system: the true base of what we should now identify as the republican form of government.

But universal manhood suffrage does not imply, in theory or in fact, that policy can properly be determined in a democracy only through universal popular elections, or that universal popular elections have or should have the capacity to make any and all decisions of democratic government without limits or delays of any kind. Representative government is, after all, a legitimate form of democracy, through which the people delegate to their elected representatives in legislatures, or in executive offices, some but not necessarily all of their powers, for a period of years. Neither the town meeting nor the Swiss referendum is an indispensable feature of democratic decision-making.

The object of the men who established the American Constitution, like the object of democratic theorists in all countries, and at all times, was not omnicompetent popular government, but the freedom of man as an individual being within a free society whose policies are based ultimately upon his consenting will. The Constitution did not give Congress the full powers of the British Parliament. If that had been the Founders' idea, no written constitution would have been necessary. On the contrary, the Constitution provided for a federal system of divided and delegated powers. Not only the courts, but the desirable friction of contending authority—the President versus the Congress, the states versus the nation—were relied upon to help preserve an equilibrium and thus to enforce the grand design of the Constitution.

For the highest aim of our Constitution is that it seeks to

protect the freedom and dignity of man by imposing severe and enforceable limitations upon the freedom of the state. Americans thought then, and their wisdom is confirmed by all our subsequent experience, that man can be free, that political processes can in truth be democratic only when, and only because, the state is not free.

Every plan for democratic government, and every democratic constitution, contains vital elements beyond its ultimate derivation from the will of a majority. The Constitution provides a significant self-limitation upon the amendatory powers of the people—that no constitutional amendment can deny a state its equal suffrage in the Senate without its consent.[5] Every democracy divides issues of policy into several categories, to be settled by different means. Some decisions are made, without violating the principle of ultimate popular sovereignty, by appointed officials to whom important powers are delegated; e.g., to the boards which license doctors and lawyers, innkeepers and chiropodists; to the Federal Reserve Board or the Tariff Commission, the armed forces and the Department of Agriculture. The President has wide authority in the conduct of foreign relations. Other classes of decisions in all systems of democracy are remitted to legislative or judicial bodies, or are reserved for decision to regular or special elections, or to constituent assemblies. Still others, in most democratic societies, are set apart and protected against the risk of hasty decision—issues of policy which are regarded as essential in assuring the division of functions among the branches of government, and the democratic character, over the long run, of the decision-making process itself. Even a classic Vermont town meeting knows limits on its jurisdiction. The town meeting can fix the tax rate, embark on a school lunch

5. U.S. Const., Art. V.

program, or decide to buy a fire engine or a snow plow. But it cannot abolish the town meeting, nor delegate its powers to the selectmen. It cannot deny a resident citizen his right to vote, nor confiscate the land of a Democrat, nor impose a sentence of exile, nor try a law suit over boundaries or the habits of cattle. Any change in the basic procedures through which policy is made requires a longer and more carefully considered series of votes.

This pattern for decision-making is characteristic of all democratic communities, whatever devices they may use for accomplishing the goal. And it is a pattern entirely consistent with their democratic character. Laws fixing different procedures for different kinds of elections do not deny the people their ultimate power. The reason for practices of this kind is a fundamental one. For democracy is more, much more, than a commitment to popular sovereignty. It is also, and equally, a commitment to popular sovereignty under law. Sometimes the precautionary devices to assure the legality of particular classes of decisions by particular elections are declared in a written constitution. Sometimes they are enforced only by the pattern of custom, the weight of tradition, or the influence and the residual powers of institutions of special prestige, like the crown in Great Britain and Sweden, or the presidency in France, Germany, and other countries.

Under our practice, limitations of this character determine the contours of the Constitution.

We often fall back, as Mr. Justice Frankfurter has recently and eloquently done, upon Chief Justice Marshall's pregnant dictum: "It is a constitution we are expounding."[6] Marshall's comment is usually read, and properly read, to stress the need for flexibility in constitutional interpreta-

6. "John Marshall and the Judicial Function," in *Government under Law* 6, 8 (A. E. Sutherland ed. 1956).

tion. In this perspective, emphasis is put on the fact that the Constitution provides a plan for government designed to last for centuries. Such an arrangement must bend, we are reminded, if it is not to break. It must give all the elected branches of government wide-ranging areas of discretion so that society may, by its own democratic decisions, adapt itself to circumstances and stresses vastly different from those of the isolated agricultural communities which put down their roots along the Atlantic coast during the seventeenth and eighteenth centuries.

All this is true enough. But Chief Justice Marshall's dictum cuts the other way with equal force. It is indeed a constitution we are expounding, a document to assure continuity as well as flexibility, boundaries of power as well as freedom of choice. Congress and the President must have enough authority under the Constitution to govern effectively, and they must be able to exercise their own political judgment in selecting among the alternative means available for dealing with the emergent problems of each new age. But it has never been supposed that elected officials had untrammeled discretion. The Constitution sets limits on their ambit of choice, and some of its limits can be enforced by the courts. For until the people change it, the Constitution is a document intended to assure them that their representatives function within the borders of their offices, and do not roam at will among the pastures of power; that certain essential values in our public life be preserved, not ignored; and, in government's choice among the instruments of action, that those be selected which advance the cause of human freedom and those eschewed which threaten it. The idea was expressed by Bryce in these terms:

> The Supreme Court is the living voice of the Constitution—that is, of the will of the people expressed in

the fundamental law they have enacted. It is, therefore, as some one has said, the conscience of the people, who have resolved to restrain themselves from hasty or unjust action by placing their representatives under the restriction of a permanent law. It is the guarantee of the minority, who, when threatened by the impatient vehemence of a majority, can appeal to this permanent law, finding the interpreter and enforcer thereof in a Court set high above the assaults of faction.[7]

We are not so naïve as to suppose that the ideas of the eighteenth century survive unchanged and by their own force fix both the limits of governmental power and the definition of men's political and social rights, privileges, and immunities in relation to government. We have all long since agreed that judges are men, not automatons—if indeed there ever was much doubt about it. Most judges are men who have had a lifetime of experience, or of study, in the world of the constitutional process. They come to their posts from the Senate or the courts, from the bar, or politics, or the law schools, with a considerable exposure to the role of the Constitution as a guiding force in American public life. Inevitably they bring different views to the Court—not differing personal and idiosyncratic views of what the Constitution might have been, but differing views, as constitutional lawyers, as to what the Constitution is, and what it ought to become, in terms of its own animating premises.

The nub of the present conflict over the Supreme Court concerns certain parts of the Constitution intended to have continuity—its definition of the ends to be sought by government through flexibly adapted means. There are two

7. *The American Commonwealth* 273 (1913). I am indebted to Dean Joseph O'Meara of the Notre Dame Law School for recalling this passage to my attention.

broad categories of issues in this realm: those of federalism and the division of powers on the one hand, and those dealing with the civil and political rights of persons on the other. While recent years have produced important cases dealing with the first of these two classes of problems, the stress in the current debate is certainly on the second—on the meaning, that is to say, which the Court has given to the constitutional guarantees of due process and of the equal protection of the laws in the relationships between the individual and the state. During the balance of this presentation, my attention will mainly be directed to such problems of civil rights under the Constitution.

It has occasionally been suggested that the reason for the extraordinarily rich and significant development of constitutional doctrine recently in the civil rights area is that wilful judges have beeen appointed to the Court, bent on legislating their personal opinions into the corpus of the law. The charge is unfair and untrue. By and large, the Supreme Court has not gone past the frontier of its power, nor taken on issues beyond its duty to decide, in its recent cycle of constitutional cases.

Why then, have there been so many civil rights cases recently, and why have they been so strongly libertarian?

Several basic factors lie behind the current flood of civil rights litigation. Along with the element of chance in the process of appointment to the bench, these factors also account for the character and quality of the trend of doctrine.

The first is that since the 1930s, and more acutely since World War II, the United States has been seeking to deal with novel and difficult problems of totalitarian aggression. Fifth column activity was an experience which stimulated anxiety. The massive and uncompromising threat of communism is a reality beyond debate. It has caused, and will rightly continue to cause, grave anxiety as we seek to protect our national security against the challenging growth of communism as a force in world politics. Some of the numerous means selected to deal with problems of internal security have raised serious questions of constitutional right. It was inevitable and proper that these regulations, directly affecting the status and reputation of thousands of citizens, should be tested in the courts and ultimately presented for adjudication to the Supreme Court. There is nothing abnormal in this sequence, any more than it should have been considered abnormal for the Court after the Civil War to have faced the problems of *Ex parte Milligan*[8] and *Ex parte Garland*.[9] In addition, a variety of problems affecting the personal rights of citizens have naturally arisen out of the conduct of the war—like that of the *Korematsu* case[10]—and the presence abroad of American troops and their families. It was to be expected that many cases concerning the relation of military and civil authority should emerge in a period when we have more men under arms than ever before in peacetime.

The second general reason for the recent concentration of cases under the Bill of Rights on the docket of the Court is the process of social development in the United States, and especially the changing status of the Negro. The circumstances of world politics have given an important special accent to that development and have forcibly reminded us that we have been remiss in making good the pledge of equality for the Negro which we made in the Thirteenth, Fourteenth and Fifteenth Amendments to the Constitution. But this cycle of change would have proceeded of its own

8.  71 U.S. (4 Wall.) 2 (1866). See infra, pp. 249–57, for further discussion of this case.

9.  71 U.S. (4 Wall.) 333 (1867).

10.  Korematsu v. United States, 323 U.S. 214 (1944). See infra, p. 193, for further discussion of this case.

momentum, even without the stimulus of Soviet propaganda and the emergence all over the world of new and proud nations composed largely of colored peoples. The advance of the American Negro, since the end of slavery less than one hundred years ago, is a story of progress as well as of passivity; of blind resistance, but of inspiring efforts, too, carried on against the pressure of real and deep-seated psychological difficulty. Now the pace of development has quickened. More and more Negroes are receiving educational opportunities, and a larger proportion of the Negro group is being educated. In steadily increasing numbers, Negroes are succeeding in the occupations and professions of the middle class. They are gaining and keeping better employment opportunities throughout the nation, helped by periodic shortages of labor, the influence of legislation, and the spread of principle. The experience of the war posed the moral dilemma of the Negro's position with a clarity which has impressed many anew. And Negroes have become a political force in many elections. Changes of this order inevitably carry with them an intensification of the Negro's rightful demand that he be treated as a citizen of equal dignity in the public life of the United States. There is no brooking, and no blinking, the reality of this tide.

The third general reason for the current importance of civil rights problems in our constitutional law has been the growth of the law itself, and the character of public opinion, public fears, and public attitudes at this point in American history. The simple sentences of the Bill of Rights take on new meaning as they are used, case after case, court after court, Congress after Congress, in what is after all the biological process of life itself. These are not dead words on a piece of paper, but the seeds of living plants. And at this moment, the soil strongly favors vigorous growth for the tree of liberty.

The quickened zeal of the American people for the protection of their civil rights is hardly a surprising response to the circumstances of life in this century. Two brutal wars have had their impact. In many areas of the world, fascist and communist tyrannies of great power and influence have ruthlessly destroyed the rights of man and have degraded and humiliated man himself. The development of huge organizations of business, labor, and government has been accelerated by the circumstances of the Cold War, which requires apparently perpetual semi-mobilization. The fear that man as an individual will be submerged, coordinated, organized, and brainwashed into a social robot has been added to the other fears of the time. A mass egalitarian culture carries its own threat, at best. Against this background, it is healthy and natural that our powerful and continuous libertarian tradition has been so strongly reasserted. The spirit of the country has been not only to resist the conformity of a garrison society, but to counterattack where possible. In that process of thesis and antithesis, the Supreme Court has played a leading part. The great opinions of Chief Justice Hughes, of Justice Sutherland in the *Scottsboro* case,[11] of Justices Brandeis, Holmes, Stone, and Cardozo, are yielding now their intended fruit. In our common law approach to the problem of constitutional construction, one case leads to another as lawyers see new vistas opening and develop new possibilities for their clients within the ambit of evolving doctrine. And the Court has thus been an educational force, along with many others, in helping to mold a state of opinion far more sensitive to civil liberties than that which prevailed in the United States thirty or fifty years ago.

Timid men see danger in this development. They fear that by striking down the decisions of powerful legislators,

11. Powell v. Alabama, 287 U.S. 45 (1932).

the courts will weaken their authority and expose the judicial institution itself to attacks which may sweep it away. From time to time, indeed, such attacks have developed, and one is now being mounted. So far, happily, all such threats to the power of the Court have been defeated, on sober reflection, by the historic confidence of the American people in the Supreme Court as a detached agency of the Constitution itself, one remove at least from what Judge Learned Hand recently called "the pressure of public hysteria, public panic and public greed."[12]

The question remains, however, whether the Court, in its own wisdom, as one among the instruments of democratic American government, should continue on its present course or retreat prudently from the field, leaving the constitutional guarantees of personal and political freedom largely to the discretion of legislatures and presidents.

The beloved and respected Judge Learned Hand expressed himself again to this general effect in his Holmes Lectures at the Harvard Law School.[13] These lectures modify in important ways the views he had previously advanced on the subject. A few years ago, he seemed to be urging that the broad, general commandments of the Bill of Rights should not be enforced at all by the courts, but should be left as moral admonitions to the conscience of legislators and other public officials.[14] In his Holmes Lectures, he takes a long step forward. In the realm of the Bill of Rights, as in other realms, he says, the courts should annul statutes or other acts of government which are

> outside the grant of power to the grantee, and should not include a review of how the power has been exer-

12. Hand, *The Bill of Rights* 68 (1958).
13. *The Bill of Rights* (1958).
14. Hand, "The Contribution of an Independent Judiciary to Civilization," in *The Spirit of Liberty* 155–65 (Dilliard ed. 1952).

cised. This distinction in the case of legislation demands an analysis of its component factors. These are
an estimate of the relevant existing facts and a forecast
of the changes that the proposed measure will bring
about. In addition it involves an appraisal of the values
that the change will produce, as to which there are no
postulates specific enough to serve as guides on concrete
occasions. In the end all that can be asked on review by
a court is that the appraisals and the choice shall be impartial. The statute may be far from the best solution
of the conflicts with which it deals; but if it is the result of an honest effort to embody that compromise or
adjustment that will secure the widest acceptance and
most avoid resentment, it is "Due Process of Law" and
conforms to the First Amendment. In theory any statute is always open to challenge upon the ground that
it was not in truth the result of an impartial effort, but
from the outset it was seen that any such inquiry was
almost always practically impossible, and moreover it
would be to the last degree "political."[15]

I am at a loss to understand the Judge's argument. Any
breach of his rule, he says, moves the judges across the subtle
boundary between the judicial and the legislative function.
By seeking to apply the vague and general ideas of the Bill
of Rights to concrete situations, and especially by taking one
step beyond what he seems to regard as the easy issue of ultra

15. *The Bill of Rights* 66–67 (1958). My colleague Alexander M. Bickel
does not read *The Bill of Rights* as modifying in any substantial sense the
views which Judge Learned Hand expressed in his earlier essay, referred to
in note 14. I freely admit that there is difficulty in construing the judge's
eloquent and elegant, but sometimes impressionistic nonjudicial prose. It
is, as always, a delight to read; but in this case it is hard to parse. Mr. Bickel
may well be right, that what Judge Hand seems to concede on certain pages,
he takes away on others. But the note of concession is there. See, especially,
pp. 30, 33, 56, 64.

vires, the Court would in effect exercise the suspensive veto of the House of Lords. In the face of such conduct, he says, we should lose the bracing privilege of self-government and submit to the overlordship of judges as a bevy of Platonic Guardians, a state of affairs he finds irksome and repugnant to his staunch democratic principles.[16]

Judge Hand would be the first to recognize that in applying a statute or a clause of the Constitution the judges must often make the law while they interpret it. Yet the heart of his argument seems to rest on a deceptively simple distinction between the judicial and the legislative functions. He defines "A" as not being "B." Legislators make certain decisions after weighing and balancing a series of conflicting interests, including their own interpretation of the constitutional limitations on their authority. The judicial function, by his definition, should be nonlegislative in character. The crucial leap in his syllogism is the passage from this proposition to the thought that the judges must rigidly exclude from their minds consideration of the factors which influenced the legislative decision. The only exception he admits is that the courts may review the legislative decision on the constitutional question whether the legislature had the power to act at all in a given realm, and may go further, along a path whose implications I for one do not pretend to understand, and enquire whether the legislative decision was honest and impartial.

The distinction does not correspond to the realities of either the judicial or the legislative process. The Court's function is recognizably different from that of the legislature or of the executive, even when it must weigh the same considerations in the scales. The forum is different. The time is different, so that the pressure of contending interests appears in a different perspective. And the constitutional

16. Id. at 67–73.

issues are not peripheral, as often must be the case in legislative or executive decisions, but central to the problem before the Court. The judges may be foolhardy or prudent, in error or in doubt, grasping for power or circumspect in the exercise of their duty. Yet the Court, as a Court, must consider many of the problems previously evaluated by the institutions of action. Judge Hand's attempt to draw a line which would neatly exclude from the Court's view all the issues passed upon by the legislature or the executive fails, as all such attempts have failed in the past. Even in determining whether a given set of circumstances sufficiently affects the national economy to justify the invocation of the commerce power—a function which Judge Hand concedes is proper—the judges cannot escape reviewing some aspects of the substance of Congress' prior decision. They may call that decision "arbitrary," or the connection "insubstantial," or go further, according to Judge Hand, and find it not "impartial." These various verbal formulas are all unconvincing in identifying what the courts must in fact do in exercising the limited, Handian power of judicial review. That function cannot be distinguished, as a function, from what the judges do in interpreting statutes, some of which are as general as constitutional prescriptions, or in deciding common law cases in the light of what they conceive to be the ultimate social purposes of the received tradition.

The judges do not, of course, have complete freedom to make the Constitution what they say it is, despite the breadth of its language. But they cannot escape this part of their judicial function—their work as lawmakers in applying the words and history of the Constitution to new situations, often unknown in the eighteenth century, in the interest of preserving and protecting the social values the Constitution was designed to assure. In doing this part of their job, Judge Hand says, they should be concerned only with the existence of the legislative or executive power, not with substituting their judgment for that of the legislature or the executive as to whether the power has been rightly used. This is true, but the distinction is not very useful, however often repeated. The trouble with Judge Hand's test is that it fails to deal with the problem the judges in fact face, and denounces them instead for various crimes they could not well commit. It is rare, indeed impossible, to catch a judge openly "substituting" his legislative judgment for that of the Congress. His problems are in another realm. Many of them arise as slippery verbal issues of qualification or classification. In terms of the record, have the defendants practiced coercion or persuasion? Did Congress punish for a crime, or merely regulate foreign affairs? Collisions between the exercise of two conceded powers, or a clash between two clauses of the Constitution which must be reconciled in a given situation, raise most of the remaining difficulty.

Let me propose an example, in the interest of testing Judge Hand's thesis by the classic maneuver of the case method. The Securities Act of 1933 makes it unlawful for those who issue, underwrite, or deal in securities to use any means of communication in interstate commerce, or of the mails, to sell certain kinds of securities unless a registration statement meeting the requirements of the Act is in effect, and unless they duly deliver a formal and approved prospectus to their potential customers.[17] Comparable restrictions on freedom of speech can be found in the Labor Management Relations Act,[18] dealing with what employers can say

17. 48 Stat. 77 (1933), 15 U.S.C. §§ 77(d), (e) (1951). Subsequent amendments have not altered the character of the conflict presented. 15 U.S.C.A. § 77(e) (1957).

18. 49 Stat. 452, § 8 (1935), as amended, 61 Stat. 142, § 8(c) (1947), 29 U.S.C. § 158 (1956). Mr. Justice Douglas discusses the problem briefly in *The Right of the People* 56 (1958).

to their employees in the context of a dispute about union recognition, and in certain other statutes dealing with the distribution of securities, proxy fights, and reorganizations. Congress has power to regulate interstate commerce, a rubric which includes a large part of securities transactions and labor relations. And it is under the flat injunction of the First Amendment: Congress shall make no law abridging the freedom of speech. Extended investigations, committee reports, and legislative debates preceded the passage both of the Securities Act and of the basic federal labor legislation. Presumably Congress weighed the rival claims of freedom and of order in these realms and took into account the prohibition of the First Amendment.

Suppose the issue came before the Supreme Court. The Court is bound by its history to enforce the First Amendment. Judge Hand says that the case for wide judicial review is strongest where freedom of speech is threatened, although he disapproves of much, perhaps all, that has been done by the courts in this area in the name of judicial review.[19] In such a case, the Court would face an apparent conflict between the policies of the First Amendment and that of congressional action based on the commerce power.

Of what help is Judge Hand's rule in such a case? Can the Court stop by saying that its role is to determine the boundaries of power, and that it will not consider in any way whether the exercise of power is justifiable—whether, that is, the situation calling for legislation was serious, whether the regulation in question was necessary or only incidental, whether the legitimate goal of the legislation could have been achieved without the restriction on freedom of speech, etc.? It could hardly evade the question by saying that the restraint on freedom of speech is not in fact an "abridge-

19. Hand, op. cit. supra note 13, at 69.

ment" of that freedom, or that the First Amendment deals only with political speech, not commercial speech. No such loopholes are available. What meaning is there in the charge that the Court would be taking over the "legislative" function and going beyond its role as "judicial" arbiter of the Constitution, if in this case it did what has to be done—to weigh and balance the relative importance of the two considerations equally involved, Congress' judgment that the protection of commerce made it desirable to impose a "prior" restraint on speech, and the apparent absolutism of the First Amendment?

Or, alternatively, should we read Judge Hand's approach —although it is not posed in such terms—as implying a special rule for the judicial review of the Bill of Rights, on the ground that in this area the constitutional phrases are so vague that they give the judges no footing sufficiently assured to permit a rational exercise of the judicial method? Is the language of the Bill of Rights so different from that of other clauses in the Constitution, or from the broad language of many statutes, as to make the judicial function here utterly indistinguishable from that of a legislature? The difficulties which the Courts have encountered in construing many, many clauses of the Constitution—those dealing, for example, with treason, with the privileges and immunities of citizenship, the commerce clause, or the taxing powers—cast doubt upon the thought that there is a tenable distinction of kind or of degree to be drawn between the Bill of Rights and the rest of the Constitution on this ground. And of course the weight of history stands heavily against so easy an escape from the burden of duty.

I submit that Judge Hand's formula would not permit the most restrained judge to escape the reality of the Court's task in passing on the constitutionality of the Securities Act and a thousand comparable cases. Nor, equally, would it help him to see, describe, and understand the problem he does face. To take Marshall's dictum in still another sense, it *is* a Constitution the Court is expounding, a single document whose various parts must often be interpreted together, like those of other legal instruments, to give effect to the purpose of the Constitution as a whole. I, for one, can see no way on the Court's part to evade the necessity for such an evaluation in a case of this kind—not as a third chamber, but as the Court charged with responsibility to the people for interpreting their Constitution. The Court may say that one interest or the other prevails. It may be right or wrong in the eyes of law professors, the Congress, or the people. Its decision may be reversed by a later Court, altered by Congress, or overturned by constitutional amendment. But it does not advance clarity or exactness of thought to say that the Court's construction of the Constitution is not a judicial, but a legislative act.

Mr. Justice Douglas puts the issue faced by the Court in cases of this order more realistically in his recent lectures at Franklin and Marshall College.[20] In his chapter on freedom of expression, for example, he contrasts the opposing claims the Court must weigh in several groups of cases. Even the seeming absolutism of the First Amendment occasionally yields, in his survey, despite the weight he gives to the value it represents, in favor of civil order itself. Thus he would permit official restraint of speech where a sensational newspaper threatened the possibility of a fair trial; where picketing was an integral part of a breach of the peace or an antitrust violation; or where an employer's words addressed to his employees sought not merely to persuade but to coerce.[21] The results advocated in his survey are not as important, for present purposes, as the method he uses.

20. *The Right of the People* (1958).
21. Ibid., Lecture 1.

For he does analyze, as Judge Hand does not, the issues which the Court must determine in situations of this kind: the classification of factual situations with respect to constitutional categories; the delineation of the boundaries of power; and the resolution of conflicts between interests and powers of seemingly equal dignity, in the light of a theory of the Constitution as a whole.

It is on this phase of the problem that Judge Hand's critique of the present Court is most vulnerable. For he would subordinate the Bill of Rights as an effective working part of the constitutional universe. The language of the Bill of Rights, he says, is vague and general. Its application to highly charged situations of conflict is almost always full of political dynamite. Therefore he urges that the Bill be confined to the narrowest possible scope. In the case of freedom of speech, freedom of religion, and the due process clause, review should be limited to one issue: legislation should be upheld if it comes within a granted power, unless the Court is satisfied that the statute or regulation was not the product of an effort "impartially to balance the conflicting values."[22] As to the other provisions of the first eight amendments, Judge Hand says,

> except perhaps the last [they] are all addressed to specific occasions and have no such scope as those I have mentioned. Many of them embody political victories of the seventeenth century over the Crown, and carry their own nimbus of precedent. So far as they do, any extension beyond their historical meaning seems to me unwarranted, though that limitation is not always observed. It is true that at times they may present issues

22. Hand, op. cit. supra note 12, at 61. See also pp. 37–55. I have never before heard it suggested that the decisions of a political and partisan body like the Congress of the United States could be impeached if a court concludes that the Congressmen were not "impartial."

not unlike those that arise under the First Amendment and the "Due Process Clause," and in such cases I cannot see why courts should intervene, unless it appears that the statutes are not honest choices between values and sacrifices honestly appraised.[23]

These prescriptions seem to me to be utterly wrong as maxims of construction for a Constitution designed to help preserve an essential continuity in our legal tradition through long periods of time. They derive, as Judge Hand frankly admits, from his qualified, but still strongly held, conviction that the exercise of the power of judicial review is undemocratic in character, and is therefore to be confined as severely by judicial self-restraint as strong-willed men find it possible to do.

The contrary view seems to me by far the stronger, both in theory and as an interpretation of our history. The dominance of the popular will through the mechanisms of our system of government is achieved in large part by having the courts enforce limitations on the power of elected officials, in the name of constitutional provisions which only the people can alter by amendment. Those limitations are of peculiar importance where the individual is being protected against the pervasive influence of the modern state. If the individual is to have a considerable scope for personal freedom in the American society of the future, he will have to continue to rely on the courts to see to it that people are treated by the state in ways which conform to constitutional standards of democratic propriety. The weight of history is evidence that the people do expect the courts to interpret, declare, adapt, and apply these constitutional provisions, as one of their main protections against the possibility of abuse by Presidents and legislatures. This history leaves no

23. Id. at 65–66.

room, it seems to me, for a thesis like Judge Hand's, that the courts should refuse to exercise their constitutional powers, especially in the area of civil rights.

The Chief Justice's recent answer, somber and simple, perhaps even simplistic, reverts to the position of Hamilton in No. 78 of *The Federalist:*

> we are mindful of the gravity of the issue inevitably raised whenever the constitutionality of an Act of the National Legislature is challenged. No member of the Court believes that in this case the statute before us can be construed to avoid the issue of constitutionality. That issue confronts us, and the task of resolving it is inescapably ours. This task requires the exercise of judgment, not the reliance upon personal preferences. Courts must not consider the wisdom of statutes but neither can they sanction as being merely unwise that which the Constitution forbids.
>
> We are oath-bound to defend the Constitution. This obligation requires that congressional enactments be judged by the standards of the Constitution. The Judiciary has the duty of implementing the constitutional safeguards that protect individual rights. When the Government acts to take away the fundamental right of citizenship, the safeguards of the Constitution should be examined with special diligence.
>
> The provisions of the Constitution are not time-worn adages or hollow shibboleths. They are vital, living principles that authorize and limit governmental powers in our nation. They are the rules of government. When the constitutionality of an Act of Congress is challenged in this Court, we must apply those rules. If we do not, the words of the Constitution become little more than good advice.

When it appears that an Act of Congress conflicts with one of these provisions, we have no choice but to enforce the paramount commands of the Constitution. We are sworn to do no less. We cannot push back the limits of the Constitution merely to accommodate challenged legislation. We must apply those limits as the Constitution prescribes them, bearing in mind both the broad scope of legislative discretion and the ultimate responsibility of constitutional adjudication. We do well to approach this task cautiously, as all our predecessors have counseled. But the ordeal of judgment cannot be shirked. In some 81 instances since this Court was established it has determined that congressional action exceeded the bounds of the Constitution. It is so in this case.[24]

Thus I should conclude that there can be no justification for treating the essential canons of the Bill of Rights as more static, more narrowly confined to their eighteenth-century meaning, than other clauses of the Constitution— the commerce clause or the war power, for example. On the contrary, these aspects of the Constitution are the very soul of the document. As my colleague Charles L. Black, Jr., has recently said:

There is an even deeper reason for the creative and broad construction of the civil liberties guarantees in the Constitution. Consider the place of these phrases— "equal protection," "freedom of speech," and the rest —in the moral life of our nation. They state our highest aspirations. They are our political reason for being; they are the things we talk about when we would persuade ourselves or others that our country deserves well of history, deserves to be rallied to in its present strug-

24. Trop v. Dulles, 356 U.S. 86, 103–04 (1958).

gle with a system in which "freedom of speech" is freedom to say what is welcome to authority, and "equal protection" is the equality of the cemetery. Surely such words, standing where they do and serving such a function, are to be construed with the utmost breadth. The proper office of legal acumen is to give them new scope and life, rather than to prune them down to whatever may currently be regarded as harmlessness. Yet, we must not forget that, if they are to be construed broadly, the Court has no choice but to apply them broadly, even against legislation, and if the Court applies them narrowly, its only justification must be that their scope is narrow.[25]

There is another reason for having the Court approach its problems under the Bill of Rights in the spirit of the common law judges, elaborating certain simple ideas, in response to the pressure of changing fact situations, into the splendor of their full potential. The ideas of the Constitution about the relation of man to the state are positive, as well as negative. There is more to the Constitution than a set of limitations and prohibitions. These rules are not meant merely to confine governmental agencies, but strongly to influence the development of society and of men's ideas.

As the men of the eighteenth century knew well, following Locke and Montesquieu, the law is a continuing force in the process of public life. It has consequences, as well as causes. The changing dispositions of law respond to changing conditions in society itself. But in turn they profoundly influence the character of men and of their society. The law is not a mere artifact, reflecting the pressure of events. It

25. "Old and New Ways in Judicial Review," *Bowdoin College Bulletin* 11 (1957).

is and should be a vital element in the movement of society toward its ultimate goals. In this perspective, the constitutional decisions of the Court are more than a factor of continuity in protecting the democratic character of our political arrangements and in protecting the individual against arbitrary action by the state. They are also among the significant forces influencing the evolution of our constitutional ideal itself. Montesquieu defined the ideal of law for each culture as the spirit of its laws—the cultural norm toward which each society aspires in the day-to-day processes of its lawmaking. But, he pointed out, that spirit was not fixed and immutable even for a given culture. It could and did evolve through time, for better or for worse, toward tyranny or toward the ideal of responsible freedom. And the principal function of law, in his view, is to serve as one of the educational and formative influences of the culture, not merely in bringing the law in action up to the standard of the existing goal of law, but in perfecting the goal of the law. Thus, in construing and enforcing the basic purposes of the Bill of Rights, the Court is a leading participant in the endless striving of our culture to approach the values of dignity and freedom for the individual whose grandeur dominates our Constitution. To preserve, to enrich, to further these ideas of the highest good in the experience of our people is one of the first aims of the Constitution.

It will not do to say that in construing these provisions of the Constitution the Court should be limited to the meaning the terms had when they were written. The broad general purposes of the Founding Fathers abide, as aspirations, as guidelines to the interpreters of the future. But the circumstances to which their words refer are gone. The context is changed. The old perspective cannot be recaptured, because it no longer exists. The scope and meaning of the provisions of the Bill of Rights evolve, like the meaning of other constitutional terms and other terms in law. They are stages in the organic process by which ideas flourish or languish as new generations find for themselves new and valid meanings for the old words. Our constitutional doctrines do not grow quite as freely as do those of Great Britain, for the written constitution has its own powerful limiting influence. But they grow in the same soil of history. As the Court said in 1914, "the provisions of the Constitution are not mathematical formulas having their essence in their form. . . . Their significance is vital, not formal; it is to be gathered not simply by taking the words and a dictionary, but by considering their origin and the line of their growth."[26] These words, Justice Frankfurter has well said, are "purposely left to gather meaning from experience."[27] Each Justice of the Court meets his highest challenge in seeking to interpret these words in ways which contribute to the advancement of the rule of law, and to the advancement of the law itself. Thus can the Court help in the education of opinion and play its part in the colloquium through which the ideas of the community about law and justice are formed.

For the people, and not the courts, are the final interpreters of the Constitution. The Supreme Court and the Constitution it expounds cannot survive unless the people are willing, by and large, to live under it. And this is the ultimate issue to consider, as we review the relationship between the work of the Court and the state of public opinion. For in a political system resting on popular sovereignty, obedience to the law is not a sufficient rule.

The nature of the problem is most starkly presented by the present reaction of some of our fellow citizens in the

26. Gompers v. United States, 233 U.S. 604, 610 (1914).

27. National Mut. Ins. Co. v. Tidewater Transfer Co., 337 U.S. 582, 646 (1949) (dissenting opinion).

South to the opinions of the federal courts in the cases holding racial segregation in various forms a violation of the Fourteenth Amendment. They find these decisions disturbing, contrary to their customs, and threatening in many acute ways. They believe the decisions represent a usurpation of power by the judges. They realize that these cases could not possibly be reversed by a constitutional amendment. Yet many are resolved to disobey the law of the Constitution as declared by the Court. The potentialities of this conflict are far more serious than those presented by the Jenner Bill and the Butler amendments to it. Law can retain its vitality even though it is not instantly or completely obeyed. But it cannot survive if it is openly and generally defied. In handling the first great public manifestation of civil disobedience, in Little Rock, President Eisenhower put his action squarely and exclusively on the issue of law enforcement: the undoubted obligation of the executive to see to it that court orders are obeyed.

This proposition, however weighty, calls up some disturbing and fundamental echoes in a democratic society, where citizen responsibility goes beyond that implicit in the electoral process itself. A hundred years ago, in the decade before the Civil War, the problem of civil disobedience was debated throughout the land. Thoreau had helped stir up the issue with his writings and his dramatic refusal to pay taxes to a government which tolerated human slavery. Emerson and others joined in widely supported movements to deny enforcement to the Fugitive Slave Law. And there was a great debate in Boston between Benjamin R. Curtis, later a Justice of the Supreme Court, and other leaders of the time about the citizen's duty as juror to vote for conviction in Fugitive Slave Law Cases.[28] The question whether there may be public duties that transcend the duty to obey

28. 1 Curtis, *A Memoir of Benjamin Robbins Curtis, LL.D.* 112–36 (1879).

the law has arisen in other settings: President Eisenhower, as a commanding general, signed an appeal in 1942 to the French officers in North Africa to disobey the orders of the Vichy government, which we recognized as having authority over them. In some cases before our courts of military justice, superior orders are not necessarily a justification for brutal and inhuman acts on the part of soldiers. Above all, of course, the problem is posed by the Nuremberg trials themselves.

This series of experiences raises an ultimate issue in the moral life of a democracy: the freedom of the citizen to disobey the law when his conscience is deeply engaged. I do not assert that such a *right* exists. But there are times in the history of law when the most law-abiding citizen must acknowledge that a *conflict* exists, and a serious one: when, that is, the positive law seems to be inconsistent with the mores, the purposes, even the objective will of the community. We acknowledge the reality of the problem by exempting conscientious objectors from the military service—an act of grace and civilization with far-reaching implications. Many have claimed that the ultimate difference between democracies and totalitarian systems is that a democracy recognizes the citizen's ultimate responsibility for the moral content of the law, and for his own moral ratification and acceptance of the law.

The problem can be put in another form: the relative importance of force and consent in law. Is law, as Holmes once remarked, merely what is at the end of the policeman's stick? Is such apparent positivism an adequate explanation of law? Or must there be acceptance by the community of the rightness of law, as well as the rightness of the procedures by which law is made?

We must start our consideration of the constitutional crisis precipitated by the segregation cases by sympathetically facing the fact that many of our fellow citizens in the South are deeply troubled, and that they believe these decisions are wrong.

I myself should claim that the demands of order against chaos require every government to enforce the law as the judges make it. This is true, at least, in states generally ordered by the procedures of law. But I suggest also that in a democratic society, dealing with a problem like this one, enforcement is not enough. The law must be an educational force as well as a force, and a moral force too. Official enforcement efforts do not meet the full obligation of the executive to the law unless they include something more than the use of the policeman's stick. They must assert with equal power what in this case I believe to be true—that our developing constitutional law of equality for all is right; that it expresses the strongest force in American life, our commitment to the corpus of ideals represented by the Declaration of Independence and the Constitution; and that at some level of consciousness or unconsciousness, silently or openly, all our people, including our brothers of the South, know this, believe it, and will in the end accept it.[29]

It is a test of our capacity for self-government to resolve this conflict without sacrificing the ultimate dignity of man. Does freedom in a free society ever permit, or require, a citizen to disobey the positive law? At what point might the appeal of conscience be justified against the obligation to obey? In this realm—the conflict of individual freedom and order—we must beware lest action in the name of order lose the power which in this case it so clearly has—of being action also in the highest interests of freedom.

Those who believe that the Supreme Court is right in its course must wrestle with the minds and hearts of those who

29. Black, "Paths to Desegregation," *New Republic* 10–15 (Oct. 21, 1957).

believe it is wrong, until a national consensus emerges and prevails. Lawyers, who are officers of the law, and government officials charged with enforcement responsibility cannot leave the task of persuasion exclusively to the federal judges, who have so firmly led the way. Each should accept his share in the process of education which is indispensable if the law is to be vindicated, in the end, by our people's willing acceptance of its rightness, not merely by their sullen acquiescence in the principle of order alone.

# 5

# *The Democratic Character of Judicial Review (I)*

*It would require an uncommon portion of fortitude in the judges to do their duty as faithful guardians of the Constitution, where legislative invasions of it had been instigated by the major voice of the community.*—ALEXANDER HAMILTON[1]

A THEME of uneasiness, and even of guilt, colors the literature about judicial review. Many of those who have talked, lectured, and written about the Constitution have been troubled by a sense that judicial review is undemocratic. Why should a majority of nine Justices appointed for life be permitted to outlaw as unconstitutional the acts of elected officials or of officers controlled by elected officials? Judicial review, they have urged, is an undemocratic shoot on an otherwise respectable tree. It should be cut off, or at least kept pruned and inconspicuous. The attack has gone further. Reliance on bad political doctrine, they say, has produced bad political results. The strength of the courts has weakened other parts of the government. The

1. *The Federalist*, No. 78 at 509 (Modern Library ed. 1937).

The substance of this essay was originally given in talks before The Club in New Haven and the Yale Law School Alumni Association of Boston during the spring of 1952. First published in 66 *Harvard Law Review* 193 (1952), copyright 1952 by The Harvard Law Review Association.

judicial censors are accused of causing laxness and irresponsibility in the state and national legislatures, and political apathy in the electorate. At the same time, we are warned, the participation of the courts in this essentially political function will inevitably lead to the destruction of their independence and thus compromise all other aspects of their work.

## I

The idea that judicial review is undemocratic is not an academic issue of political philosophy. Like most abstractions, it has far-reaching practical consequences. I suspect that for some judges it is the mainspring of decision, inducing them in many cases to uphold legislative and executive action which would otherwise have been condemned. Particularly in the multiple opinions of recent years, the Supreme Court's self-searching often boils down to a debate within the bosoms of the Justices over the appropriateness of judicial review itself.

The attack on judicial review as undemocratic rests on the premise that the Constitution should be allowed to grow without a judicial check. The proponents of this view would have the Constitution mean what the President, the Congress, and the state legislatures say it means.[2] In this way,

2. Many writers have distinguished the authority of the Supreme Court to deny effect to an unconstitutional act of the Congress or the President from its duty under Art. VI to declare unconstitutional provisions of state constitutions or statutes, although Art. VI declares even federal statutes to be "the supreme Law of the Land" only when made in pursuance of the Constitution. Holmes, "Law and the Court" in *Collected Legal Papers* 291, 295–96 (1920); Jackson, *The Struggle for Judicial Supremacy* 15 et seq. (1941); Thayer, "The Origin and Scope of the American Doctrine of Constitutional Law" in *Legal Essays* 1, 35–41 (1908); Thayer, *John Marshall* 61–65 (1901); Haines, *The American Doctrine of Judicial Supremacy* 131–35, 511–12 (2d ed. 1932).

they contend, the electoral process would determine the course of constitutional development, as it does in countries with plenipotentiary parliaments.

But the Constitution of the United States does not establish a parliamentary government, and attempts to interpret American government in a parliamentary perspective break down in confusion or absurdity. One may recall, in another setting, the anxious voice of the *Washington Post* urging President Truman to resign because the Republican Party had won control of the Congress in the 1946 elections.

It is a grave oversimplification to contend that no society can be democratic unless its legislature has sovereign powers. The social quality of democracy cannot be defined by so rigid a formula. Government and politics are after all the arms, not the end, of social life. The purpose of the Constitution is to assure the people a free and democratic society. The final aim of that society is as much freedom as possible for the individual human being. The Constitution provides society with a mechanism of government fully competent to its task, but by no means universal in its powers. The power to govern is parceled out between the states and the nation and is further divided among the three main branches of all governmental units. By custom as well as constitutional practice, many vital aspects of community life are beyond the direct reach of government—for example, religion, the press, and, until recently at any rate, many phases of educational and cultural activity. The separation of powers under the Constitution serves the end of democracy by limiting the roles of the several branches of government and protecting the citizen, and the various parts of the state itself, against encroachments from any source.

The power of constitutional review, to be exercised by some part of the government, is implicit in the conception of a written constitution delegating limited powers. A written constitution would promote discord rather than order in society if there were no accepted authority to construe it, at the least in cases of conflicting action by different branches of government or of constitutionally unauthorized governmental action against individuals. The limitation and separation of powers, if they are to survive, require a procedure for independent mediation and construction to reconcile the inevitable disputes over the boundaries of constitutional power which arise in the process of government. British Dominions operating under written constitutions have had to face the task pretty much as we have, and they have solved it in similar ways. Like institutions have developed in other federal systems.

As far as the American Constitution is concerned, there can be little real doubt that the courts were intended from the beginning to have the power they have exercised. The *Federalist* papers are unequivocal; the Debates as clear as debates normally are. The power of judicial review was commonly exercised by the courts of the states, and the people were accustomed to judicial construction of the authority derived from colonial charters.[3] Constitutional interpretation by the courts, Hamilton said, does not

> by any means suppose a superiority of the judicial to the legislative power. It only supposes that the power of the people is superior to both; and that where the will of the legislature, declared in its statutes, stands in opposition to that of the people, declared in the Constitution, the judges ought to be governed by the latter rather than the former. They ought to regulate their

3. The evidence is reviewed in Thayer, "The Origin and Scope of the American Doctrine of Constitutional Law" in *Legal Essays* 1, 3–7 (1908); Beard, *The Supreme Court and the Constitution* (1912); and Haines, op. cit. supra note 2, at 44–59, 88–121. A useful bibliography appears in Dodd, *Cases on Constitutional Law* 8–18 (3d ed. 1941).

decisions by the fundamental laws, rather than by those
which are not fundamental.[4]

Hamilton's statement is sometimes criticized as a verbal
legalism.[5] But it has an advantage too. For much of the discussion has complicated the problem without clarifying it.
Both judges and their critics have wrapped themselves so
successfully in the difficulties of particular cases that they
have been able to evade the ultimate issue posed in the
*Federalist* papers.

Whether another method of enforcing the Constitution
could have been devised, the short answer is that no such
method has developed. The argument over the constitutionality of judicial review has long since been settled by
history. The power and duty of the Supreme Court to declare statutes or executive action unconstitutional in appropriate cases is part of the living Constitution. "The
course of constitutional history," Mr. Justice Frankfurter
recently remarked, has cast responsibilities upon the Supreme Court which it would be "stultification" for it to
evade.[6] The Court's power has been exercised differently
at different times: sometimes with reckless and doctrinaire
enthusiasm; sometimes with great deference to the status
and responsibilities of other branches of the government;
sometimes with a degree of weakness and timidity that
comes close to the betrayal of trust. But the power exists,
as an integral part of the process of American government.
The Court has the duty of interpreting the Constitution
in many of its most important aspects, and especially in
those which concern the relations of the individual and the

4. *The Federalist*, No. 78 at 506 (Modern Library ed. 1937).

5. See Thayer, *John Marshall* 96 (1901); Thayer, "The Origin and Scope
of the American Doctrine of Constitutional Law" in *Legal Essays* 1, 12–15
(1908); Haines, op. cit. supra note 2, at 518–27.

6. Rochin v. California, 342 U.S. 165, 173 (1952).

state. The political proposition underlying the survival of the power is that there are some phases of American life which should be beyond the reach of any majority, save by constitutional amendment. In Mr. Justice Jackson's phrase, "One's right to life, liberty, and property, to free speech, a free press, freedom of worship and assembly, and other fundamental rights may not be submitted to vote; they depend on the outcome of no elections."[7] Whether or not this was the intention of the Founding Fathers, the unwritten Constitution is unmistakable.

If one may use a personal definition of the crucial word, this way of policing the Constitution is not undemocratic. True, it employs appointed officials, to whom large powers are irrevocably delegated. But democracies need not elect all the officers who exercise crucial authority in the name of the voters. Admirals and generals can win or lose wars in the exercise of their discretion. The independence of judges in the administration of justice has been the pride of communities which aspire to be free. Members of the Federal Reserve Board have the lawful power to plunge the country into depression or inflation. The list could readily be extended. Government by referendum or town meeting is not the only possible form of democracy. The task of democracy is not to have the people vote directly on every issue, but to assure their ultimate responsibility for the acts of their representatives, elected or appointed. For judges deciding ordinary litigation, the ultimate responsibility of the electorate has a special meaning. It is a responsibility for the quality of the judges and for the substance of their instructions, never a responsibility for their decisions in particular cases. It is hardly characteristic of law in democratic society to encourage bills of attainder or to allow appeals

7. West Virginia State Board of Educ. v. Barnette, 319 U.S. 624, 638 (1943).

from the courts, in particular cases, to legislatures or to mobs. Where the judges are carrying out the function of constitutional review, the final responsibility of the people is appropriately guaranteed by the provisions for amending the Constitution itself and by the benign influence of time, which changes the personnel of courts. Given the possibility of constitutional amendment, there is nothing undemocratic in having responsible and independent judges act as important constitutional mediators. Within the narrow limits of their capacity to act, their great task is to help maintain a pluralist equilibrium in society. They can do much to keep it from being dominated by the states or the federal government, by Congress or the President, by the purse or the sword.

In the execution of this crucial but delicate function, constitutional review by the judiciary has an advantage thoroughly recognized in both theory and practice. The power of the courts, however final, can only be asserted in the course of litigation. Advisory opinions are forbidden, and reefs of self-limitation have grown up around the doctrine that the courts will determine constitutional questions only in cases of actual controversy, when no lesser ground of decision is available and when the complaining party would be directly and personally injured by the assertion of the power deemed unconstitutional. Thus the check of judicial review upon the elected branches of government must be a mild one, limited not only by the detachment, integrity, and good sense of the Justices, but by the structural boundaries implicit in the fact that the power is entrusted to the courts. Judicial review is inherently adapted to preserving broad and flexible lines of constitutional growth, not to operating as a continuously active factor in legislative or executive decisions.

The division and separation of governmental powers

within the American federal system provides the community with ample power to act, without compromising its pluralist structure. The Constitution formalizes the principle that a wide dispersal of authority among the institutions of society is the safest foundation for social freedom. It was accepted from the beginning that the judiciary would be one of the chief agencies for enforcing the restraints of the Constitution. In a letter to Madison, Jefferson remarked of the Bill of Rights:

> In the arguments in favor of a declaration of rights, you omit one which has great weight with me; the legal check which it puts into the hands of the judiciary. This is a body, which, if rendered independent and kept strictly to their own department, merits great confidence for their learning and integrity. In fact, what degree of confidence would be too much, for a body composed of such men as Wythe, Blair and Pendleton? On characters like these, the *"civium ardor prava pubentium"* would make no impression.[8]

Jefferson, indeed, went further. He regretted the absence in the Constitution of a direct veto power over legislation entrusted to the judiciary, and wished that no legislation

8. Jefferson, *Life and Selected Writings* 462 (Modern Library ed. 1944). This passage, Griswold comments, "suggests that while [Jefferson] relied on the Court to safeguard the Bill of Rights, he was also counting on the bill to ensure a long-run democratic tendency on the part of the Court. History has borne out the acumen of this thought . . . . The Court's vested responsibility for our civil liberties has kept it anchored to democratic fundamentals through all kinds of political weather." A. W. Griswold, "Jefferson's Republic—The Rediscovery of Democratic Philosophy," *Fortune* 130 (April 1950). Later in life, of course, Jefferson strongly differed with many of the decisions and opinions of the Supreme Court and expressed his disagreement in terms which sometimes seemed to repudiate the constitutionality of judicial review itself.

could take effect for a year after its final enactment.[9] Within such constitutional limits, Jefferson believed, American society could best achieve its goal of responsible self-government. "I have no fear," he wrote, "but that the result of our experiment will be, that men may be trusted to govern themselves without a master."[10]

Democracy is a slippery term. I shall make no effort at a formal definition here. Certainly as a matter of historical fact some societies with parliamentary governments have been and are "democratic" by standards which Americans would accept, although it is worth noting that almost all of them employ second chambers, with powers at least of delay, and indirect devices for assuring continuity in the event of a parliamentary collapse, either through the crown or some equivalent institution, like the presidency in France. But it would be scholastic pedantry to define democracy in such a way as to deny the title of "democrat" to Jefferson, Madison, Lincoln, Brandeis, and others who have found the American constitutional system, including its tradition of judicial review, well adapted to the needs of a free society.[11] As Mr. Justice Brandeis said,

> the doctrine of the separation of powers was adopted by the Convention of 1787, not to promote efficiency but to preclude the exercise of arbitrary power. The purpose was, not to avoid friction, but, by means of the inevitable friction incident to the distribution of gov-

9. Jefferson, *Life and Selected Writings* 437, 441, 460 (Modern Library ed. 1944).

10. 6 *The Writings of Thomas Jefferson* 151 (Lipscomb and Bergh ed. 1904).

11. See, e.g., Lincoln, "First Inaugural Address" in 6 *Messages and Papers of the Presidents* 5–12 (Richardson ed. 1897); Wilson, *Constitutional Government in the United States* c. 6 (1911).

ernmental powers among three departments, to save the people from autocracy.[12]

It is error to insist that no society is democratic unless it has a government of unlimited powers, and that no government is democratic unless its legislature has unlimited powers. Constitutional review by an independent judiciary is a tool of proven use in the American quest for an open society of widely dispersed powers. In a vast country, of mixed population, with widely different regional problems, such an organization of society is the surest base for the hopes of democracy.[13]

## II

There is another fundamental aspect of the sustained attack on the legitimacy of judicial review. Men like James Bradley Thayer have urged that if the propertied classes come to regard the courts as their protectors against popular

12. Myers v. United States, 272 U.S. 52, 293 (1926) (dissenting opinion).
13. See Cardozo, *The Nature of the Judicial Process* 92–94 (1921):
The great ideals of liberty and equality are preserved against the assaults of opportunism, the expediency of the passing hour, the erosion of small encroachments, the scorn and derision of those who have no patience with general principles, by enshrining them in constitutions, and consecrating to the task of their protection a body of defenders. By conscious or subconscious influence, the presence of the restraining power, aloof in the background, but none the less always in reserve, tends to stabilize and rationalize the legislative judgment, to infuse it with the glow of principle, to hold the standard aloft and visible for those who must run the race and keep the faith. I do not mean to deny that there have been times when the possibility of judicial review has worked the other way. Legislatures have sometimes disregarded their own responsibility, and passed it on to the courts. Such dangers must be balanced against those of independence from all restraint, independence on the part of public officers elected for brief terms, without the guiding force of a continuous tradition. On the whole, I believe the latter dangers to be the more formidable of the two. Great maxims, if they may be violated with impunity, are honored often with lip-service,

government they will neglect government. Local and national government, shorn of power, will be indifferently conducted. The people will fail to meet their political responsibilities.[14] This position is translated by some judges into the doctrine that they serve the cause of democracy by refusing to decide important questions of a political cast, thus forcing the elected agencies of government to settle or postpone them.

This contention has been belied by the course of history: legislatures today, despite almost sixty more years of considerable pressure from their judicial censors, are a good deal less "belittled" and "demoralized" than they were at the end of the nineteenth century when Thayer wrote.[15]

---

which passes easily into irreverence. The restraining power of the judiciary does not manifest its chief worth in the few cases in which the legislature has gone beyond the lines that mark the limits of discretion. Rather shall we find its chief worth in making vocal and audible the ideals that might be otherwise silenced, in giving them continuity of life and expression, in guiding and directing choice within the limits where choice ranges. This function should preserve to the courts the power that now belongs to them, if only the power is exercised with insight into social values, and with suppleness of adaptation to changing social needs.

14. See Thayer, "The Origin and Scope of the American Doctrine of Constitutional Law" in *Legal Essays* 1, 39–41 (1908); Haines, *The American Doctrine of Judicial Supremacy* 500–40 (2d ed. 1932); L. Hand, "The Contribution of an Independent Judiciary to Civilization" in *The Spirit of Liberty* 172 (Dilliard ed. 1952); Commager, *Majority Rule and Minority Rights* 57–83 (1943), Wyzanski, Book Review, 57 *Harv. L. Rev.* 389 (1944); Clark, "The Dilemma of American Judges," 35 *A.B.A.J.* 8 (1949). For other views of the proper extent of judicial review, see M. Cohen, "Constitutional and Natural Rights" in *The Faith of a Liberal* 175 (1946); Pekelis, *Law and Social Action* 194–203 (1950); Curtis, *Lions under the Throne* 24–34 (1947); Freund, *On Understanding the Supreme Court* 37–41 (1949); Braden, "The Search for Objectivity in Constitutional Law," 57 *Yale L.J.* 571 (1948).

15. Thayer, "The Origin and Scope of the American Doctrine of Constitutional Law" in *Legal Essays* 1, 39 (1908), originally published in 1893 in 7 *Harv. L. Rev.* 129.

Nor does it stand up as a persuasive argument even in the terms Thayer and his followers used. The existence of the power of judicial review is hardly an adequate explanation for the lapses of legislatures, then or now. The election of petty and irresponsible men to state and national legislatures reflects cultural and sociological forces of far greater significance and generality. Political apathy and ignorance can hardly be explained by the hypothesis that the mass of nonvoting citizens, or the larger mass who accept and support government by bosses, are comfortably relying on the courts to protect them. The reasons for the occasional low estate of legislators and Congressmen must be sought in the history and development of American society—the ways in which the population has grown, the deplorable level of popular education, the nature of political tradition, the acceptance of graft, the concentration of American energies in business and other nonpolitical activities. It is certainly not true today, and was not true in 1893, that dependence on the courts leads people to

> become careless as to whom they send to the legislature; too often they cheerfully vote for men whom they would not trust with an important private affair, and when these unfit persons are found to pass foolish and bad laws, and the courts step in and disregard them, the people are glad that these few wiser gentlemen on the bench are so ready to protect them against their more immediate representatives.[16]

Actually Thayer's papers on constitutional law were written in the setting of different problems from those which face American public life today. It is doubtful whether his views would have had the same emphasis if applied to the

16. Thayer, *John Marshall* 104 (1901).

constitutional issues of the 1950s that he gave them in discussing those of the last years of the nineteenth century. Thayer was preoccupied with the cycle of cases after the Civil War through which, in Mr. Justice Holmes' phrase, the Court wrote Herbert Spencer's *Social Statics* into the Constitution. He was resisting the practice of declaring all sorts of regulatory legislation illegal as unreasonable in the light of the due process clause of the Fourteenth Amendment or as outside the scope of the commerce power. There is little if any reference in his writings to the function of the courts in enforcing the civil rights listed in the Constitution and the Bill of Rights. He quoted with approval Chief Justice Marshall's statement that the Court on which he served "never sought to enlarge the judicial power beyond its proper bounds, nor feared to carry it to the fullest extent that duty required." "That," Professor Thayer remarked, "is the safe twofold rule; nor is the first part of it any whit less important than the second; nay, more; today it is the part which most requires to be emphasized."[17]

In our time, however, the problem has changed. The constitutional revolution which began in 1937 has had its unmistakable impact. There is little or no risk that the present Supreme Court will become again a third chamber annulling a wide variety of regulatory legislation. The breadth of the commerce power, the freedom of the states to legislate in the realm of business, the wide discretionary powers of administrative bodies, state and national—these features of the constitutional scene are not the subject of significant disagreement among the Justices. And public opinion has become acutely conscious of the fact that state and national legislatures have enormous powers which are frequently exercised. While the problems of the future may provoke a new constitutional crisis over the powers of government,

17. Id. at 106.

today the people are well aware that their own political exertions, and not the long arm of the Supreme Court, must be their chief reliance in molding the body of regulatory legislation to their heart's desire.

The risk today, and it is a real one, is that the Supreme Court is not giving sufficient emphasis to the second part of Marshall's "twofold rule." The freedom of the legislatures to act within wide limits of constitutional construction is the wise rule of judicial policy only if the processes through which they act are reasonably democratic. Chief Justice Stone put emphasis on the fact that in many instances legislative acts are directed against interests which are not or cannot be represented in the legislature: out-of-state interests, where the purpose of legislation is local economic protection, or politically impotent minorities, where the thrust of the act is discrimination or repression. This line of thought led him to the arresting conclusion that statutes which affected interests beyond political protection, or which limited the full democratic potentialities of political action, were not to be approached by the Court with the deference it usually accorded legislative decisions, by way of "presumption" or otherwise.[18]

18. Building on a suggestion in McCulloch v. Maryland, 17 U.S. [4 Wheat.] 316, 428 (1819), and other early cases, Chief Justice Stone contended that the Court should give less than the normal weight to the legislative judgment where the normal electoral safeguards against legislative abuse are not present or where the legislative act would itself tend to restrict the effectiveness of "those political processes which can ordinarily be expected to bring about the repeal of undesirable legislation . . . ." United States v. Carolene Products Co., 304 U.S. 144, 152 n.4 (1938). See also McGoldrick v. Berwind-White Coal Mining Co., 309 U.S. 33, 46 (1940); South Carolina State Highway Dep't v. Barnwell Bros., Inc., 303 U.S. 177, 185 (1938); Southern Pacific Co. v. Arizona, 325 U.S. 761, 767–68 (1945); Minersville School District v. Gobitis, 310 U.S. 586, 603–07 (1940) (dissenting opinion); Dowling, "The Methods of Mr. Justice Stone in Constitutional Cases," 41 *Colum. L. Rev.* 1160, 1171–79 (1941); Wechsler, "Stone and the Constitution," 46 *Colum. L. Rev.* 764, 785–800 (1946).

Chief Justice Stone's distinction brings out an element which cannot easily be dismissed or disregarded in determining the weight to be given the constitutional judgment of the legislature in a judicial decision as to the constitutionality of its action. After all, the form and character of our present legal attack on communism and "disloyalty" is largely determined by the impotence of communism as a domestic political force. France or Italy, confronting communist parties to which one-third of the electorate is loyal, could not consider the kind of direct legal proceedings against communism which we have undertaken. Dealing with an infinitely more serious threat, the French and Italian governments must rely only on police action, in the narrower sense, and on political struggle in the marketplace of ideas.

## III

The argument that action by the courts in protecting the liberties of the citizens is futile in bad times and unnecessary in good ones is fundamentally wrong. Judge Learned Hand has given the contrary view its strongest and most eloquent form. In a speech called "The Contribution of an Independent Judiciary to Civilization,"[19] he reviews the main tasks of judges. In applying "enacted law"—commands of an organ of government "purposely made responsive to the pressure of the interests affected"—he believes that the judiciary should pursue a course of "unflinching" independence in seeking loyally to enforce the spirit of the enactment as it

19. Address on 250th anniversary of the Supreme Judicial Court of Massachusetts, Nov. 21, 1942, reprinted in *The Spirit of Liberty* 172 (Dilliard ed. 1952). See also Freund, "The Supreme Court and Civil Liberties," 4 *Vand. L. Rev.* 533, 551–54 (1951).

was made.[20] In a society which makes law by the procedures of democratic and representative government, "enacted laws" are always compromises of competing forces, and "to disturb them by surreptitious, irresponsible and anonymous intervention imperils the possibility of any future settlements and pro tanto upsets the whole system." The power of the judges to legislate in the field of customary law he regards as an anomaly which could not exist in "a pitilessly consistent democracy." Moreover, he points out, modern legislatures can pass laws more readily than ancient parliaments. But as long as the judges live by "a self-denying ordinance which forbids change in what has not already become unacceptable," the old system works out very well as it is, "for the advantages of leaving step by step amendments of the customary law in the hands of those trained in it, outweigh the dangers." As to the constitutional functions of the American judiciary, he makes a distinction. Insofar as the Constitution is "an instrument to distribute political power," he would defend entrusting its construction to an independent judiciary, as in the case of interpreting "enacted law." Conflicts over authority are inevitable in a system of divided power. It was "a daring expedient" to have them settled by

> judges deliberately put beyond the reach of popular pressure. And yet, granted the necessity of some such authority, probably independent judges were the most likely to do the job well. Besides, the strains that decisions on these questions set up are not ordinarily dangerous to the social structure. For the most part the

20. This and the following quotations, until otherwise indicated, are from L. Hand, "The Contribution of an Independent Judiciary to Civilization" in *The Spirit of Liberty* 172–81 (Dilliard ed. 1952). This is not the occasion to comment on these remarks as the starting point for a theory of statutory construction.

interests involved are only the sensibilities of the officials whose provinces they mark out, and usually their resentments have no grave seismic consequences.

Judge Hand's use of "ordinarily," "for the most part," and "usually" in the two preceding sentences may be appropriate as a matter of statistics, but it conceals some dramatic exceptions, of which the explosions of 1937 are only the most recent instance.

The next part of his lecture, however, distinguishes another class of constitutional questions and advances to the attack:

> American constitutions always go further. Not only do they distribute the powers of government, but they assume to lay down general principles to insure the just exercise of those powers. This is the contribution to political science of which we are proud, and especially of a judiciary of Vestal unapproachability which shall always tend the Sacred Flame of Justice. Yet here we are on less firm ground.

In a passage of Browningesque passion and obscurity, he advances the thesis that the judiciary will lose the independence it needs for its other functions unless it resolutely refuses to decide constitutional questions of this order. The general constitutional commands of fairness and equality, which he nowhere identifies in detail, are "moral adjurations, the more imperious because inscrutable, but with only that content which each generation must pour into them anew in the light of its own experience. If an independent judiciary seeks to fill them from its own bosom, in the end it will cease to be independent." If the judges are "intransigent but honest, they will be curbed; but a worse fate will befall them if they learn to trim their sails to the prevailing winds." The price of judicial independence, he concludes, is that the judges

> should not have the last word in those basic conflicts of "right and wrong—between whose endless jar justice resides." You may ask what then will become of the fundamental principles of equity and fair play which our constitutions enshrine; and whether I seriously believe that unsupported they will serve merely as counsels of moderation. I do not think that anyone can say what will be left of those principles; I do not know whether they will serve only as counsels; but this much I think I do know—that a society so riven that the spirit of moderation is gone, no court *can* save; that a society where that spirit flourishes, no court *need* save; that in a society which evades its responsibility by thrusting upon the courts the nurture of that spirit, that spirit in the end will perish.

This gloomy and apocalyptic view is a triumph of logic over life. It reflects the dark shadows thrown upon the judiciary by the Court-packing fight of 1937. Judge Hand is preoccupied with a syllogism. The people and the Congress have the naked power to destroy the independence of the courts. Therefore the courts must avoid arousing the sleeping lion by venturing to construe the broad and sweeping clauses of the Constitution which would "demand the appraisal and balancing of human values which there are no scales to weigh." Presumably he would include in this catalogue of forbidden issues problems of freedom of speech, the separation of church and state, and the limits, if any, to which "the capable, the shrewd or the strong" should "be allowed to exploit their powers." Are we to read the last phrase as encompassing the right of habeas corpus, the central civil liberty and the most basic of all protections against the authority of the state? Would it deny the possibility of constitutional review by the courts for laws denying the vote to Negroes, for searches and seizures without warrant, for bills of attainder or test oaths?

In the first place, the judicial decisions which brought on the storm in 1937 were not in this area at all. They concerned the division of power between the states and the nation,[21] and between Congress and the President[22]—issues which Judge Hand regards as inescapably within the province of the courts and not likely in any event to have "seismic consequences." Further, it is important to reiterate the obvious but sometimes forgotten fact that the historic conception of the Supreme Court's duties, however challenged in 1937, prevailed in that struggle. In the end that idea of the Court's function was sustained against the reluctant and half-hearted opposition of a Congress which did not really believe in President Roosevelt's proposal and took its first opportunity to abandon it.

The possibility of judicial emasculation by way of popular reaction against constitutional review by the courts has not in fact materialized in more than a century and a half of American experience. When the Court has differed from the Congress and the President in its notions of constitutional law—whether in the realm of the eternal verities or in interpreting the scope of the commerce power—time has unfailingly cured the conflicts, such as they were. Against that history, should we weigh the chance that Congress would suppress or intimidate the Supreme Court as ominously as Judge Hand does? Is it a reason for denying the Court competence in the broader reaches of constitutional law, or a bogeyman?

21. See, e.g., United States v. Butler, 297 U.S. 1 (1936).
22. See, e.g., Schechter Poultry Corp. v. United States, 295 U.S. 495 (1935). See also Youngstown Sheet & Tube Co. v. Sawyer, 343 U.S. 579 (1952).

If the courts persist, Judge Hand warns, in seeking to impose their ideas as to the higher law of the Constitution upon the litigants before them, the end will be the destruction of society. The independence of the courts will be compromised, and social life will "relapse into the reign of the tooth and claw."[23] Is this dire vision justified? If the courts, for example, refused to defend the rights of Negroes in the name of the Fourteenth Amendment, or the right of political groups to assemble and make speeches, would the result be more order or more disorder in society? While no statistical answer to such questions is possible, I, for one, believe that the defense of civil rights by the courts is a force not only for democratic values but for social order. If repressed by those who control the local police, the social and political aspirations of the people would often spill over into rioting or sullen disaffection, which would be worse. Nothing has destroyed the essential solidarity of a people more effectively than policies of repression imposed by the strong on the weak. Such policies, not those of open discussion and political equality, have led modern societies to the rule of the tooth, the claw, and the tommy gun.

It may of course be true that no court can save a society bent on ruin. But American society is not bent on ruin. It is a body deeply committed in its majorities to the principles of the Constitution and both willing and anxious to form its policy and programs in a constitutional way. Americans are, however, profoundly troubled by fears—intense and real fears, raised by unprecedented dangers and by the conduct of perilous tasks unprecedented in the history of the government. It is difficult for legislators confronting the menace of the world communist movement to reject any proposals which purport to attack communism or to protect

23. L. Hand, "Chief Justice Stone's Concept of the Judicial Function," in *The Spirit of Liberty* 201, 208 (Dilliard ed. 1952).

the community from it. This does not mean, however, that the President and the Congress would refuse to obey the Supreme Court's rulings on the constitutionality of some of the means with which they have chosen to attack—and often, alas, merely to exorcise—the evil. Ruin can come to a society not only from the furious resentments of a crisis. It can be brought about in imperceptible stages by gradually accepting, one after another, immoral solutions for particular problems. The "relocation camps" conducted during World War II for Japanese residents and for Americans of Japanese descent are the precedent for the proposal that concentration camps be established for citizens suspected of believing in revolutionary ideas.[24] Thus can the protection of the writ of habeas corpus be eroded, and the principle lost that criminal punishment can be inflicted only for criminal behavior and then only after a trial by jury conducted according to the rules of the Bill of Rights. Thus can we be led to accept the ideas and techniques of the police state.

Nor, more broadly, is it true as a matter of experience that a vigorous lead from the Supreme Court inhibits or weakens popular responsibility in the same area. The process of forming public opinion in the United States is a continuous one with many participants—Congress, the President, the press, political parties, scholars, pressure groups, and so on. The discussion of problems and the declaration of broad principles by the courts is a vital element in the community experience through which American policy is made. The Supreme Court is, among other things, an educational body, and the Justices are inevitably teachers in a vital national

24. See Subchapter II of the Internal Security Act of 1950, 64 Stat. 1019, 50 U.S.C. §§ 811–26 (Supp. 1952); see O'Brian, "Changing Attitudes toward Freedom," 9 *Wash. & Lee L. Rev.* 157 (1952).

seminar. The prestige of the Supreme Court as an institution is high, despite the conflicts of the last twenty years, and the members of the Court speak with a powerful voice.

Can one doubt, for example, the immensely constructive influence of the series of decisions in which the Court is slowly asserting the right of Negroes to vote and to travel, live, and have a professional education without segregation? These decisions have not paralyzed or supplanted legislative and community action. They have precipitated it. They have not created bigotry. They have helped to fight it. The cycle of decisions in these cases—influential because they are numerous, cumulative, and, on the whole, consistent—have played a crucial role in leading public opinion and encouraging public action toward meeting the challenge and burden of the Negro problem as a constitutional—that is, as a moral[25]—obligation. The Court's stand has stimulated men everywhere to take action, by state statutes, by new corporate or union policies, in local communities, on university faculties, in student fraternities, on courts, and in hospitals. The Negro does not yet have equality in American society or anything approaching it. But his position is being improved, year by year. And the decisions and opinions of the Supreme Court are helping immeasurably in that process.

The Court's lead has also been constructive, on the whole, in reforming state criminal procedures—here again in a long series of decisions which year by year are having their effect on the conduct of police officers and on the course of trials.[26] This slow and evolutionary process re-

25. See Myrdal, *An American Dilemma* (1944).

26. See, e.g., Boskey and Pickering, "Federal Restrictions on State Criminal Procedure," 13 *U. Chi. L. Rev.* 266 (1946); Frank, "The United States Supreme Court, 1950–51," 19 *U. Chi. L. Rev.* 165, 201–09 (1952), and earlier surveys cited at 165; Comment, 58 *Yale L.J.* 268 (1949).

quires a good deal of litigation: a single bolt from the blue could not overcome the inertia of long years of bad practice nor the natural desire of policemen and prosecutors to win their cases. The pressure of the Court's opinions in this area requires thought and action in every state legislature and, indeed, in every court and police station of the land. The Court has not stilled or prevented responsible democratic action on these problems. It has required it. Lawless police action has not yet been banished from American life, but the most primitive police sergeant is learning that third degree methods may backfire.

Other examples, both of action and of inaction, could readily be listed. Even the tortuous and often maddening cases in which the Court considers whether state action unduly burdens or discriminates against the national commerce or conflicts with national legislation in the same field impose some limits on the degree of economic autarchy states can practice, and provide ammunition to those who urge the preservation of the national economy as a single continental market.[27]

In the field of civil rights itself, the libertarian cases of the early 1930s helped prevent during the Second World War many of the repressive and unnecessary acts which distinguished the course of public policy during and after the First World War. Where the Court failed to follow its own traditions, as in the Japanese-American cases, the results were painful. I have elsewhere contended that earlier decisions[28] required new trials, at the least, in the *Korematsu* and *Hirabayashi* cases.[29] Even there, Congress has in part

27. See "The Price of Federalism," infra, p. 289.

28. Reaffirmed in Sterling v. Constantin, 287 U.S. 378 (1932).

29. Korematsu v. United States, 323 U.S. 214 (1944), and Hirabayashi v. United States, 320 U.S. 81 (1943), discussed in "The Japanese American Cases—A Disaster," infra, p. 193.

atoned for the weakness of the Supreme Court.[30] And in *Duncan v. Kahanamoku*[31] the Court itself has come some distance toward repairing the rent in its doctrines.

The reciprocal relation between the Court and the community in the formation of policy may be a paradox to those who believe that there is something undemocratic in the power of judicial review. But the work of the Court can have, and when wisely exercised does have, the effect not of inhibiting but of releasing and encouraging the dominantly democratic forces of American life. The historic reason for this paradox is that American life in all its aspects is an attempt to express and to fulfill a far-reaching moral code. Some observers find this a handicap to coldly realistic policy-making.[32] Others see in it the essential greatness and appealing power of America as an idea and a world force.[33] The prestige and authority of the Supreme Court derive from the fact that it is accepted as the ultimate interpreter of the American code in many of its most important applications.

30. ". . . to redress these loyal Americans in some measure for the wrongs inflicted upon them . . . would be simple justice." H.R. Rep. No. 732, 80th Cong., 1st Sess. 5 (1947). See 62 Stat. 1231 (1948), 50 U.S.C. App. §§ 1981 et seq. (Supp. 1952).

31. 327 U.S. 304 (1946).

32. See Kennan, *American Diplomacy, 1900–1950,* 95–103 (1951), McDougal, Book Review, 46 *A.B.A.J.* 102 (1952).

33. See Myrdal, *An American Dilemma* 3–6 (1944).

PART III

*Toward an Affirmative Constitutional Theory*
*of Judicial Action*

# 6

# *The Democratic Character of Judicial Review (II)*

THE DISTRUST of judicial review has been reflected in several aspects of the Supreme Court's work, but nowhere more clearly than in its consideration of politically sensitive issues. One of the central responsibilities of the judiciary in exercising its constitutional power is to help keep the other arms of government democratic in their procedures. The Constitution should guarantee the democratic legitimacy of political decisions by establishing essential rules for the political process. It provides that each state should have a republican form of government. And it gives each citizen the political as well as the personal protection of the Bill of Rights and other fundamental constitutional guarantees. The enforcement of these rights would assure Americans that legislative and executive policy would be formed out of free debate, democratic suffrage, untrammeled political effort, and full inquiry.

A series of modern cases in the Supreme Court throws doubt on the zeal with which the present-day Court will insist on preserving the personal and political liberties essential to making political decisions democratic. The language and reasoning of the Justices' opinions are full of unresolved doubts about the extent—and indeed the propriety

—of their powers. Contradictory and obscure, they represent not the final word, but a hesitant step toward the formulation of a constitutional doctrine adequate to the needs of American society in its present state of siege.

The contradictions and inconsistencies of the constitutional ideas which occupy the minds of several of the Justices are clearly presented by Elliot Richardson in an article called "Freedom of Expression and the Function of Courts."[1] I find it difficult to be sure of the ultimate position Mr. Richardson takes on the courts' function in protecting freedom of expression. He says he is not against judicial review as such, although he quotes with enthusiasm those who strongly disapprove it. He is against "the interventionist view," but concedes to history that the courts are under a constitutional obligation to strike down "clearly bad laws." "Clearly bad," he repeatedly points out, means "unconstitutional," and not merely "unwise." For it is "plainly untenable," he says, that the Constitution be considered a "source of specific directions for the solution of every issue of political wisdom," even where freedom of expression is involved. Not "every issue," but some issues. For in interpreting the limitations of the First and Fourteenth Amendments the courts must be free to disagree with the legislature and the executive sometimes, since

> once having conceded the power of the judiciary to enforce the Constitution, the very meaning of the First Amendment is that freedom of expression embodies values that must not be supplanted by short-sighted surges of bigotry and intolerance, however faithfully reflected by the legislature. The court must, therefore, having so far as possible determined what interests the

1. 65 *Harv. L. Rev.* 1 (1951). Until otherwise indicated the following quotations are from id. at 50–53.

legislature had in view, accept the responsibility of measuring their long-run importance against the values protected by the First Amendment. The courts have not yet articulated—and it is hardly to be expected that language apt for the purpose can be found—any standards of measurement. The triviality of the interests in unlittered streets, at one extreme, and the major importance of the interest in the national security, at the other, are easily recognized. Judgments in the area between must largely rest on "an intuition of experience which outruns analysis." The question is —whose intuition?[2]

The answer he gives is that in the end, the "intuition" of the judges must and does govern. The judges cannot escape the obligation of deciding matters of this kind, even when they give every degree of deference short of blind submission to the views of the legislature and the executive. Their judgment, after meticulously weighing the conflicting interests involved, will contain a final and decisive element of "wisdom" and even of "intuition"—"constitutional" wisdom and intuition, to be sure, as distinguished from the components of "legislative" judgment, but human choice nonetheless.

What standards are to guide the courts in exercising this extraordinary power, rather grudgingly conceded to exist? While I find much in Mr. Richardson's careful analysis of the elements of decision in this class of cases which helps to clarify the role and the responsibility of the judiciary, I can trace little or no connection between the conclusions of his analysis and his general philosophy of judicial review. Indeed, they seem to be in irreconcilable conflict. For his belief in the democratic character of judicial abstinence is

2. Id. at 39–40.

so strong as apparently to overcome even his distaste for decisions which fail to measure up to his standards of procedure in the exercise of the courts' constitutional function.

Whatever the exact nuance of meaning other readers will find in his article, to me the broad argument of Mr. Richardson's paper stands with the view deprecating and seeking to limit the Supreme Court's constitutional function as "undemocratic" and dangerous. The Court is not an elected body, but a bench of judges appointed for life. Therefore, he seems to be saying, it is an undemocratic institution.[3] It would be preferable in a democracy if the courts lacked the power to declare statutes or executive action unconstitutional, even in the area of civil rights. Although the power exists historically, reasons of democratic principle require that its exercise be kept to an irreducible minimum.

Although I believe that unresolved doubts on this score have led Mr. Richardson and others to tortured and untenable judgments about the work of the Court, this is not a conclusion he can admit. An inner conflict about the democratic propriety of judicial review is translated into an advocacy of extreme self-restraint in the exercise of the Court's acknowledged powers.

Few people would disagree with Mr. Richardson that in exercising their powers of judicial review, the courts should be as wise and statesmenlike as their capacities and temperaments permit—wise as judges, wise in their concern for the effectiveness of their occasional interventions into public affairs, and wise too in adapting the Constitution to changing conditions over centuries of development. The policy against judicial excess does not derive from an unhappy sense that the Supreme Court is "undemocratic," but from an awareness of the limited but vital historical place it oc-

3. See id. at 1, 54.

cupies in American public life. These limitations stem in considerable part from the fact that, as a court, it can pass only on issues presented at random in the course of litigation, often long after the action being reviewed has taken place. "The only check upon our own exercise of power," Justice Stone said, "is our own sense of self-restraint."[4] But "self-restraint," he made clear both there and elsewhere, is not an excuse for inaction. It is rooted in a respect for the dignity and high purpose of the other branches of government and a sympathetic understanding of the problems they must try to resolve.

That the Supreme Court's power is limited is perhaps the key to its extraordinary influence. Of course the Justices should give the utmost consideration to the views of other branches of the government, in civil rights as in other constitutional cases. Of course the Court should keep its powder dry and avoid wasting its ammunition in petty quarrels. Of course in the end the Court must balance even the policy in favor of freedom of speech against the right of the state to protect itself from mobs, riots in the streets, pornography, espionage, and revolution. It must consider whether means are reasonably adapted to ends; whether the government could have chosen alternative means which would raise fewer constitutional doubts; whether in fact circumstances justify the means adopted.

But when all the facts and arguments are before a court, in a suitable case and on a suitable record, it must decide, and invariably does decide, since a refusal to do so is a decision in favor of the constitutionality of the action being reviewed. The judges cannot refuse to decide cases because they personally believe the United States would be a more democratic country without judicial review. A preoccupa-

4. United States v. Butler, 297 U.S. 1, 79 (1936) (dissenting opinion).

tion with the prudent and statesmanlike exercise of their duties can hardly be allowed to deny the existence of those duties. Anxious as they may be not to compromise the Court as an institution, and to avoid when possible the intense political pressures of hard cases, they should recall too that their great power exists to be used at the right times, not lost in atrophy. The Court can be destroyed by the weakness as well as the recklessness of its members. The maxim *justitia fiat* has a place in the history of law at least as honorable as the Fabian counsel of prudence. There are times when the hard, great, politically sensitive cases do come before the bar. In times of crisis they are likely to come frequently and in acute form; indeed, if the cases were not hard, there would be little point in bringing them to the Supreme Court. It is not because people expect the Supreme Court to avoid difficult and vital cases that it has gained its peculiar prestige and authority in popular opinion. Visitors to Washington piously bring their children to the Supreme Court because they believe it is a place where vitally important rights are vindicated against all comers—where *The Law* in some primitive but meaningful sense is supreme even against the mighty forces of society.

Mr. Richardson cannot bring himself to accept Judge Learned Hand's monkish rule of complete abstinence,[5] though he quotes it with approval.[6] The courts cannot avoid some responsibility for enforcing the political and civil rights declared by the Constitution, although he warns that dependence on the courts as protectors of liberty would sap self-discipline, and lead to "suspicion, intolerance, bigotry and discrimination which the sporadic forays of the judiciary are helpless to check." While Judge Hand's state-

5. See pp. 129–37 supra.
6. Richardson, supra note 1, at 52–53. Quotations in this paragraph are from id. at 52–53.

ment should not be taken literally, it should serve as a "counsel of moderation" for judges. The transition is difficult to follow. If it destroys the spirit of self-reliance to submit large political issues to litigation, surely a little more or less of the hemlock cup will not make much difference. This is strong poison, fatal in small doses. But Mr. Richardson urges a distinction. "Ten opinions striking down ten doubtfully bad laws," he contends, "surely are not twice as effective in their educational impact as five opinions striking down five clearly bad laws. There is much to be said, in any event, for the educational value of opinions *refusing* to invalidate as unconstitutional what is merely unwise."

Since no one in recent years has revived Jefferson's proposal to make the Supreme Court a third house of the national legislature or advocated the invalidation of "doubtful" laws, this part of the argument strikes at men of straw. The question, and the only question, is what criteria the Court should employ in deciding that a statute or executive action is "clearly" contrary to one or another of the provisions of the Constitution. Unless we are to say that the Supreme Court, like a jury, should not declare statutes unconstitutional save by unanimous vote, the criterion of limiting judicial review to "clear" cases is one for the minds and souls of the Justices. Dissenters normally believe the law is just as clear as their brethren in the majority. In cases dealing with freedom of expression the Court sits as the ultimate guardian of the liberties on which the democratic effectiveness of political action depends. Their decisions in this area help to determine whether the citizen, whatever his color or his opinions, can live in dignity and security. Mr. Richardson contends, however, that even on such questions the normal presumptions in favor of the constitutionality of legislation should apply with full force. The Court must decide, he repeats over and over again, not that a statute is

179

unwise, but that its provisions fall outside the area of reasonable judgment: in other words, to paraphrase his text, that the competing considerations resolved by its enactment have been arbitrarily resolved and that the inferences from the data upon which they rest have been irrationally drawn.[7]

There are alternative ways to define the Court's task in passing on the constitutionality of legislation or official action. The language of "presumptions" is often used. And it is commonly said that the Supreme Court should not invalidate action by other branches of the government if "any" rational basis for upholding it can be found. Formulas of this kind obscure more than they illuminate. The real problem for the Court cannot be compressed into a "scintilla" rule. The Court must balance competing considerations: rights of privacy against the duty to speak; order against freedom; safety against the privileges of political action. In reaching a judgment that must accommodate society to such conflicts, the Court is hardly aided by the proposition that it must uphold the act of government if "any" rational basis for it exists. As Justice Frankfurter has said, "those liberties of the individual which history has attested as the indispensable conditions of an open as against a closed society" must be given an altogether different weight by the Court than other privileges altered by legislative or executive order.[8] Society is more deeply affected by a statute limiting political action than by a zoning ordinance, however restrictive.

However, even Mr. Richardson's formula for stating the Court's function in judicial review does not settle the cases. The difficulty under his rule comes in deciding whether

7. Id. at 50.
8. Kovacs v. Cooper, 336 U.S. 77, 95 (1949) (concurring opinion).

competing considerations have been "arbitrarily" resolved or inferences from data "irrationally" drawn.

When Mr. Richardson applies his general view of the Court's function to the cases, I find a sharp difference between the two halves of his thesis. In the *Dennis* case,[9] the jury had found the defendants guilty under the Smith Act of "teaching and advocating" the doctrine of overthrowing the state by force and of conspiring to teach and advocate such doctrines. There were strong competing interests: the right of the state to protect itself against subversion or revolution and the interest of the state and of the defendants in protecting freedom of speech, of thought, and of political organization and action. Presumably Mr. Richardson would defend the decision upholding the conviction, either as a "doubtful" case which the Court should have refused to decide, or as one where legislative and executive judgment, however unwise, clearly fell within the zone of rationality. Yet the Court had no record before it which could permit a judicial judgment on the final constitutional issue as Mr. Richardson defines it.

There was no legislative judgment that the organized promulgation of these doctrines by the Communist Party threatened the security of the state at the time of the trial. The statute underlying the prosecution was passed in 1940, with a meager and obscure legislative history, in language which has been invoked since 1798, with few variations, whenever American legislatures have become alarmed over seditious doctrines and their effect on public order.[10] The Act was hardly aimed at the Communist Party in express terms or otherwise, and in fact its first application was directed against bitter enemies of that Party. While Congress has passed many statutes against the Communist threat, it

9. Dennis v. United States, 341 U.S. 494 (1951).
10. See Chafee, *Free Speech in the United States* 439–46, 462–84 (1941).

has not declared that membership in the Communist Party is a crime. The decision to try the leaders of the Communist Party under the Smith Act was not a legislative judgment but an executive one. For the period from June 22, 1941, when Germany invaded Russia, until some time after the end of the war, presumably neither the legislative nor the executive branches of the government would have invoked the statute against the Communist Party. The development of world political pressures and the change in the policies of the Communist Party within the United States, however, led the executive branch of the government to proceed against it under the Act, although other statutes could have been chosen as more direct and appropriate bases for the prosecution.

In terms of Mr. Richardson's analysis, the Court's constitutional task should have led it to consider evidence on the probability and gravity of the evil sought to be suppressed and on the "necessity" of restricting speech in order to prevent it. In this case, the Court's examination could hardly have been aided by a presumption in favor of a legislative determination of the danger and of the necessity for the application of the legislation to the defendants, for no such legislative determinations had been made.

Judge Learned Hand, for the Court of Appeals, fell back on judicial notice for evidence that restriction of speech was necessary to protect the state against the Communist conspiracy. Reviewing the state of world politics in 1948, when the indictment was presented, he found sufficient evidence in the reality of Soviet strength and of Soviet plans for direct and indirect aggression to support the conclusion that the activities of the defendants in organizing and directing the American Communist Party were a "present danger" to the security of the United States. The conspirators did not plan to strike until war broke out or until

other circumstances presented them with a favorable opportunity. But in 1948 Soviet-American relations were such
that war could break out at any moment.

> We shall be silly dupes [Judge Hand wrote], if we for-
> get that again and again in the past thirty years, just
> such preparations in other countries have aided to
> supplant existing governments, when the time was ripe.
> Nothing short of a revived doctrine of *laissez-faire,*
> which would have amazed even the Manchester School
> at its apogee, can fail to realize that such a conspiracy
> creates a danger of the utmost gravity and of enough
> probability to justify its suppression. We hold that it is
> a danger "clear and present."[11]

The Chief Justice's opinion, formally accepting the
"clear and present danger" test as the starting point of analysis, similarly treated the case as if it were a prosecution for
conspiracy to overthrow the government by force. Since the
indictment charged only the organized teaching and advocacy of revolutionary doctrine, however, the Court was able
to avoid the historic distinctions between criminal "prepa-
rations" and criminal "attempts" which might have complicated a direct prosecution for revolutionary action. By
assuming certain facts not in the record of the trial to be
true, under the doctrine that judges can take "judicial
notice" of matters of common knowledge, the Court viewed
the defendants as guilty of a crime for which they had been
neither indicted nor convicted. On that footing, it found
that the crime charged was within the limits of what could
be done constitutionally. Both the opinion of Judge Hand
and that of the Chief Justice are at pains to indicate that
the defendants' advocacy of revolution could be made crim-

11. United States v. Dennis, 183 F.2d 201, 213 (2d Cir. 1950).

inal only because the defendants were part and parcel "of an apparatus designed and dedicated to the overthrow of the Government, in the context of world crisis after crisis. . . . It is the existence of the conspiracy which creates the danger. . . . If the ingredients of the reaction are present, we cannot bind the Government to wait until the catalyst is added."[12] Yet this crucial element, which seemed to make the "teaching and advocacy" of revolution a crime, was established by the uncontrolled process of judicial notice.

Mr. Justice Jackson, in a typical statement of the fainéant judicial philosophy he sometimes espouses, refused to put judgment on so slender a foundation. A serious application of a "clear and present danger" test, he wrote, would require the courts to assess imponderables "which baffle the best informed foreign offices and our most experienced politicians. . . . The judicial process simply is not adequate to a trial of such far-flung issues."[13] He therefore rested his vote for affirmance on the broader ground that the organized teaching and advocacy of revolutionary doctrine, without particular qualification as to surrounding circumstance, could be made criminal in the name of defending the state.

Mr. Justice Frankfurter, who also concurred in the result, did not go far into the central doctrinal and procedural problems of the case. His opinion passes off the issue with a quip. "Mr. Justice Douglas," he wrote, "quite properly points out that the conspiracy before us is not a conspiracy to overthrow the Government. But it would be equally wrong to treat it as a seminar in political theory."[14] It would be absurd, he said—despite his formal acceptance of the "clear and present danger" test—"To make the validity of legislation depend on judicial reading of events still in the

12. Dennis v. United States, 341 U.S. 494, 510–11 (1951).
13. Id. at 570.
14. Id. at 546.

womb of time . . ."[15] He would not say that a legislature was beyond the limits of its constitutional powers in concluding that under present political circumstances the "recruitment of additional members for the Party would create a substantial danger to national security."[16] While there was no reliable evidence in the record tracing acts of sabotage or espionage directly to the defendants, a report of the Canadian Royal Commission on the role of the Communist movement in Canadian espionage, and the experience of Klaus Fuchs—who, the Justice thought, had been led into the service of the Soviet Union through Communist indoctrination—were invoked to help support and justify what the Justice treated throughout his opinion as the judgment of Congress that the statute should apply to the Communist Party:

> Congress was not barred by the Constitution from believing that indifference to such experience would be an exercise not of freedom but of irresponsibility. . . . Congress has determined that the danger created by advocacy of overthrow justifies the ensuing restriction on freedom of speech. . . . Can we establish a constitutional doctrine which forbids the elected representatives of the people to make this choice? Can we hold that the First Amendment deprives Congress of what it deemed necessary for the Government's protection?[17]

For a variety of reasons drawn from his philosophy of judicial review, he shrinks from such a conclusion.

The transmutation of the "clear and present danger" test in these opinions is quite remarkable. It begins as the principle that since the First Amendment cannot be considered

15. Id. at 551.
16. Id. at 547.
17. Id. at 548–51.

to mean what it says, the Court will decide for itself whether attempted restrictions on freedom of speech are justified by evidence of an imminent and serious danger arising from a speech. Judge Learned Hand finds a present danger of a future coup d'etat in the activities of the defendants, viewed against the background of world and domestic politics in 1948. The Chief Justice's opinion says that the danger need not be one that the government will be overthrown; it is enough that an attempt may some day be made. Nor must the danger be "present" in any immediate sense. The injury to the state sought to be prevented by the Act, he indicates, is both the physical and the political damage which may be occasioned by extremist parties and their more extreme activities. Since the "clear and present danger" test in this form permits the Court to consider not only present but also possible future injuries, the problem of anticipating the future becomes inscrutable, if not insoluble, and the Court says it can find no ground for overruling the supposed judgment of Congress that the teaching and advocacy of revolution is illegal, at least in the case of the twelve leaders of the Communist Party.

To all this Justice Douglas' answer was a powerful one. The record, he urges, contains no evidence on the key factual issue of the case: whether the defendants' conspiracy to teach and advocate the communist theory of revolution constituted a clear and present danger to the nation. While the purposes and capabilities of the Soviet Union in world politics would be relevant evidence on the clear and present danger of the defendants' advocacy of revolution within the United States, they hardly exhaust the issue. The Court could not say that the defendants' conspiracy to teach revolution in the United States "is outlawed because Soviet Russia and her Red Army are a threat to world peace."[18] If

18. Id. at 588.

it were proper to approach the question on the basis of judicial notice, Mr. Justice Douglas observed, he would conclude that the Communist Party was impotent and discredited as a political force within the United States, that it had been exposed and destroyed as an effective political faction by free speech and vigorous counteraction. "Some nations less resilient than the United States, where illiteracy is high and where democratic traditions are only budding, might have to take drastic steps and jail these men for merely speaking their creed. But in America they are miserable merchants of unwanted ideas; their wares remain unsold. The fact that their ideas are abhorrent does not make them powerful."[19] The weakness of the Communist Party as a political entity is not the end of the matter, however. In determining whether their advocacy of revolution would endanger the Republic, he continued, it would be necessary to examine the extent to which they had infiltrated key areas of government and of economic life.

But the record is silent on these facts. If we are to proceed on the basis of judicial notice, it is impossible for me to say that the Communists in this country are so potent or so strategically deployed that they must be suppressed for their speech. I could not so hold unless I were willing to conclude that the activities in recent years of committees of Congress, of the Attorney General, of labor unions, of state legislatures, and of Loyalty Boards were so futile as to leave the country on the edge of grave peril. To believe that petitioners and their following are placed in such critical positions as to endanger the Nation is to believe the incredible. It is safe to say that the followers of the creed of Soviet

19. Id. at 588–89.

Communism are known to the F.B.I.; that in case of war with Russia they will be picked up overnight as were all prospective saboteurs at the commencement of World War II; that the invisible army of petitioners is the best known, the most beset, and the least thriving of any fifth column in history. Only those held by fear and panic could think otherwise.

This is my view if we are to act on the basis of judicial notice. But the mere statement of the opposing views indicates how important it is that we know the facts before we act. Neither prejudice nor hate nor senseless fear should be the basis of this solemn act. Free speech—the glory of our system of government—should not be sacrificed on anything less than plain and objective proof of danger that the evil advocated is imminent. On this record no one can say that petitioners and their converts are in such a strategic position as to have even the slightest chance of achieving their aims.[20]

Mr. Richardson is concerned with this phase of the *Dennis* case. He disagrees with Justice Frankfurter, who, he says, supports the supposed legislative judgment by taking judicial notice of facts which the legislature could not have considered when the statute was passed. He argues that

To assure that the facts of which it proposes to take notice are properly subject to notice, the court should give the defendant an opportunity to controvert these facts, although reserving to itself the final determination as to whether they are genuinely disputable. Disregard of the disputed facts may still leave an undisputed residue adequate to fill in the background of

20. Id. at 589–90.

inherent probability. If not, there would remain no alternative but to take testimony on the issue.[21]

And he is equally troubled by the failure of the Court explicitly to exercise its own judgment as to the rationality of the government's view that the defendants' organized advocacy of revolution constituted a danger to the state:

> The legislative judgment expressed in the Smith Act could not, any more than that expressed in the New York statute involved in the *Gitlow* case, foreclose the question whether the circumstances justified the suppression of any sort of "discourse" teaching or advocating violent overthrow of organized government, no matter how "redundant" and no matter how limited its circulation. Supplementing the legislative judgment in the *Dennis* case, however, in contrast with the *Gitlow* case, were the jury's findings that the conspiracy to teach and advocate embraced a systematic course of indoctrination, not a single discourse, and was to be carried out by a rigidly disciplined organization "as speedily as circumstances would permit." Both the legislative judgment and the jury's findings, moreover, were strengthened in the *Dennis* case by facts subject to judicial notice which bore on the already existing probability of the apprehended evils, while in the *Gitlow* case such facts were insignificant. But the inexplicitness of the *Dennis* affirming opinions, their differences in emphasis, and the very fact that none was able to secure a majority leaves uncertain the weight to be given in future cases to legislative judgments that

21. Richardson, "Freedom of Expression and the Function of Courts," 65 *Harv. L. Rev.* 1, 30–31 (1951).

a certain type of utterance contributes to the probability of an apprehended evil.[22]

The *Dennis* case is by any standard one of the most important and far-reaching of modern civil rights cases. In disposing of it, the Supreme Court had several alternatives. It could have reversed for a further trial on the factual justification for a conclusion that the defendants' organized advocacy of revolution gave rise to a present danger of anticipated future action to achieve that end. Such a decision would have put the Court's performance of its own function, in reviewing the constitutionality of a statute outlawing "the teaching and advocacy" of revolutionary ideas, on a more orderly and rational basis. Or it could have held that the statute, as applied to the defendants, violated the First Amendment. A result on this ground would have forced the executive to prosecute the Communists on the direct charge that the Communist Party is not a political party, but a conspiracy to subvert the state. No one doubts the constitutionality of statutes making it a crime to attempt the overthrow of the government or to conspire to that end.[23] In such a prosecution, the propaganda arms of the Communist Party would be considered as an integral part of a central conspiratorial plan before the Court in its entirety.

As the case was disposed of, however, we are left with a series of paradoxes. Insofar as the Justices' opinions can be brought into a single focus, they declare that the systematic teaching and advocacy of revolution can be made a crime, at least (and perhaps only) if the organization for spreading such ideas is an aspect of a serious and potentially important attempt to attack the government by other means. The

22. Id. at 35.
23. See Nathanson, "The Communist Trial and the Clear-and-Present Danger Test," 63 *Harv. L. Rev.* 1167 (1950).

case is confusing, however, because the qualifications of factual circumstance considered decisive of constitutionality were established entirely on the basis of judicial notice. The Court purports to accept the "clear and present danger" test of the Holmes-Brandeis dissents as prevailing law. That approach to the constitutional problem in civil rights cases is designed to give the courts considerable discretion in passing on the constitutionality of legislative or executive action. Yet the Court applies the Holmes-Brandeis formula in a way which makes it extremely difficult to conceive of a successful case against the reasonableness of the government's decision to prosecute.

In the end, the *Dennis* case is strongly colored—perhaps determined—by the view that cloistered and appointed Justices should not pit their judgment of the Constitution against that of the elected representatives of the people, who have to deal with these difficult problems at first hand. Some of the Justices, indeed, come perilously close to denying that they have any duty to review the constitutional judgment of the legislature and the executive at all. Much of the reasoning in the various opinions, like that in other cases, draws strength from the premise that the power of judicial review is somehow tainted, and of undemocratic character, and that the courts should not interfere with the attempts of Congress and the President to deal with wars and emergencies.

## II

When the Supreme Court falters, as I believe it has in this and some other civil rights cases, we need not conclude that the Constitution is dead. Mr. Justice Brandeis used to say that no case is ever finally decided until it is rightly decided. The example of the Holmes and Brandeis dissents, and their ultimate acceptance, should encourage the present dissenters on the Court to persevere. Even though all their arguments are not of equal weight, their effort and example are a force which can in time help to restore sounder views. For civil liberties in the United States are in a state of grave crisis, and I venture to hope that some of these decisions of the Supreme Court will not prove to be its lasting position. The problem of security is concededly most serious, and the state has every right to protect itself against attack. But the Court has the correlative duty to inquire whether repressive acts are reasonably adapted to the end of security. Do we really protect the state against spies and saboteurs by making professors of music take oaths and by combing through the lives of all government employees for scattered episodes of sin, enthusiasm, and folly? Is it proper to attack the Communist Party for "teaching and advocating" subversion of the state—a doctrine which could have jailed Calhoun and the participants in the Hartford Convention, and perhaps Thoreau as well—when the Party could have been prosecuted for what it was and undoubtedly is, a conspiracy to overthrow the government by force? Can the real and pressing danger of the Communist fifth column be met by police measures, as some qualified students of the problem urge,[24] or by a general movement to silence heterodoxy, create doubts in the relation of man to man, make universities hesitate to appoint young firebrands, and lead honest men to wonder whether they should continue to visit their friends?

24. Philbrick, *I Led Three Lives* 299–300 (1952).

# 7

# *The Japanese American Cases—A Disaster*

*He* [the King of Great Britain] *has affected to render the Military independent of and superior to the Civil Power.*
            —THE DECLARATION OF INDEPENDENCE

*War is too serious a business to be left to generals.*
            —CLEMENCEAU

OUR WARTIME treatment of Japanese aliens and citizens of Japanese descent on the West Coast was hasty, unnecessary, and mistaken. The course of action which we undertook was in no way required or justified by the circumstances of the war. It was calculated to produce both indi-

The following short-form citations will be used: *Tolan Committee Hearings: Hearings before House Select Committee Investigating National Defense Migration pursuant to H. Res. 113, 77th* Cong., 2d Sess. (1942); *Tolan Committee Reports (Preliminary)* and *(Fourth Interim):* H. R. Rep. No. 1911 *(Preliminary Report and Recommendations)* and H. R. Rep. No. 2124 *(Fourth Interim Report),* 77th Cong., 2d Sess. (1942); *DeWitt Final Report:* U. S. Army, Western Defense Command, *Final Report, Japanese Evacuation from the West Coast,* 1942 (1943, released 1944).

———

First published in 54 *Yale Law Journal* 489 (1945); a shortened version appeared in *Harper's Magazine* in 1945 under the title, "Our Worst Wartime Mistake."

vidual injustice and deep-seated social maladjustments of a cumulative and sinister kind.[1]

All in all, the internment of the West Coast Japanese is the worst blow our liberties have sustained in many years. Over 100,000 men, women, and children were imprisoned, some 70,000 of them citizens of the United States, without indictment or the proffer of charges, pending inquiry into their "loyalty." They were taken into custody as a military measure on the ground that espionage and sabotage were especially to be feared from persons of Japanese blood. They were removed from the West Coast area because the military thought it would take too long to conduct individual loyalty investigations on the ground. They were arrested in an area where the courts were open and freely functioning. They were held under prison conditions in uncomfortable camps, far from their homes, and for lengthy periods—several

1. See Message from the President of the United States, Segregation of Loyal and Disloyal Japanese in Relocation Centers, Report on S. Res. 166, 78th Cong., 1st Sess., S. Doc. No. 69 (1943); *Tolan Committee Reports (Preliminary* and *Fourth Interim);* McWilliams, *Prejudice* (1944); McWilliams, *What About Our Japanese Americans* (1944); Leighton, *The Governing of Men* (1945); An Intelligence Officer, "The Japanese in America: The Problem and the Solution," 185 *Harper's Mag.* 489 (1942); Miyamoto, "Immigrants and Citizens of Japanese Origin," 223 *Annals* 107 (1942); Fisher, "What Race Baiting Costs America," 60 *Christian Century* 1009 (1943); Heath, "What About Hugh Kiino?" 187 *Harper's Mag.* 450 (1943); "Issei, Nisei, Kibei," 29 *Fortune* 8 (April 1944); Bellquist, "Report on the Question of Transferring the Japanese from the Pacific Coast," 29 *Tolan Committee Hearings* 11240 (1942); La Violette, "The American-Born Japanese and the World Crisis," 7 *Can. J. Econ. & Pol. Sci.* 517 (1941); Redfield, "The Japanese-Americans," in *American Society in Wartime* 143 (Ogburn ed. 1943); Stonequist, "The Restricted Citizen," 223 *Annals* 149 (1942).

The War Relocation Authority compiled an admirable bibliography on Japanese and Japanese Americans in the United States; Parts I and II were published Nov. 7, 1942, and Part III Aug. 14, 1943. *The Pacific Citizen,* a newspaper published in Salt Lake City by the Japanese American Citizens League is an indispensable source of material on events and attitudes with respect to the process of evacuation, internment, and relocation.

years in many cases. If found "disloyal" in administrative proceedings they were confined indefinitely, although no statute makes "disloyalty" a crime; it would be difficult indeed for a statute to do so under a Constitution which has been interpreted to minimize imprisonment for political opinions, both by defining the crime of treason in extremely rigid and explicit terms, and by limiting convictions for sedition and like offenses.[2] In the course of relocation citizens suffered severe property losses, despite some custodial assistance by the government.[3] Perhaps seventy thousand persons were still in camps, "loyal" and "disloyal" citizens and aliens alike, more than three years after the programs were instituted.[4]

By the time the question reached the Supreme Court, the crisis which was supposed to justify the action had passed. The Court faced two issues: should it automatically accept the judgment of the military as to the need for the relocation program, or should it require a judicial investigation of the question? Was there factual support for the military

2. See Cramer v. United States, 325 U.S. 1 (1945) (treason). For the evidence required to justify imprisonment for attacking the loyalty of the armed forces, see Hartzel v. United States, 322 U.S. 680 (1944). It is notable that persons—citizens or aliens—who actively propagandized in favor of the Axis cause could not be convicted of sedition nor placed into protective custody, although loyal citizens of Japanese descent could be arrested and held in preventive custody for periods of more than three years. See also Keegan v. United States, 325 U.S. 478 (1945), which reversed the conviction of active members of the German-American Bund, a Nazi organization, for conspiracy to obstruct the draft. Apparently the defendants included persons of German nationality as well as of German descent, id. at 1212. As for the difficulty of obtaining individual exclusion orders against persons—usually naturalized citizens—with strong German political affiliations, see cases cited infra note 13.

3. On the handling of evacuees' property see War Relocation Authority, *A Statement on Handling of Evacuee Property* (May 1943); *DeWitt Final Report*, c. xi; *Tolan Committee Reports (Fourth Interim)* 173–97.

4. See Myer, "The WRA Says 'Thirty,'" 112 *New Republic* 867 (1945).

judgment that the course of the war required the exclusion and confinement of the Japanese American population of the West Coast? Clearly, if such steps were not necessary to the prosecution of the war, they invaded rights protected by the third article of the Constitution, and the Fifth and Sixth Amendments.

If the Court had stepped forward in bold heart to vindicate the law and declare the entire program illegal, the episode would have been passed over as a national scandal, but a temporary one altogether capable of reparation. But the Court, after timid and evasive delays, upheld the main features of the program.[5] That step converted a piece of wartime folly into political doctrine and a permanent part of the law. Moreover, it affected a peculiarly important and sensitive part of the law. The relationship of civil to military authority is not often litigated. It is nonetheless one of the two or three most essential elements in the legal structure of a democratic society. The Court's few declarations on the subject govern the handling of vast affairs. They determine the essential organization of the military establishment, state and federal, in time of emergency or of war, as well as of peace. What the Supreme Court did in these cases, and especially in *Korematsu v. United States,* was to in-

---

5. Hirabayashi v. United States, 320 U.S. 81 (1943); Korematsu v. United States, 323 U.S. 214 (1944); *Ex parte* Mitsuye Endo, 323 U.S. 283 (1944). See Fairman, *The Law of Martial Rule* 255–61 (2d ed. 1943); Dembitz, "Racial Discrimination and the Military Judgment," 45 *Colum. L. Rev.* 175 (1945); Fairman, "The Law of Martial Rule and the National Emergency," 55 *Harv. L. Rev.* 1253 (1942); Freeman, "Genesis, Exodus and Leviticus: Genealogy, Evacuation and the Law," 28 *Cornell L. Q.* 414 (1943); Graham, "Martial Law in California," 31 *Calif. L. Rev.* 6 (1942); Lerner, "Freedom: Image and Reality," in *Safeguarding Civil Liberty Today* (1945); Watson, "The Japanese Evacuation and Litigation Arising Therefrom," 22 *Ore. L. Rev.* 46 (1942); Wolfson, "Legal Doctrine, War Power and Japanese Evacuation," 32 *Ky. L. J.* 328 (1944); Comment, 51 *Yale L. J.* 1316 (1942); Note, 11 *Geo. Wash. L. Rev.* 482 (1943).

crease the strength of the military in relation to civil government. It upheld an act of military power without a factual record in which the justification for the act was analyzed. Thus it created doubt as to the standards of responsibility to which the military power will be held. For the first time in American legal history, the Court seriously weakened the protection of our basic civil right, the writ of habeas corpus. It established a precedent which may well be used to encourage attacks on the civil rights of citizens and aliens, and may make it possible for some of those attacks to succeed. It will give aid to reactionary political programs which use social division and racial prejudice as tools for conquering power. As Mr. Justice Jackson pointed out, the principle of these cases "lies about like a loaded weapon ready for the hand of any authority that can bring forward a plausible claim of an urgent need."[6]

The opinions of the Supreme Court in the Japanese American cases do not belong in the same political or intellectual universe with *Ex parte Milligan*,[7] *DeJonge v. Oregon*,[8] *Hague v. CIO*,[9] or Mr. Justice Brandeis' opinion in the *Whitney* case.[10] They threaten even more than the trial tradition of the common law and the status of individuals in relation to the state. By their acceptance of ethnic differences as a criterion for discrimination, these cases will make it more difficult to resolve one of the central problems in

6. Korematsu v. United States, 323 U.S. 214, 246 (1944).

7. 4 Wall. 2 (U.S. 1867).

8. 299 U.S. 353 (1937).

9. 307 U.S. 496 (1939).

10. Whitney v. California, 274 U.S. 357, 372–80 (1927). See Prof. Riesman's thoughtful essay, "Civil Liberties in a Period of Transition," in 3 *Public Policy* 33 (1942); Chafee, *Free Speech in the United States* (1941) passim, especially pp. 440–90; Lusky, "Minority Rights and the Public Interest," 52 *Yale L. J.* 1 (1942).

American life—the problem of minorities. They are a breach, potentially a major breach, in the principle of equality. Unless repudiated, they may encourage devastating and unforeseen social and political conflicts.

## II

What General DeWitt did in the name of military precaution within his Western Defense Command was quite different from the security measures taken in Hawaii or on the East Coast—although both places were more active theaters of war in 1942 than the states of Washington, Oregon, California, and Arizona, which comprised the Western Defense Command.

On the East Coast, and in the United States generally, enemy aliens were controlled without mass arrests or evacuations, despite a considerable public agitation in favor of violent action. A registration of aliens had been accomplished under the Alien Registration Act of 1940, and the police authorities had compiled information about fascist sympathizers among the alien population, as well as about those who were citizens. "On the night of December 7, 1941," the Attorney General reported, "the most dangerous of the persons in this group were taken into custody; in the following weeks a number of others were apprehended. Each arrest was made on the basis of information concerning the specific alien taken into custody. We have used no dragnet techniques and have conducted no indiscriminate, large-scale raids."[11] Immediately after Pearl Harbor restric-

11. *Annual Report of the Attorney General for Fiscal Year Ended June 30, 1942* at 14 (1943). In the first few weeks of war, 2,971 enemy aliens were taken into custody, 1,484 Japanese, 1,256 Germans and 231 Italians. See *N.Y. Times*, Jan. 4, 1942, § IV, p. 8, col. 3. The basic Presidential proclamations on the treatment of enemy aliens appear in 6 *Fed. Reg.* 6321, 6323, 6324 (1941). Regulations under them were issued from time to time by the

tions were imposed upon the conduct of all enemy aliens over fourteen years of age. They were forbidden the Canal Zone and certain restricted military areas thereafter to be specified. They were not to leave the country, travel in a plane, change their place of abode, or travel about outside their own communities without special permission. They were forbidden to own or use firearms, cameras, short-wave radio sets, codes, ciphers, or invisible ink. The district attorneys were given broad discretion to allow aliens of enemy nationality to carry on their usual occupations, under scrutiny, but without other restriction. A new registration of aliens of enemy nationality was conducted. The basic object of the control plan was to keep security officers informed, but otherwise to allow the aliens almost their normal share in the work and life of the community.

Aliens under suspicion, and those who violated the regulations, were subject to summary arrest on Presidential warrant. "The law," the Attorney General said, "does not require any hearing before the internment of an enemy alien. I believed that nevertheless, we should give each enemy alien who had been taken into custody an opportunity for a hearing on the question whether he should be interned."[12] Those arrested were therefore promptly examined by voluntary Alien Enemy Hearing Boards, consisting of citizens appointed for the task by the Attorney General. These Boards could recommend that individuals be interned,

Attorney General. See, e.g., 7 *Fed. Reg.* 844 (1942). See *Tolan Committee Reports (Fourth Interim)* 25; Biddle, "Taking No Chances," *Collier's*, March 21, 1942, p. 21; Lasker, "Friends or Enemies?" 31 *Survey Graphic* 277 (1942); Rowe, "The Alien Enemy Program—So Far," 2 *Common Ground* 19 (Summer 1942); Bentwich, "Alien Enemies in the United States," 163 *Contemp. Rev.* 225 (1943); Comment, 51 *Yale L. J.* 1316 (1942).

12. *Annual Report of the Attorney General for Fiscal Year Ended June 30, 1942* at 14 (1943).

paroled, or released unconditionally. This operation was smoothly conducted, with a minimal interference with the standards of justice in the community. Of the 1,100,000 enemy aliens in the United States, 9,080 had been examined by the end of the fiscal year 1943; 4,119 were then interned, 3,705 paroled, 1,256 released, and 9,341 were still in custody. On June 30, 1944, the number in custody had been reduced to 6,238. The number of those interned was then 2,525, those paroled, 4,840, and those released, 1,926.[13]

In Hawaii a somewhat different procedure was followed, but one less drastic than the evacuation program pursued on the West Coast. Immediately after Pearl Harbor martial law was declared in Hawaii, and the commanding general assumed the role of military governor. Courts were reopened for some purposes shortly after the bombing raid, but the return of civil law to Hawaii was a slow, controversial process. During the period of three and a half years after Pearl Harbor, military power was installed in Hawaii, con-

---

13. The number in custody was greater than the number interned by reason of the inclusion of members of internees' families who requested internment, as well as certain alien enemy seamen and alien enemies held for Central and South American countries. See *Annual Report of the Attorney General for Fiscal Year Ended June 30, 1944* at 8 (1945).

A small number of citizens and enemy aliens suspected of a propensity for espionage or sabotage by reason of their political opinions were ordered removed from designated security areas both on the East and West Coasts under the statute of March 21, 1942, cited infra note 27. This process met with notable judicial resistance. Schueller v. Drum, 51 F. Supp. 383 (E. D. Pa. 1943); Ebel v. Drum, 52 F. Supp. 189 (D. Mass. 1943); Scherzberg v. Maderia, 57 F. Supp. 42 (E. D. Pa. 1944). Cf. Labedz v. Kramer, 55 F. Supp. 25 (D. Ore. 1944); Ochikubo v. Bonesteel, 57 F. Supp. 513 (S. D. Calif. 1944). See also United States v. Meyer, 140 F. 2d 652 (2nd Cir., 1944); Alexander v. DeWitt, 141 F. 2d 573 (9th Cir., 1944). The standards developed in these cases to justify the exclusion of persons from military areas as dangerous now closely correspond to those applied in sedition cases. Exclusion will be sustained, that is, only on a showing of "clear and present danger," of aid to the enemy, something more than opinions alone.

stitutionally or not, and the normal controls against arrest on suspicion were not available.[14] The population of Hawaii was then 500,000, of whom some 160,000, or 32 per cent, were of Japanese descent. Despite the confusions of the moment in Hawaii, only 700 to 800 Japanese aliens were arrested and sent to the mainland for internment. In addition, fewer than 1,100 persons of Japanese ancestry were transferred to the mainland to relocation centers. These Japanese were arrested on the basis of individual suspicion, resting on previous examination or observed behavior, or they were families of interned aliens, transferred voluntarily. Of those transferred from Hawaii to the mainland, 912 were citizens, the rest aliens.[15] Even under a regime of martial law, men were arrested as individuals, and safety was assured without mass arrests.

These procedures compare favorably in their essential character with the precautions taken in Britain and France. The British procedure was the model for our general practice in dealing with enemy aliens. The British government began in 1939 by interning only those enemy aliens who were on a "security list." Others were subjected to minor police restrictions, pending their individual examination by especially established tribunals. One hundred and twelve

14. See Fairman, *The Law of Martial Rule* 239–55 (2d ed. 1943); Lind, *The Japanese in Hawaii under War Conditions* (1942); Anthony, "Martial Law in Hawaii," 30 *Calif. L. Rev.* 371 (1942), 31 *Calif. L. Rev.* 477 (1943); Frank, "Ex parte Milligan v. The Five Companies: Martial Law in Hawaii," 44 *Colum. L. Rev.* 639 (1944); Coggins, "The Japanese-Americans in Hawaii," 187 *Harper's Mag.* 75 (1943); Fisher, "Our Two Japanese American Policies," 60 *Christian Century* 961 (1943); Henderson, "Japan in Hawaii," 31 *Survey Graphic* 328 (1942); Horne, "Are the Japs Hopeless?" *Sat. Eve. Post* 16 (Sept. 9, 1944); Lind, *Economic Succession and Racial Invasion in Hawaii* (1936); Lind, *An Island Community* (1938); Smith, "Minority Groups in Hawaii," 223 *Annals* 36 (1942).

15. Communication from the Hon. Abe Fortas, Under Secretary of the Interior, June 28, 1945.

such tribunals were set up, under citizens with legal experience, to examine all enemy aliens in Britain. There was an appeals advisory committee to advise the Home Secretary in disputed cases. Aliens were divided into three classes: those judged dangerous were interned; if judged doubtful in their loyalty, they were subjected to certain continuing restrictions, especially as to travel, and the ownership of guns, cameras, and radios; those deemed entirely loyal to the Allied cause were freed without further restraint. At first 2,000 enemy aliens on a blacklist were interned. But the entire group was then examined individually, and by March 1940 only 569 of approximately 75,000 aliens were ordered interned. During the panic period of 1940, a new screening was undertaken, to intern all those of doubtful loyalty, and other measures of mass internment were undertaken. Beginning as early as July 1940, however, the policy of wholesale internment was modified, and releases were granted, either generally or on certain conditions—the proved politics of the internee, his joining the Auxiliary Pioneer Corps, his emigration, and so on.[16] The maximum number interned during July 1940 was about 27,000 of a total enemy alien population (German, Austrian, and Italian) of about 93,000. By September 1941, the number of internees dropped to about 8,500. At the same time, the British undertook to arrest certain British subjects on suspicion alone, under the Emergency Powers Act of 1939. A constitutional storm was aroused by this procedure, which

16. "Report, The Position of Aliens in Great Britain During the War," 31 *Tolan Committee Hearings* 11861 (1942); Koessler, "Enemy Alien Internment: With Special Reference to Great Britain and France," 57 *Pol. Sci. Q.* 98 (1942); Kempner, "The Enemy Alien Problem in the Present War," 34 *Am. J. Int'l L.* 443 (1940); Cohn, "Legal Aspects of Internment," 4 *Modern L. Rev.* 200 (1941); Feist, "The Status of Refugees," 5 *Modern L. Rev.* 51 (1941).

was finally resolved in favor of the government.[17] The general pattern of British security practice was thus to treat enemy aliens on an individual basis and to arrest British subjects of Fascist tendencies in a limited number, and then only on strong personal suspicion.

In France all men enemy aliens between the ages of 17 and 65 were interned in 1939. After a good deal of confusion and complaint, and a vigorous parliamentary protest, many were screened out, either upon joining the Foreign Legion or, for older men, upon examination and sponsorship by French citizens. Further parliamentary criticism in December 1939 led to relief for the internees, but the crisis of May and June 1940 produced mass internment. In France, though less effectively than in Britain, the principle of internment on an individual basis was the objective of policy, if not always its norm.[18]

But on the West Coast the security program was something else again. A policy emerged piecemeal, apparently without sponsors or forethought. By May 1, 1942, it had become a policy of evacuating all persons of Japanese ancestry from the West Coast and confining them indefinitely in camps located away from the coastal area. After some hesitation, General DeWitt proposed evacuation. Quite clearly, a conflict took place between the military authorities on the West Coast and some of the representatives of the Department of Justice over the justification for such

17. Liversidge v. Anderson [1942] A. C. 206; Greene v. Secretary of State [1942] A. C. 284; Keeton, "Liversidge v. Anderson," 5 *Modern L. Rev.* 162 (1942); Allen, "Regulation 18B and Reasonable Cause," 58 *L. Q. Rev.* 232 (1942); Goodhart, Notes, 58 *L. Q. Rev.* 3, 9 (1942), and "A Short Replication," 58 *L. Q. Rev.* 243 (1942); Holdsworth, Note, 58 *L. Q. Rev.* 1 (1942); Carr, "A Regulated Liberty," 42 *Colum. L. Rev.* 339 (1942), and "Crisis Legislation in Britain," 40 *Colum. L. Rev.* 1309 (1940).

18. See Koessler, supra note 16, at 114 et seq.

action.[19] But no one in the government would take the responsibility for overruling General DeWitt and the War Department, which backed him up.

The dominant factor in the development of this policy was not a military estimate of a military problem, but familiar West Coast attitudes of race prejudice. The program of excluding all persons of Japanese ancestry from the coastal area was conceived and put through by the organized minority whose business it has been for forty-five years to increase and exploit racial tensions on the West Coast. The Native Sons and Daughters of the Golden West and their sympathizers were lucky in their general, for General De-Witt amply proved himself to be one of them in opinion and values. As events happened, he became the chief policy-maker in the situation, and he caused more damage even than General Burnside, whose blunderings with Vallandigham, the Ohio Copperhead, in 1863, were the previous high in American military officiousness.[20]

In the period immediately after Pearl Harbor there was no special security program on the West Coast for persons of Japanese extraction, and no general conviction that a special program was needed.[21] Known enemy sympathizers

19. See *DeWitt Final Report* at 3, 7, 19. Mr. Justice Clark (then in the Justice Department) stated that mass evacuation was not contemplated as necessary on Feb. 23, 1942. 29 *Tolan Committee Hearings* 11164.

20. See 2 Sandburg, *Abraham Lincoln, The War Years* 160–65 (1939). President Lincoln wrote to General Burnside, "All the Cabinet regretted the necessity of arresting for instance Vallandigham—some perhaps doubting that there was a real necessity for it, but being done all were for seeing you through with it." Lincoln arranged to have Vallandigham passed through the Confederate lines and banished. Randall, *Constitutional Problems under Lincoln* 176–79 (1926). The text of Lincoln's remarks is given somewhat differently by Sandburg and Randall. See also Klaus, *The Milligan Case,* 12–16 (1929).

21. See Rowell, "Clash of Two Worlds," 31 *Survey Graphic* 9, 12 (1942); McWilliams, *Prejudice* 108–14 (1944); *Tolan Committee Reports (Fourth Interim)* 154–56; An Intelligence Officer, "The Japanese in America: The Problem and the Solution," 185 *Harper's Mag.* 489 (1942).

among the Japanese, like white traitors and enemy agents, were arrested. There was no sabotage on the part of persons of Japanese ancestry, either in Hawaii or on the West Coast. There was no reason to suppose that the 112,000 persons of Japanese descent on the West Coast, 1.2 per cent of the population, constituted a greater menace to safety than such persons in Hawaii, 32 per cent of the Territory's population. Their access to military installations was not substantially different in the two areas; their status in society was quite similar; their proved record of loyalty in the war was the same. Although many white persons were arrested and convicted as Japanese agents, no resident Japanese American was convicted of sabotage or espionage as an agent of Japan.[22]

After a month's silence, the professional anti-Oriental agitators of the West Coast began a comprehensive campaign. There had been no sabotage in the area, although there was evidence of radio signaling from unknown persons within the area to enemy ships at sea. The West Coast Congressional delegation, led by Senator Hiram Johnson, memorialized the Administration in favor of excluding all persons of Japanese lineage from the coastal area. Anti-Oriental spokesmen appeared as witnesses before the Tolan Committee,[23] and later the Dies Committee,[24] and they explained the situation as they conceived of it to General DeWitt.[25] Some of the coast newspapers, and particularly those owned by William Randolph Hearst, took up the cry. Politicians, fearful of an unknown public opinion, spoke out for white supremacy. Tension was intensified, and doubters,

22. See McWilliams, *Prejudice* 111 (1944).

23. 29 *Tolan Committee Hearings* 10973, 11061, 11068, 11087, 11111; 30 id. at 11303–06, 11314–21, 11325; 31 id. at 11642.

24. *Hearings before Special Committee on Un-American Activities on H. Res. 282*, 78th Cong., 1st Sess. (1943), vols. 15, 16.

25. 31 *Tolan Committee Hearings* 11643; *Hearings before Special Committee on Un-American Activities*, supra note 24, vol. 15, p. 9207.

worried about the risks of another Pearl Harbor, remained silent, preferring too much caution to too little. An opinion crystallized in favor of evacuating the Japanese. Such action was at least action, promising greater relief from tension than the slow, patient work of military preparation for the defense and counterattack. German and Italian aliens were too numerous to be arrested or severely confined, and they were closely connected with powerful blocs of voters. There were too many Japanese Americans in Hawaii to be moved. The 100,000 persons of Japanese descent on the West Coast thus became the chief available target for the release of frustration and aggression.

Despite the nature of the emergency, the military refused to act without fuller legal authority. Executive Order No. 9066 was issued on February 19, 1942, authorizing the Secretary of War, and military commanders he might designate, to prescribe "military areas" in their discretion, and either to exclude any or all persons from such areas or to establish the conditions on which any or all such persons might enter, remain in, or leave such areas.[26] Lieutenant General J. L. DeWitt, head of the Western Defense Command, was ordered on February 20, 1942, to carry out the policy of the Executive Order. During the first two weeks of March, more than three months after Pearl Harbor, General DeWitt issued orders in which he announced that he would subsequently exclude "such persons or classes of persons as the situation may require" from the area.

But the Army's lawyers wanted more authority than the Executive Order. With inevitable further delays, a statute was therefore obtained prescribing that

> whoever shall enter, remain in, leave, or commit any act in any military area or military zone prescribed,

26. 7 *Fed. Reg.* 1407 (1942).

under the authority of an Executive order of the President, by the Secretary of War, or by any military commander designated by the Secretary of War, contrary to the restrictions applicable to any such area or zone or contrary to the order of the Secretary of War or any such military commander, shall, if it appears that he knew or should have known of the existence and extent of the restrictions or order and that his act was in violation thereof, be guilty of a misdemeanor and upon conviction shall be liable to a fine of not to exceed $5,000 or to imprisonment for not more than one year, or both, for each offense.[27]

The statute thus authorized the exclusion of people from the military areas. It said nothing about their subsequent confinement in camps. This omission was seized upon in *Ex parte Endo* as a crucial fact limiting the power of the government to hold persons shifted under military orders to relocation centers.[28]

Starting on March 27, 1942, almost four months after Pearl Harbor, the first actual restrictions were imposed. A policy of encouraging the Japanese to move away on a voluntary and individual basis had shown signs of producing confusion and irritation.[29] It was decided to have a uniform and comprehensive program of governmentally controlled migration. At first Japanese aliens and citizens of Japanese ancestry were subjected to the same controls applied to German and Italian aliens. Citizens of German and Italian descent were left free. Early in April, the first of a series of civilian exclusion orders were issued. They applied only to Japanese aliens and citizens of Japanese descent, who were

27. 56 Stat. 173 (1942), 18 U.S.C. § 97a (Supp. 1943).
28. *Ex parte* Mitsuye Endo, 323 U.S. 283, 300–01 (1944).
29. See *DeWitt Final Report*, c. ix. But see Fisher, "Japanese Colony: Success Story," 32 *Survey Graphic* 41 (1943).

to be excluded altogether from West Coast areas, ordered to report to control stations, and then confined in camps conducted by the newly organized War Relocation Authority, which became an agency of the Department of the Interior on February 16, 1944.[30]

The rules and policies of these camps were perhaps the most striking part of the entire program. Despite the humanitarian character of the WRA, which was from the beginning intrusted to high-minded and well-meaning men, a policy for discharging Japanese was developed which encouraged lawlessness and refused support to the simplest constitutional rights of citizens and aliens. It was originally thought that the camps would give temporary haven to some Japanese refugees from the West Coast who could not easily arrange new homes, jobs, and lives for themselves. Then it was decided to make a stay in the camps compulsory, so as to facilitate the loyalty examinations which were supposed to have been too difficult and prolonged to conduct on the West Coast. Further, it was wisely decided that a loyalty "screening" would facilitate relocation and combat anti-Japanese agitation. The fact that all released evacuees had been approved, as far as loyalty was concerned, gave practical support to their position in new communities. Japanese aliens and citizens of Japanese origin found by this administrative process to be disloyal were confined indefinitely in a special camp. Persons of Japanese descent found to be loyal were to be released from the camps upon the satisfac-

30. Public Proclamations No. 1, 7 *Fed. Reg.* 2320 (1942), No. 2, 7 *Fed Reg.* 2405 (1942), No. 3, 7 *Fed. Reg.* 2543 (1942), and other public proclamations established restrictions on travel, residence, and activities for enemy aliens and citizens of Japanese extraction. Civilian Exclusion Order No. 1, March 24, 1942, 7 *Fed. Reg.* 2581 (1942), and subsequent exclusion orders established the basis of evacuation. Civilian Exclusion Order No. 34, 7 *Fed. Reg.* 3967 (1942), was the basis of Korematsu's case. The War Relocation Authority was established by Executive Order 9102, 7 *Fed. Reg.* 2165 (1942).

tion of certain conditions. As applied to citizens especially, those conditions upon the right to live and travel in the United States are so extraordinary as to require full statement:

> In the case of each application for indefinite leave, the Director, upon receipt of such file from the Project Director, will secure from the Federal Bureau of Investigation such information as may be obtainable, and will take such steps as may be necessary to satisfy himself concerning the applicant's means of support, his willingness to make the reports required of him under the provisions of this part, the conditions and factors affecting the applicant's opportunity for employment and residence at the proposed destination, the probable effect of the issuance of the leave upon the war program and upon the public peace and security, and such other conditions and factors as may be relevant. The Director will thereupon send instructions to the Project Director to issue or deny such leave in each case, and will inform the Regional Director of the instructions so issued. The Project Director shall issue indefinite leaves pursuant to such instructions.

> (f) A leave shall issue to an applicant in accordance with his application in each case, subject to the provisions of this Part and under the procedures herein provided, as a matter of right, where the applicant has made arrangements for employment or other means of support, where he agrees to make the reports required of him under the provisions of this Part and to comply with all other applicable provisions hereof, and where there is no reasonable cause to believe that applicant cannot successfully maintain employment and residence at the proposed destination, and no reasonable

ground to believe that the issuance of a leave in the particular case will interfere with the war program or otherwise endanger the public peace and security.

(g) The Director, the Regional Director, and the Project Director may attach such special conditions to the leave to be issued in a particular case as may be necessary in the public interest.[31]

In other words, loyal citizens were required to have official approval of their homes, jobs, and friends before they were allowed to move. They had to report subsequent changes of address and remain under scrutiny almost amounting to parole. Officials were required to ascertain that community sentiment was not unfavorable to the presence of such citizens before they were permitted to enter the community. The briefs in behalf of the United States

31. War Relocation Authority, "Issuance of Leave for Departure from a Relocation Area," 7 *Fed Reg.* 7656, 7657 (1942). These regulations were revised in detail from time to time, but their basic policy was not substantially altered. See War Relocation Authority, Administrative Notice No. 54 (Summary of Leave Clearance Procedures), March 28, 1944. The basic security data on an evacuee was provided by the FBI and other intelligence agencies, not by independent investigation. This data was supplemented by his answers to questionnaires, particularly as to his loyalty to the United States, and by field investigations in doubtful cases. These field investigations included interviews with the evacuee. An appeal was provided to a Board of Appeals for leave clearance, consisting of citizens not employed by the War Relocation Authority. This Board had the power to advise the Director. Actually, leave was granted *pending inquiry* in cases where the applicant did not have an adverse FBI record; had answered the loyalty questions affirmatively; was not a Shinto priest; and had not spent the larger part of his life in Japan. Thus in fact Japanese Americans were given permission to leave the camps and, after the decision in the *Endo* case, to return to their homes, on the basis of very little information, beyond their answers to questionnaires, which was not available on the West Coast in 1942. Administrative Notice No. 54, supra. See discussion of issues in the report of the House Special Committee on Un-American Activities, H. R. Rep. No. 717, 78th Cong., 1st Sess. 13–16, 25 (1943).

before the Supreme Court in the *Korematsu* and *Endo* cases explain the kind of evidence regarded as sufficient to uphold a finding of unfavorable community sentiment and a suspension of the relocation process: the introduction of anti-Japanese bills in the local legislature, the occurrence of riots or other lawless episodes, and similar expressions of minority opinion.[32]

This policy played a part in encouraging the growth and violent expression of race antagonisms in American society. The forces of the national government were not devoted to protecting and vindicating what *Edwards v. California* had recently upheld as the privilege of a United States citizen, or indeed of any resident, to move freely from state to state without interference.[33] Local lynch spirit was not controlled and punished by the agencies of law enforcement. On the contrary, it was encouraged to manifest itself in words and unpunished deeds. The threat of lawlessness was allowed to frustrate the legal rights of colored minorities unpopular with small and articulate minorities of white citizens. In March 1943, a small number of Japanese returned to their homes in Arizona, which had been removed from the military zone, without substantial incident.[34] In the spring of 1945, however, the Ku Klux Klan spirit in California had been manifested in at least twenty major episodes of arson

32. Brief for United States, pp. 35–36, *Ex parte* Mitsuye Endo, 323 U.S. 283 (1944); Brief for United States, p. 15, Korematsu v. United States, 323 U.S. 214 (1944).

33. Edwards v. California, 314 U.S. 160 (1941). Justices Douglas, Black, Murphy, and Jackson concurred specially on the ground that California's ban on indigent migrants from the Southwest was not only an unconstitutional interference with commerce, but a violation of privileges and immunities of national citizenship. See Myers, "Federal Privileges and Immunities: Application to Ingress and Egress," 29 *Cornell L. Q.* 489 (1944).

34. See *Encyclopaedia Britannica Book of the Year:* 1944 at 47.

or intimidation.[35] The War Relocation Authority was consistently and effectively on the side of facilitating resettlement and combatting race prejudice. Yet the terms of its leave regulations constituted an extraordinary invasion of citizens' rights, as the Supreme Court later held. They were

35. "Are Japs Wanted?" *Newsweek,* May 28, 1945, p. 33. Including minor episodes, there were 59 such incidents by the end of April 1945. See *N.Y. Times,* May 6, 1945, § IV, p. 7, col. 4. Some of the episodes were terroristic shooting by night riders; others were arson, the desecration of cemeteries, posting of opprobious handbills, etc.; still others were commercial boycotts, like the refusal of Portland, Ore., vegetable merchants (largely of Italian descent) to buy farm produce from a Japanese American farmer. See *Pacific Citizen,* May 5, 1945, p. 5, col. 4. See also *N.Y. Times,* Jan. 11, 1945, p. 4, col. 7; id., Jan. 21, 1945, p. 4, col. 3; id., Feb. 17, 1945, p. 2, col. 5; id., Feb. 25, 1945, p. 26, col. 4; id., March 18, 1945, p. 17, col. 1. Both West Coast judges and juries tended to acquit persons charged with violence directed against the Japanese, often after confessions by defendants and inflammatory appeals by defense counsel. See *Pacific Citizen,* April 28, 1945, p. 1, col. 4; p. 4, col. 1 ("This is a white man's country"); 160 *The Nation* 531, 598 (1945). Labor leaders, historically one of the strongest anti-Japanese groups in West Coast life, were in the forefront of resistance to the return of the Japanese to their homes. See, e.g., the position of Dave Beck, reported in the *Pacific Citizen,* April 21, 1945, p. 4, col. 2; p. 5, col. 4.

Strong reactions of opinion and of citizens groups in favor of protecting the rights of Japanese Americans were manifested, led by Secretary of War Stimson, Secretary of the Interior Ickes, and the staff of the War Relocation Authority. See *Pacific Citizen,* April 7, 1945, p. 1, col. 1, quoting Secretary Ickes' forceful statement of April 4, 1945; *Pacific Citizen,* April 14, 1945, p. 2, col. 1 (Secretary Stimson's remarks at press conference of April 5). Many West Coast groups were organized to oppose the Klan movement in the Far West. See *Pacific Citizen,* April 28, 1945, p. 7, col. 1; id., April 21, 1945, p. 3, col. 1. See excellent speech of Attorney General Robert W. Kenny of California, delivered to a convention of California sheriffs, calling on law enforcement officers to protect the legal rights of returning Japanese Americans. *N.Y. Times,* March 18, 1945, p. 17, col. 1; *Pacific Citizen,* March 24, 1945, p. 1, col. 4; id., March 31, 1945, p. 5, col. 1 (partial text of Mr. Kenny's speech); Beshoar, "When Good Will Is Organized," 5 *Common Ground* 19 (Spring 1945); *Pacific Citizen,* March 3, 1945, p. 6, col. 1 (speech by Joe E. Brown before Commonwealth Club of San Francisco in behalf of fair play for Japanese Americans); *Time,* May 28, 1945, p. 13 (Quakers aid returned evacuees in Oregon).

a practical compromise, under the circumstances, but a compromise nonetheless, with social forces which might better have been opposed head-on.

Studies have appeared about conditions within the camps. They make it plain that the camps were in fact concentration camps, where the humiliation of evacuation was compounded by a regime which ignored citizens' rights and the amenities which might have made the relocation process more palatable.[36]

Thus there developed a system for the indefinite confinement and detention of Japanese aliens and citizens of Japanese descent, without charges or trial, without term, and without visible promise of relief. By May 1942, it was compulsory and self-contained. On pain of punishment under the Act of March 21, 1942, all had to leave the West Coast through Assembly Centers and the Relocation Centers. Counsel in the *Hirabayashi* case called it slavery; Mr. Justice Jackson said it was attainder of blood.[37] The Japanese radio discussed it at length, finding in the system ample propaganda material for its thesis that American society was incapable of dealing justly with colored peoples.

### III

Attempts were made at once to test the legality of the program. The district courts and the circuit courts of appeals had a good deal of difficulty with the issues. Although troubled, they generally upheld both the exclusion of Japanese aliens and citizens from the West Coast, and at least their temporary confinement in WRA camps.[38]

36. See Leighton, op. cit. supra note 1.

37. Brief for Northern California Branch of the American Civil Liberties Union, p. 93; Korematsu v. United States, 323 U.S. 214, 243 (1944).

38. See, e.g., United States v. Yasui, 48 F. Supp. 40 (D. Ore. 1942); Korematsu v. United States, 140 F. 2d 289 (9th Cir., 1943).

The question of how and on what grounds the Supreme Court should dispose of the cases was one of broad political policy. Would a repudiation of the Congress, the President, and the military in one aspect of their conduct of the war affect the people's will to fight? Would it create a campaign issue for 1944? Would it affect the power, status, and prestige of the Supreme Court as a political institution? How would a decision upholding the government influence civil liberties and the condition of minorities? A bench of sedentary civilians was reluctant to overrule the military decision of those charged with carrying on the war. Conflicting loyalties, ambitions, and conceptions of the Court's duty undoubtedly had their part in the positions the Justices took.

The issue first came before the Supreme Court in May 1943, and the first cases, *Hirabayashi v. United States* and *Yasui v. United States,* were decided on June 21, 1943.[39] No Japanese submarines had been detected off the West Coast for many months. Midway was won; Libya, Tripolitania, and Tunisia had been conquered. Guadalcanal and a good deal of New Guinea were in Allied hands. The posture of the war had changed profoundly in a year. We had suffered no defeats since the fall of Tobruk in July 1942, and we had won a long series of preliminary victories. Our forces were poised for the offensive. The phase of aggressive deployment was over.

The problem presented to the Supreme Court was thus completely different from that which confronted worried legislators and officials in the bleak winter and spring of 1942. Invalidation of the exclusion and confinement programs would do no possible harm to the prosecution of the war. The Court could afford to view the issues in full perspective. The war powers of the legislature and executive

39. 320 U.S. 81 and 115 (1943).

must of course be amply protected. But the special concerns of the Supreme Court for the development of constitutional law as a whole could be given proper weight, free of the pressure of the Pearl Harbor emergency.

It was only half the truth to say that the cases had to be decided as if the date of decision were February 1942. It was not in fact the date of decision and could not be made so. The issue was not only whether the military should have excluded the Japanese in the spring of 1942, but whether the Court should now validate what had been done. As many episodes in the history of the United States eloquently attest, these are different issues. The problem of the Court in the *Hirabayashi* case was not that of General DeWitt in 1942, but an infinitely more complex one. Whether it faced the issues or tried to ignore them, whether it decided the cases frankly or obliquely, by decision or evasion, the Court could not escape the fact that it was the Supreme Court, arbiter of a vast system of rules, habits, customs, and relationships. No matter how inarticulate, its decision could not be confined in its effect to the United States Reports. It would necessarily alter the balance of forces determining the condition of every social interest within range of the problems of the cases—the power of the military and the police; our developing law of emergencies, which is beginning to resemble the French and German law of the state of siege; the status of minorities and of groups which live by attacking minorities; the future decision of cases in police stations and lower courts, involving the writ of habeas corpus, the equal rights of citizens, the protection of aliens, the segregation of racial groups, and like questions.

In a bewildering and unimpressive series of opinions, relieved only by the dissents of Mr. Justice Roberts and of Mr. Justice Murphy in *Korematsu v. United States*,[40] the Court

40. 323 U.S. 214, 225, 233 (1944).

chose to assume that the main issue of the cases—the scope and method of judicial review of military decisions—did not exist. In the political process of American life, these decisions were a negative and reactionary act. The Court avoided the risks of overruling the government on an issue of war policy. But it weakened society's control over military authority—one of the polarizing forces on which the organization of our society depends. And it solemnly accepted and gave the prestige of its support to dangerous racial myths about a minority group, in arguments which can be applied easily to any other minority in our society.

The cases are worth separate statement, for they are by no means alike. In *Hirabayashi v. United States* the Court considered a conviction based on the Act of March 21, 1942, for violating two orders issued by General DeWitt under authority of the Executive Order of February 19, 1942. Gordon Hirabayashi, a citizen of the United States and a senior in the University of Washington, was sentenced to three months in prison on each of two counts, the sentences running concurrently. The first count was that Hirabayashi failed to report to a control station on May 11 or May 12, 1942, for exclusion from the duly designated military area including Seattle, his home. The first count thus raised the legality of the compulsory transportation of an American citizen from one of the military areas to a WRA camp, and of his indefinite incarceration there. The second count was that on May 9, 1942, he had violated a curfew order by failing to remain at home after 8 P.M., within a designated military area, in contravention of a regulation promulgated by the military authority. The Court considered the violation of the second count first, upheld the curfew order and the sentence imposed for violating it. Since the two sentences were concurrent, it said, there was no need to consider the conviction on the first count.

In fact, of course, the Court was entirely free to consider the first count if it wanted to. It would have been normal practice to do so. Its refusal to pass on the more serious controversy cannot be put down to wise and forbearing judicial statesmanship. This was not the occasion for prudent withdrawal on the part of the Supreme Court, but for affirmative leadership in causes peculiarly within its sphere of primary responsibility. The social problems created by the exclusion and confinement of the Japanese Americans of the West Coast states increased in seriousness with every day of their continued exclusion. The rabble-rousers of California now were demanding the permanent exclusion of all persons of Japanese ancestry from the West Coast area. They were living at peace, altogether free of the threat of Japanese invasion. Yet they were still successful in their efforts to keep the Japanese out. The business and professional capital of the Japanese was being profitably used by others. Intelligent and resourceful competitors had been removed from many markets. At the expense of the Japanese, vested interests were being created, entrenched, and endowed with political power. All these interests would resist the return of the Japanese by law if possible, if not, by terror. The refusal of the Supreme Court to face the problem was itself a positive decision on the merits. It gave strength to the anti-Oriental forces on the West Coast and made a difficult social situation more tense. A full assertion of the ordinary rights of citizenship would have shamed and weakened the lynch spirit. It would have fortified the party of law and order. Instead, that party was confused and weakened by the vacillation of the Court.[41]

The reasoning of the Court itself contributed to the intensification of social pressure.

41. See materials cited supra note 34.

## Toward a Theory of Judicial Action

In the *Hirabayashi* case the Court held that its problem
was the scope of the war power of the national government.
The extent of Presidential discretion was not presented as
a separate issue, because the statute of March 21, 1942, and
appropriation acts under it, were passed with full knowledge of the action taken and proposed by General DeWitt,
and thus fully authorized the curfew. Both Congress and
the executive were held to have approved the curfew as a
war measure, required in their judgment because espionage
and sabotage were especially to be feared from persons of
Japanese origin or descent on the West Coast during the
spring of 1942.

The premise from which the Court's argument proceeded
was the incontestable proposition that the war power is the
power to wage war successfully. The state must have every
facility and the widest latitude in defending itself against
destruction. The issue for the Court, the Chief Justice said,
was whether at the time "there was any substantial basis for
the conclusion" that the curfew as applied to a citizen of
Japanese ancestry was "a protective measure necessary to
meet the threat of sabotage and espionage which would
substantially affect the war effort and which might reasonably be expected to aid a threatened enemy invasion."[42]
The formulation of the test followed the lines of the Court's
familiar doctrine in passing on the action of administrative
bodies: was there "reasonable ground" for those charged
with the responsibility of national defense to believe that
the threat was real and the remedy useful? The orders of
the commander, the Court held, were based on findings of
fact which supported action within the contemplation of
the statute. The findings were based on an informed appraisal of the relevant facts in the light of the statutory

42. 320 U.S. 81, 95 (1943).

standard, and published as proclamations. The circumstances, the Court said, afforded a sufficiently rational basis for the decision made.

The "facts" which were thus held to "afford a rational basis for decision" were that in time of war "residents having ethnic affiliations with an invading enemy may be a greater source of danger than those of different ancestry," and that in time of war such persons could not readily be isolated and dealt with individually.[43] This is the basic factual hypothesis on which all three cases rest.

The first part of this double-headed proposition of fact is contrary to the experience of American society, in war and peace.[44] Imagine applying an ethnic presumption of disloyalty in the circumstances of the Revolution or the Civil War! In World War I and in World War II, soldiers who had ethnic affiliations with the enemy—German, Austrian, Hungarian, Finnish, Romanian, Bulgarian, Japanese, and Italian—fought uniformly as Americans in our armed forces, without any suggestion of group disloyalty. As a generalization about the consequences of inheritance, as compared with experience, in determining political opinions, the Supreme Court's doctrine of ethnic disloyalty belongs with folk proverbs—"blood is thicker than water"—and the pseudo-genetics of the Nazis. It is flatly contradicted by the evidence of the biological sciences, of cultural anthropology, sociology, and every other branch of systematic social study, both in general and with specific reference to the position of Japanese groups on the West Coast. The most important driving urge of such minority groups is to conform, not to rebel. This is true even for the American minorities which are partially isolated from the rest of so-

43. Id. at 101–02.

44. Compare the opinion of Mr. Justice Black, for a unanimous Court, in *Ex parte* Kumezo Kawato, 317 U.S. 69, 73 (1942).

ciety by the bar of color.[45] The desire to conform is stronger than resentments and counter-reactions to prejudice and discrimination. Insecure and conscious of the environment as a threat, such minorities seek to establish their status by proving themselves to be good Americans. The younger generation rejects the language, customs, and attitudes of the older. The exemplary combat records of the Japanese American regiments in Italy and in France are a normal symbol of their quest for security within the environment. It is an expected part of the process of social adjustment, repeated again and again in our experience with minorities within American society. By and large, men and women who grow up in the American cultural community are Americans in outlook, values, and basic social attitudes. This is the conclusion of the scientific literature on the subject. It has been the first tenet of American law, the ideal if not always the practice of American life.

To support its contrary opinion, the Supreme Court undertook a review of its own intuitions, without a judicial record before it and without serious recourse to available scientific studies of the problem. Kiplingesque folklore about East and West is close to the heart of the opinions.

45. Cf. infra, pp. 244–46 and materials cited supra notes 1 and 14; Wirth, "The Problem of Minority Groups," in *The Science of Man in the World Crisis* 347 (Linton ed. 1945); Myrdal, *An American Dilemma* cc. 3, 33–39, app. 10 (1944); Sherman, *Basic Problems of Behavior* 289–91 (1941); Mead, *And Keep Your Powder Dry* cc. 3, 46 (1942); Warner and Srole, *The Social Systems of American Ethnic Groups* 283–84 (1945); Benedict, *Patterns of Culture* especially cc. 1–3, 7, 8 (1934); Benedict, *Race: Science and Politics* (1940); *When Peoples Meet* cc. 7–12 (Locke and Stern ed. 1942); Miyamoto, *Social Solidarity among the Japanese in Seattle* (1939); Dollard, *Caste and Class in a Southern Town* cc. 12–16 (1937); *Race Relations and the Race Problem* (Thompson ed. 1939); Stonequist, *The Marginal Man, a Study in Personality and Culture Conflict* cc. 3–4, particularly pp. 101–06 (1937); Cox, "Race and Caste: A Distinction," 50 *Am. J. Soc.* 360, 365–66 (1945); *Group Relations and Group Antagonisms* pt. 1 (MacIver ed. 1944).

The Japanese, the Court said, had been imperfectly assimilated; they constituted an isolated group in the community; their Japanese language schools might be sources of Japanese propaganda. Moreover, the discriminatory way in which the Japanese on the West Coast were treated may have been regarded as contributing to Japanese solidarity, preventing their assimilation and increasing in many instances their attachments to Japan and its institutions.[46]

There was no testimony or other evidence in the record as to the facts which governed the judgment of the military in entering the orders in question. They were not required to support the action they had taken by producing evidence as to the need for it. Nor were they exposed to cross-examination. By way of judicial research and notice the Court wrote four short paragraphs to explain "some of the many considerations" which in its view might have been considered by the military in making their decision to institute a discriminatory curfew.[47]

The second part of the Court's basic premise of fact was that it was impossible to investigate the question of loyalty individually. As to the validity of this proposition there was neither evidence in the record nor even discussion by the Court to indicate a basis for the conclusion which might appeal to a reasonable man or even to a choleric and harassed general faced with the danger of invasion and the specter of his own court-martial. The issue was dismissed in a sentence. "We cannot say that the war-making branches of the Government did not have ground for believing that in a critical hour such persons could not readily be isolated and separately dealt with, and constituted a menace to the national defense and safety, which demanded that prompt and ade-

46. 320 U.S. 81, 98 (1943). See infra, pp. 242–44. Such fears arising from sentiments of guilt are of special interest to the student of social psychology.

47. Id. at 99.

quate measures be taken to guard against it."[48] In view of the history of security measures during the war, it would not have been easy to establish strong grounds for such a belief. There were about 110,000 persons subject to the exclusion orders, 43 per cent of them being over 50 or under 15.[49] At the time of the exclusion orders, they had lived in California without committing sabotage for five months after Pearl Harbor. The number of persons to be examined was not beyond the capacities of individual examination processes, in the light of experience with such security measures both in the United States and abroad.[50] The fact was that the loyalty examinations finally undertaken in the Relocation Authority camps consisted in large part of filling out a questionnaire, and little more, except in cases of serious doubt as to loyalty. Most of those released from the camps were given their freedom on the basis of little information which was not available on the West Coast in 1942.[51]

Actually, the exclusion program was undertaken not because the Japanese were too numerous to be examined individually, but because they were a small enough group to be punished by confinement. It would have been physically impossible to confine the Japanese and Japanese Americans in Hawaii, and it would have been both physically and politically impossible to undertake comparable measures against the 690,000 Italians or the 314,000 Germans living in the United States. The Japanese were being attacked because for some they provided the only possible outlet and expression for sentiments of group hostility. Others were unable or unwilling to accept the burden of urging the re-

48. Ibid.
49. *DeWitt Final Report,* at 403–04.
50. See supra, pp. 202–04.
51. See note 31 supra.

pudiation of a general's judgment which he placed on grounds of military need.

The *Hirabayashi* case states a rule which permits some judicial control over action purporting to be taken under military authority. It proposes that such action be treated in the courts like that of administrative agencies generally, and upheld if supported by "facts" which afford "a rational basis" for the decision. For all practical purposes, it is true, the *Hirabayashi* case ignores the rule; but the Court did go to great lengths to assert the principle of protecting society against unwarranted and dictatorial military action. *Korematsu v. United States* seems sharply to relax even the formal requirement of judicial review over military conduct. Korematsu, an American citizen of Japanese descent, was convicted under the Act of March 21, 1942, for violating an order requiring his exclusion from the coastal area. The Court held the problem of exclusion to be identical with the issue of discriminatory curfew presented in the *Hirabayashi* case. There, it said, the Court had decided that it was not unreasonable for the military to impose a curfew in order to guard against the special dangers of sabotage and espionage anticipated from the Japanese group. The military had found, and the Court refused to reject the finding, that it was impossible to bring about an immediate segregation of the disloyal from the loyal. According to Mr. Justice Black, the exclusion orders merely applied these two findings—that the Japanese were a dangerous lot and that there was no time to screen them individually. Actually, there was a new "finding" of fact in this case, going far beyond the situation considered in the *Hirabayashi* case. The military had "found" that the curfew provided inadequate protection against the danger of sabotage and espionage. Therefore the exclusion of all Japanese, citizens and aliens alike, was thought to be a reasonable way to protect the coast against sabotage and espionage. Mr. Justice Black does not pretend to review even the possible foundations of such a judgment. There is no attempt in the *Korematsu* case to show a reasonable connection between the factual situation and the program adopted to deal with it.

The Court refused to regard the validity of the detention features of the relocation policy as raised by the case. Korematsu had not yet been taken to a camp, and the Court would not pass on the issues presented by such imprisonment. Those issues, the Court said, are "momentous questions not contained within the framework of the pleadings or the evidence in this case. It will be time enough to decide the serious constitutional issues which petitioner seeks to raise when an assembly or relocation order is applied or is certain to be applied to him, and we have its terms before us."[52] This is a good deal like saying in an ordinary criminal case that the appeal raises the validity of the trial and verdict, but not the sentence, since the defendant may be out on probation or bail. It is difficult to understand in any event why this consideration did not apply equally to the evidence before the Court on the issue which the Court conceded was raised by the pleadings, i.e., the decision of the General to exclude all Japanese from the Defense Area. On this problem there was literally no trial record or other form of evidence in the case.

There were four other opinions in *Korematsu v. United States*. Mr. Justice Roberts and Mr. Justice Murphy dissented on the merits, in separate opinions. Mr. Justice Roberts said that while he might agree that a temporary or emergency exclusion of the Japanese was a legitimate exercise of military power, this case presented a plan for imprisoning the Japanese in concentration camps solely be-

52. 323 U.S. 214, 222 (1944).

cause of their ancestry and "without evidence or inquiry" as to their "loyalty and good disposition towards the United States."[53] Such action, he said, was clearly unconstitutional.

Mr. Justice Murphy's substantial opinion did not join issue with the opinion of the Court on the central problem of how to review military decisions, but it did contend that the military decisions involved in this case were unjustified in fact. The military power, he agreed, must have wide and appropriate discretion in carrying out military duties. But,

> like other claims conflicting with the asserted constitutional rights of the individual, the military claim must subject itself to the judicial process of having its reasonableness determined and its conflicts with other interests reconciled. . . .
>
> The judicial test of whether the Government, on a plea of military necessity, can validly deprive an individual of any of his constitutional rights is whether the deprivation is reasonably related to a public danger that is so "immediate, imminent, and impending" as not to admit of delay and not to permit the intervention of ordinary constitutional processes to alleviate the danger. . . . Civilian Exclusion Order No. 34, banishing from a prescribed area of the Pacific Coast "all persons of Japanese ancestry, both alien and non-alien," clearly does not meet that test. Being an obvious racial discrimination, the order deprives all those within its scope of the equal protection of the laws as guaranteed by the Fifth Amendment. It further deprives these individuals of their constitutional rights to live and work where they will, to establish a home where they choose and to move about freely. In excommunicating them without

53. Id. at 226.

benefit of hearings, this order also deprives them of all their constitutional rights to procedural due process. Yet no reasonable relation to an "immediate, imminent, and impending" public danger is evident to support this racial restriction which is one of the most sweeping and complete deprivations of constitutional rights in the history of this nation in the absence of martial law.[54]

The action taken did not meet such a test, Justice Murphy argued, because there was no reasonable ground for supposing that all persons of Japanese blood have a tendency to commit sabotage or espionage, nor was there any ground for supposing that their loyalty could not have been tested individually where they lived. A review of statements made by General DeWitt before Congressional committees and in his Final Report to the Secretary of War clearly reveals that the basis of his action was "an accumulation of much of the misinformation, half-truths and insinuations that for years have been directed against Japanese Americans by people with racial and economic prejudices."[55] These are compared with the independent studies of experts and shown to be nonsensical. The supposed basis for the exercise of military discretion disappears, and the case for the order falls.

Mr. Justice Jackson wrote a fascinating and fantastic essay in nihilism. Nothing in the record of the case, he said very properly, permitted the Court to judge the military reasonableness of the order. But even if the orders were permissible and reasonable as military measures, he said, "I deny that it follows that they are constitutional."[56]

54. Id. at 234–35.
55. Id. at 239. See discussion infra, pp. 242–47.
56. Id. at 245.

I should hold that a civil court cannot be made to enforce an order which violates constitutional limitations even if it is a reasonable exercise of military authority. The courts can exercise only the judicial power, can apply only law, and must abide by the Constitution, or they cease to be civil courts and become instruments of military policy.

Of course the existence of a military power resting on force, so vagrant, so centralized, so necessarily heedless of the individual, is an inherent threat to liberty. But I would not lead people to rely on this Court for a review that seems to me wholly delusive. The military reasonableness of these orders can only be determined by military superiors. If the people ever let command of the war power fall into irresponsible and unscrupulous hands, the courts wield no power equal to its restraint. The chief restraint upon those who command the physical forces of the country, in the future as in the past, must be their responsibility to the political judgments of their contemporaries and to the moral judgments of history.

My duties as a justice as I see them do not require me to make a military judgment as to whether General DeWitt's evacuation and detention program was a reasonable military necessity. I do not suggest that the courts should have attempted to interfere with the Army in carrying out its task. But I do not think that they may be asked to execute a military expedient that has no place in law under the Constitution. I would reverse the judgment and discharge the prisoner.[57]

Thus the Justice proposes to refuse enforcement of the statute of March 21, 1942. Apparently, in this regard at

57. Id. at 247–48.

least, the statute would be treated as unconstitutional. The prisoner would then be taken to the camp and kept there by the military, and all judicial relief would be denied him.

It is hard to imagine what courts are for if not to protect people against unconstitutional arrest. If the Supreme Court washed its hands of such problems, for what purposes would it sit? The idea that military officers whose only authority rests on that of the President and the Congress, both creatures of the Constitution, can be considered to be acting "unconstitutionally" when they carry out concededly legitimate military policies is Pickwickian, to say the least. For judges to pass by on the other side, when men are imprisoned without charge or trial, suggests a less appealing analogy. The action of Chief Justice Taney in *Ex parte Merryman* is in a more heroic tradition of the judge's responsibility.[58]

What Justice Jackson is saying seems to be this: Courts should refuse to decide hard cases, for in the hands of foolish judges they make bad law. The ark of the law must be protected against contamination. Therefore law should not be allowed to grow through its application to the serious and intensely difficult problems of modern life, such as the punishment of war criminals or the imprisonment of Japanese Americans. It should be kept in orderly seclusion and confined to problems like the logical adumbration of the full faith and credit clause and other lawyers' issues.[59] The problems which deeply concern us should be decided out-

58. *Ex parte* Merryman, 17 Fed. Cas. 144, No. 9487 (D. Md. 1861). See Swisher, *Roger B. Taney*, c. 26 (1935).

59. See Jackson, "Full Faith and Credit—The Lawyer's Clause of The Constitution," 45 *Colum. L. Rev.* 1 (1945). See also Northwestern Bands of Shoshone Indians v. United States, 65 Sup. Ct. 690, 700–02 (U.S. 1945); Jackson, "The Rule of Law among Nations," 31 *A. B. A. J.* 290, 292–93 (1945). Compare his report to the President on trials for war criminals, *N.Y. Times,* June 8, 1945, p. 4.

side the courts, even when they arise as the principal and inescapable issues of law suits. Judges are thus to be relieved of the political responsibilities of their citizenship and their office. They will be allowed to pretend that the judicial function is to "interpret" the law, and that law itself is a technical and antiquarian hobby, not the central institution of a changing society.

Mr. Justice Frankfurter concurred specially, answering Mr. Justice Jackson's dissent. "To talk about a military order that expresses an allowable judgment of war needs by those entrusted with the duty of conducting war as 'an unconstitutional order' is to suffuse a part of the Constitution with an atmosphere of unconstitutionality," he said.[60] But one of the first issues of the case was whether or not the military order in question did express an "allowable judgment of war needs." That was the question which the Court was compelled to decide and did decide, without benefit of the testimony of witnesses or a factual record and without substantial independent study on its own motion.

*Ex parte Endo* was the next stage in the judicial elucidation of the problem.[61] In *Ex parte Endo,* decided on December 18, 1944, an adjudication was finally obtained on about one half the question of the validity of confining Japanese aliens and citizens in camps. The case was a habeas corpus proceeding in which an American citizen of Japanese ancestry sought freedom from a War Relocation Center where she was detained, after having been found loyal, until the Authority could place her in an area of the country where local disorder would not be anticipated as a result of her arrival. The Court held that the statute, as rather strenuously construed, did not authorize the detention of persons in the petitioner's situation, although temporary

60. 323 U.S. 214, 224–25 (1944).
61. 323 U.S. 283 (1944).

detention for the purpose of investigating loyalty was assumed to be valid as an incident to the program of "orderly" evacuation approved in the *Korematsu* case.

The purpose of the statute under which exclusion and detention were accomplished, the Court said, was to help prevent sabotage and espionage. The act talked only of excluding persons from defense areas. It did not mention the possibility of their detention. While the Court assumed that an implied power of temporary detention could be accepted as an incident in the program of exclusion, for the purpose of facilitating loyalty examinations, such an implied power should have been narrowly confined to the precise purpose of the statute in order to minimize the impact of the statute on the liberties of the individual citizen. The authority to detain a citizen as a measure of protection against sabotage and espionage was exhausted when his loyalty was established. The persistence of community hostility to citizens of Japanese descent was not, under the statute, a ground for holding them in camp. The disclosure of the full scope of the detention program to various committees of the Congress, including appropriation committees, was held not to support a ratification by the Congress of what was done. The basis of this conclusion was the extraordinarily technical proposition that the appropriation acts which might have been considered to ratify the entire program were lump-sum appropriations, and were not broken down by items to earmark a specific sum for the specific cost of detaining citizens found to be loyal pending their relocation in friendly communities. In this respect the reasoning of the Court was contrary to that in the *Hirabayashi* case, where congressional ratification of the plans of the executive branch was established in a broad and common-sense way. Justices Roberts and Murphy concurred specially, urging that the decision be based on the constitutional grounds stated in their opinions in the *Korematsu* case, rather than on the statutory interpretation underlying Justice Douglas' opinion.

## IV

The many opinions of the three Japanese cases did not consider the primary constitutional issues raised by the West Coast anti-Japanese program as a whole. This was a program which included (a) a discriminatory curfew against Japanese persons; (b) their exclusion from the West Coast; (c) their confinement pending investigations of loyalty; and (d) the indefinite confinement of those persons found to be disloyal. These measures were proposed and accepted as military necessities. Their validity as military measures was an issue in litigation. By what standards are courts to pass on the justification for such military action? Were those standards satisfied here?

The conception of the war power under the American Constitution rests on the experience of the Revolution and the Civil War. It rests on basic political principles which men who endured those times of trouble fully discussed and carefully articulated. The chief architects of the conception were men of affairs who participated in war and had definite and sophisticated ideas about the role of the professional military mind in the conduct of war.

The first and dominating proposition about the war power under the Constitution is that the Commander in Chief of the armed forces is a civilian and must be a civilian, elected and not promoted to his office. The subordination of the military to the civil power is thus primarily assured. In every democracy the relationship between civil and military power is the crucial social and political issue on which its capacity to survive a crisis ultimately depends. Inadequate analysis of this problem, and inadequate measures to deal with it, led to the downfall of the Spanish Republic and gravely weakened the Third French Republic. British experience, especially during the First World War, puts the problem in dramatic perspective.[62] In its own proper sphere of tactics, the professional military judgment is decisive. In waging war the larger decisions—the choice of generals, the organization of command, the allocation of forces, the political, economic, and often strategic aspects of war—these have to be made by responsible civilian ministers.[63] Clemenceau's famous remark, quoted at the head of this article, is not a witticism, but the first principle of organizing democracy for war. It reflects a balanced view of the proper relation in policy-making between the expert and the practical man. It expresses a keen sense of the supremacy of civil power in a republic. The image of Napoleon is never far from the surface of French political consciousness. France's experience with Pétain has once more underscored the danger. In our own national life recurring waste and incompetence in the handling of war problems—in the Mexican War, the Civil War, and the Spanish-American War— led to important reforms in the organization of the War

62. See *War Memoirs of David Lloyd George* (1933–37), c. 10 ("Some Reflections on the Functions of Governments and Soldiers Respectively in a War"); vol. 1, cc. 5, 6, 9, 10, 14, 15; vol. 2, cc. 8–10, 17–19; vol. 3, cc. 3–6, 9–11; vol. 4, cc. 9–11, 13; vol. 5, cc. 6, 8; Churchill, *The World Crisis* cc. 4, 19, 38, pp. 733–45 (1931); Wilkinson, *War and Policy* 259–300 (1910); Wright, *At the Supreme War Council* (1921); Rogers, "Civilian Control of Military Policy," 18 *Foreign Affairs* 280 (1940).

63. See Palmer, *Washington, Lincoln, Wilson, Three War Statesmen* 224–27, 282–83 (1930); Palmer, *America in Arms* 145–46 (1941); De Weerd, "Civilian and Military Elements in Modern War," in Clarkson and Cochran, *War as a Social Institution* 95 (1941). See also McKinley, *Democracy and Military Power* (2d ed. 1941); Vagts, *A History of Militarism* (1937).

Department under Elihu Root, and further developments under later Secretaries of War.[64] The process of achieving adequate organization and control is by no means complete.

The second political principle governing the exercise of the war power in a democracy is that of responsibility. Like every other officer of government, soldiers must answer for their decisions to the system of law, and not to the Chief of Staff alone. Where, as in the Japanese exclusion program, military decisions lead to conflicts between individuals and authority, the courts must adjudicate them. Even if Mr. Justice Jackson's doctrine of the judicial function is accepted, the courts will adjudicate nonetheless, by refusing relief, and thus decide cases in favor of the military power. The problem is the scope of the military power and means for assuring its responsible exercise. It is not a problem which can be avoided by any verbal formula.

Most occasions for the exercise of authority in the name of military need will not present justiciable controversy. When a general attacks or retreats in the field, sends his troops to the right or to the left, he may have to justify his decision to a court-martial, but not often to a court. On the other hand some steps deemed to be required in war do raise the kind of conflict over property or personal rights which can be presented to the courts. A factory or business may be taken into custody, prices and wages may be established, whole classes of activity, like horse-racing, temporarily forbidden. Without stopping for an over-nice definition of the terms, these are justiciable occasions—situations in which courts have customarily decided controversies and determined the legality of official action when such prob-

64. See 1 Jessup, *Elihu Root* 240–64 (1938); Root, *The Military and Colonial Policy of the United States* (1916); Rogers, op. cit. supra note 62, at 288–91.

lems were implicit in the conflicts presented to them.[65] It is essential to every democratic value in society that official action taken in the name of the war power be held to standards of responsibility under such circumstances. The courts have not in the past, and should not now, declare the whole category of problems to be political questions beyond the reach of judicial review. The present Supreme Court is dominated by the conviction that in the past judicial review has unduly limited the freedom of administrative action. But surely the permissible response to bad law is good law, not no law at all. The Court must review the exercise of military power in a way which permits ample freedom to the executive, yet assures society as a whole that appropriate standards of responsibility have been met.

The issue for judicial decision in these cases is not lessened or changed by saying that the war power includes any steps required to win the war. The problem is still one of judgment as to what helps win a war. Who is to decide whether there was a sensible reason for doing what was done? Is it enough for the General to say that at the time he acted he honestly thought it was a good idea to do what he did? Is this an example of "expertise," to which the courts must give blind deference?[66] Or must there be "objective" evidence, beyond the General's state of mind, to show "the reasonable ground for belief" which the *Hirabayashi* case says is necessary?[67] Should such evidence be avail-

65. See, e.g., Block v. Hirsh, 256 U.S. 135 (1921); Bowles v. Willingham, 321 U.S. 503 (1944); Home Building & Loan Ass'n v. Blaisdell, 290 U.S. 398 (1934); Yakus v. United States, 321 U.S. 414 (1944); Montgomery Ward & Co. v. United States, 150 F. 2d 369, vacated for mootness, 326 U.S. 690 (1945).

66. Railroad Commission of Texas v. Rowan & Nichols Oil Co., 310 U.S. 573 (1940), *mod.*, 311 U.S. 614 (1941); Railroad Commission v. Rowan & Nichols Oil Co., 311 U.S. 570 (1941). *Cf.* Thompson v. Consolidated Gas Corp., 300 U.S. 55 (1937); Note, 51 *Yale L. J.* 680 (1942).

67. See note 17 supra. For recent treatments of administrative and executive findings by various Justices of the Supreme Court in cognate, if not

able before the action is taken? Should the rule be a procedural one that a general has to consider evidence and then come to a decision, or should it be only that at the subsequent trial suitable evidence must be available to justify the result? As the Chief Justice remarked, the Constitution "does not demand the impossible or the impractical."[68] The inquiry should be addressed to the rationality of the general's exercise of his judgment as a general, not as a master in chancery. It should give full and sympathetic weight to the confusion and danger which are inevitable elements in any problem presented for military decision.

Unless the courts require a showing, in cases like these, of an intelligible relationship between means and ends, society has lost its basic protection against the abuse of military power. The general's good intentions must be irrelevant. There should be evidence in court that his military judgment had a suitable basis in fact. As Colonel Fairman, a strong proponent of widened military discretion, points out: "When the executive fails or is unable to satisfy the court of the evident necessity for the extraordinary measures it has taken, it can hardly expect the court to assume it on faith."[69]

-------

directly comparable situations, see Schneiderman v. United States, 320 U.S. 118 (1943); ICC v. Inland Waterways, 319 U.S. 671 (1943); FPC v. Hope Natural Gas Co., 320 U.S. 591 (1944); Connecticut Light & Power Co. v. FPC, 324 U.S. 515 (1945); Bridges v. Wixon, 326 U.S. 135 (1945).

68. Hirabayashi v. United States, 320 U.S. 81, 104 (1943).

69. Fairman, *The Law of Martial Rule* 217–18 (2d ed. 1943). See also id. at 47–49, 103–07; Fairman, "The Law of Martial Rule and the National Emergency," 55 *Harv. L. Rev.* 1253, 1259–61, 1272 (1942). The test is put by Wiener, *A Practical Manual of Martial Law* 26–27 (1940), for "the hapless Guardsman who commands the troops," as "What can you justify afterwards?". See Comment, 45 *Yale L. J.* 879 (1936). The statute of March 21, 1942, should be interpreted to pose the same issue, despite its broad language.

# Toward a Theory of Judicial Action

The *Hirabayashi* case proposes one test for the validity of an exercise of military power. Even though that test is not applied in the *Hirabayashi* case, and is roughly handled in the *Korematsu* case, it is not hopelessly lost. As the Court said in *Sterling v. Constantin,* the necessity under all the circumstances for a use of martial power "is necessarily one for judicial inquiry in an appropriate proceeding directed against the individuals charged with the transgression."[70]

Perhaps the closest judicial precedent and analogy for the Japanese American cases is *Mitchell v. Harmony,* which arose out of the Doniphan raid during the Mexican War. The plaintiff was a trader, whose wagons, mules, and goods were seized by the defendant, a lieutenant colonel of the United States Army, during the course of the expedition. The plaintiff, who wanted to leave the Army column and trade with the Mexicans, was forced to accompany the troops. All his property was lost on the march and in battle. The action was of trespass, for the value of the property taken, and for damages. The defenses were that the control of the trader and the destruction of his property were a military necessity, justified by the circumstances of the situation. After a full trial, featured by depositions of the commanding officers, the jury found for the plaintiff.

> The defence has been placed . . . on rumors which reached the commanding officer and suspicions which he appears to have entertained of a secret design in the plaintiff to leave the American forces and carry on an illicit trade with the enemy, injurious to the interests

70. 287 U.S. 378, 398 (1932). Id. at 401: "What are the allowable limits of military discretion, and whether or not they have been overstepped in a particular case, are judicial questions." Certain cases, though technically distinguishable, seem to proceed from different hypotheses. Martin v. Mott, 12 Wheat. 19 (U.S. 1827); The Prize Cases, 2 Black 635 (U.S. 1862); Moyer v. Peabody, 212 U.S. 78 (1909).

of the United States. And if such a design had been shown, and that he was preparing to leave the American troops for that purpose, the seizure and detention of his property, to prevent its execution, would have been fully justified. But there is no evidence in the record tending to show that these rumors and suspicions had any foundation. And certainly mere suspicions of an illegal intention will not authorize a military officer to seize and detain the property of an American citizen. The fact that such an intention existed must be shown; and of that there is no evidence.

The 2d and 3d objections will be considered together, as they depend on the same principles. Upon these two grounds of defence the Circuit Court instructed the jury, that the defendant might lawfully take possession of the goods of the plaintiff, to prevent them from falling into the hands of the public enemy; but in order to justify the seizure the danger must be immediate and impending, and not remote or contingent. And that he might also take them for public use and impress them into the public service, in case of an immediate and pressing danger or urgent necessity existing at the time, but not otherwise.

In the argument of these two points, the circumstances under which the goods of the plaintiff were taken have been much discussed, and the evidence examined for the purpose of showing the nature and character of the danger which actually existed at the time or was apprehended by the commander of the American forces. But this question is not before us. It is a question of fact upon which the jury have passed, and their verdict has decided that a danger or necessity, such as the court described, did not exist when the property of the plaintiff was taken by the defendant.

And the only subject for inquiry in this court is whether the law was correctly stated in the instruction of the court; and whether any thing short of an immediate and impending danger from the public enemy, or an urgent necessity for the public service, can justify the taking of private property by a military commander to prevent it from falling into the hands of the enemy or for the purpose of converting it to the use of the public.

The instruction is objected to on the ground, that it restricts the power of the officer within narrower limits than the law will justify. And that when the troops are employed in an expedition into the enemy's country, where the dangers that meet them cannot always be foreseen, and where they are cut off from aid from their own government, the commanding officer must necessarily be intrusted with some discretionary power as to the measures he should adopt; and if he acts honestly, and to the best of his judgment, the law will protect him. But it must be remembered that the question here, is not as to the discretion he may exercise in his military operations or in relation to those who are under his command. His distance from home, and the duties in which he is engaged, cannot enlarge his power over the property of a citizen, nor give to him, in that respect, any authority which he would not, under similar circumstances, possess at home. And where the owner has done nothing to forfeit his rights, every public officer is bound to respect them, whether he finds the property in a foreign or hostile country, or in his own.

There are, without doubt, occasions in which private property may lawfully be taken possession of or destroyed to prevent it from falling into the hands of the public enemy; and also where a military officer, charged with a particular duty, may impress private property into the public service or take it for public use. Unquestionably, in such cases, the government is bound to make full compensation to the owner; but the officer is not a trespasser.

But we are clearly of opinion, that in all of these cases the danger must be immediate and impending; or the necessity urgent for the public service, such as will not admit of delay, and where the action of the civil authority would be too late in providing the means which the occasion calls for. It is impossible to define the particular circumstances of danger or necessity in which this power may be lawfully exercised. Every case must depend on its own circumstances. It is the emergency that gives the right, and the emergency must be shown to exist before the taking can be justified.

In deciding upon this necessity, however, the state of the facts, as they appeared to the officer at the time he acted, must govern the decision; for he must necessarily act upon the information of others as well as his own observation. And if, with such information as he had a right to rely upon, there is reasonable ground for believing that the peril is immediate and menacing, or the necessity urgent, he is justified in acting upon it; and the discovery afterwards that it was false or erroneous, will not make him a trespasser. But it is not sufficient to show that he exercised an honest judgment, and took the property to promote the public service; he must show by proof the nature and character of the emergency, such as he had reasonable grounds to believe it to be, and it is then for a jury to say, whether it was so pressing as not to admit of delay; and the occasion such, according to the information upon which he acted, that private rights must for the time give way to the common and public good.

But it is not alleged that Colonel Doniphan was deceived by false intelligence as to the movements or strength of the enemy at the time the property was taken. His camp at San Elisario was not threatened. He was well informed upon the state of affairs in his rear, as well as of the dangers before him. And the property was seized, not to defend his position, nor to place his troops in a safer one, nor to anticipate the attack of an approaching enemy, but to insure the success of a distant and hazardous expedition, upon which he was about to march.

The movement upon Chihuahua was undoubtedly undertaken from high and patriotic motives. It was boldly planned and gallantly executed, and contributed to the successful issue of the war. But it is not for the court to say what protection or indemnity is due from the public to an officer who, in his zeal for the honor and interest of his country, and in the excitement of military operations, has trespassed on private rights. That question belongs to the political department of the government. Our duty is to determine under what circumstances private property may be taken from the owner by a military officer in a time of war. And the question here is, whether the law permits it to be taken to insure the success of any enterprise against a public enemy which the commanding officer may deem it advisable to undertake. And we think it very clear that the law does not permit it.[71]

Applied to the circumstances of the Japanese exclusion cases, these precedents require that there be a showing to

71. Mitchell v. Harmony, 13 How. 115, 133-35 (U.S. 1851).

the trial court of the evidence upon which General DeWitt acted, or evidence which justifies his action under the statute and the Constitution. Nor will it do to say that there need be only enough evidence to prove his good faith or to provide a possible basis for the decision. This was the contention expressly overruled in *Mitchell v. Harmony*.[72] The varying formulas about presumptions, and the quantum of proof required in different classes of cases, merely conceal the court's problem. There must be evidence enough to satisfy the court as to the need for the grave and disagreeable action taken—arrest on vague suspicion, denial of trial, and permanent incarceration for opinions alone. The standard of reasonableness, here as elsewhere, is one requiring a full evaluation of all circumstances. But the law is not neutral. It has a positive preference for protecting civil rights where possible, and a long-standing suspicion of the military mind when acting outside its own sphere. In protecting important social values against frivolous or unnecessary interference by generals, the court's obligations cannot be satisfied by a scintilla of evidence or any other mechanical rule supposed to explain the process of proof. There must be a convincing and substantial factual case, in Colonel Fairman's phrase, to satisfy the court of "the evident necessity" for the measures taken.

No matter how narrowly the rule of proof is formulated, it could not have been satisfied in either the *Hirabayashi* or the *Korematsu* cases. Not only was there insufficient evidence in those cases to satisfy a reasonably prudent judge or a reasonably prudent general: there was no evidence whatever by which a court might test the responsibility of General DeWitt's action, either under the statute of March 21, 1942, or on more general considerations. True, in the

72. Id. at 119–20.

*Hirabayashi* case the Court carefully identified certain of General DeWitt's proclamations as "findings," which established the conformity of his actions to the standard of the statute—the protection of military resources against the risk of sabotage and espionage. But the military proclamations record conclusions, not evidence. And in both cases the record is bare of testimony on either side about the policy of the curfew or the exclusion orders. There was every reason to have regarded this omission as a fatal defect, and to have remanded in each case for a trial on the justification of the discriminatory curfew and of the exclusion orders.

Such an inquiry would have been illuminating. General DeWitt's Final Report and his testimony before committees of the Congress clearly indicated that his motivation was ignorant race prejudice, not facts to support the hypothesis that there was a greater risk of sabotage among the Japanese than among residents of German, Italian, or any other ethnic affiliation. The most significant comment on the quality of the General's report is contained in the government's brief in *Korematsu v. United States*. There the Solicitor General said that the report was relied upon "for statistics and other details concerning the actual evacuation and the events that took place subsequent thereto. We have specifically recited in this brief the facts relating to the justification for the evacuation, of which we ask the Court to take judicial notice, and we rely upon the Final Report only to the extent that it relates such facts."[73] Yet the Final Report

73. Brief for United States, p. 11, n. 2, Korematsu v. United States, 323 U.S. 214 (1944). See Brief for United States, p. 23, *Ex parte* Mitsuye Endo, 322 U.S. 233 (1944). It was peculiarly inappropriate to decide these cases on the basis of judicial notice alone. Borden's Farm Products Co., Inc. v. Baldwin, 293 U.S. 194 (1934); United States v. Carolene Products Co., 304 U.S. 144 (1938); Polk Co. v. Gloser, 305 U.S. 5 (1938). See Comment, 49 *Harv. L. Rev.* 631 (1936).

embodied the basic decision under review and stated the reasons why it was actually undertaken. General DeWitt's Final Recommendation to the Secretary of War, dated February 14, 1942, included in the Final Report, was the closest approximation we have in these cases to an authoritative determination of fact. In that Recommendation, General DeWitt said:

> In the war in which we are now engaged racial affinities are not severed by migration. The Japanese race is an enemy race and while many second and third generation Japanese born on United States soil, possessed of United States citizenship, have become "Americanized," the racial strains are undiluted. To conclude otherwise is to expect that children born of white parents on Japanese soil sever all racial affinity and become loyal Japanese subjects, ready to fight and, if necessary, to die for Japan in a war against the nation of their parents. That Japan is allied with Germany and Italy in this struggle is no ground for assuming that any Japanese, barred from assimilation by convention as he is, though born and raised in the United States, will not turn against this nation when the final test of loyalty comes. It, therefore, follows that along the vital Pacific Coast over 112,000 potential enemies, of Japanese extraction, are at large today. There are indications that these are organized and ready for concerted action at a favorable opportunity. The very fact that no sabotage has taken place to date is a disturbing and confirming indication that such action will be taken.[74]

74. *DeWitt Final Report* at 34. See also id. at vii, 7–24. Some of the reasoning used to justify the discriminatory treatment of the Japanese Americans can only be described as astounding in its terms and in its refusal to consider or to evaluate available sociological data. See, e.g., Fairman, *The*

In his Final Report to the Secretary of War General De-Witt adduced somewhat more evidence than the absence of sabotage to prove its special danger. His report, and the briefs for the United States in *Hirabayashi v. United States* and *Korematsu v. United States* emphasized these points as well: The Japanese lived together, often concentrated around harbors and other strategic areas. They had been discriminated against, and it was suggested that their resentment at such treatment might give rise to disloyalty. Japanese clubs and religious institutions played an important part in their social life. Japanese language schools were maintained to preserve for the American-born children something of the cultural heritage of Japan. The Japanese government, like that of Italy, France, and many other countries, asserted a doctrine of nationality which was thought to result in claims of dual citizenship, and thus to cast doubt on the loyalty of American citizens of Japanese descent. There were some 10,000 Kibei among the population of the West Coast—Japanese Americans who had returned to Japan for an important part of their education and who were thought to be more strongly affiliated with Japan in their political outlook than the others.[75]

Much of the suspicion inferentially based on these statements disappears when they are more closely examined. In many instances the concentration of Japanese homes around strategic areas had come about years before and for entirely innocent reasons. Japanese fishing and cannery workers,

---

*Law of Martial Rule* 260 (2d ed. 1943) ("Fundamental differences in mores have made them inscrutable to us"); Watson, "The Japanese Evacuation and Litigation Arising Therefrom," 22 *Ore. L. Rev.* 46, 47 (1942) ("Their mental and emotional responses are understood by but few of our people and in general the Japanese presents an inscrutable personality").

75. See *Tolan Committee Reports (Preliminary)* 16. Such persons were of course individually known, through travel records and otherwise.

for example, were compelled by the canneries to live on the waterfront, in order to be near the plants in which they worked. Japanese truck gardeners rented land in the industrial outskirts of large cities in order to be as close as possible to their markets. They rented land for agricultural purposes under high tension lines—regarded as a very suspicious circumstance—because the company could not use the land for other purposes. The initiative in starting the practice came from the utility companies, not from the Japanese.[76] Despite discrimination against the Japanese, many had done well in America. They were substantial property owners. Their children participated normally and actively in the schools and universities of the West Coast. Their unions and social organizations had passed resolutions of loyalty in great number, before and after the Pearl Harbor disaster.[77] It is difficult to find real evidence that either religious or social institutions among the Japanese had successfully fostered Japanese militarism, or other dangerous sentiments, among the Japanese American population. The Japanese language schools, which the Japanese Americans themselves had long sought to put under state control, seem to have represented little more than the familiar desire of many immigrant groups to keep alive the language and tradition of the "old country"; in the case of Japanese Americans, knowledge of the Japanese language was of particular economic importance, since so much of their working life was spent with other Japanese on the West Coast.[78]

76. See McWilliams, *Prejudice* 119–21 (1944); 29 *Tolan Committee Hearings* 11225.

77. See *Tolan Committee Reports (Preliminary)* 15 ("We cannot doubt, and everyone is agreed, that the majority of Japanese citizens and aliens are loyal to this country"); An Intelligence Officer, "The Japanese in America: The Problem and the Solution," 185 *Harper's Mag.* 489 (1942).

78. See McWilliams, *Prejudice* 121–22 (1944).

There were of course suspicious elements among the Japanese. They were known to the authorities, which had for several years been checking the security of the Japanese American population. Many had been individually arrested immediately after Pearl Harbor, and the others were under constant surveillance. We had many intelligence officers who knew both the language and the people well. As far as the police were concerned, there was no substance to the man-in-the-street's belief that all Orientals "look alike."[79] On the contrary, the Japanese were a small and conspicuous minority on the West Coast, both individually and as a group. They would have been an unlikely source of sabotage agents for an intelligent enemy in any case.

Apart from the members of the group known to be under suspicion, there was no evidence beyond the vaguest fear to connect the Japanese on the West Coast with the unfavorable military events of 1941 and 1942. Both at Pearl Harbor and in sporadic attacks on the West Coast the enemy had shown that he had knowledge of our dispositions. There was some signaling to enemy ships at sea, both by

79. See, e.g., 31 *Tolan Committee Hearings* 11631; Denman, J., dissenting, Korematsu v. United States, 140 F. 2d 289, 302–03 (9th Cir., 1943). As for the knowledge of the situation possessed by security officers, see 31 *Tolan Committee Hearings* 11697–702; An Intelligence Officer, loc. cit. supra note 77. A considerable percentage—perhaps 19%—of the evacuees gave negative answers to the loyalty questions in their questionnaires. Many of those answers expressly referred to the treatment the Japanese had received in being uprooted and imprisoned. It is estimated that many more of the answers were directly or indirectly referable to the shock of evacuation and confinement. See *Hearings before Committee on Immigration and Naturalization on H. R. 2701, 3012, 3489, 3446, and 4103,* 78th Cong., 1st Sess. 36–43 (1944). Basically, of course, the issue is to a considerable extent irrelevant. Disloyalty is not a crime, even in the aggravated form of enthusiastic propaganda for the Axis cause. See note 2 supra. At most, it is a possible ground for interning enemy aliens, see *N.Y. Times,* June 27, 1945, p. 15, col. 7, but hardly a sufficient ground for excluding individuals from strategic areas. See note 13 supra.

radio and by lights, along the West Coast. It was said to be difficult to trace such signals because of limitations on the power of search without warrant. There had been several episodes of shelling the coast by submarine, although two of the three such episodes mentioned by General DeWitt as tending to create suspicion of the Japanese Americans had taken place after their removal from the Coast. These were the only such items in the Final Report which were not identified by date.[80] And it was positively known that no suspicions attached to the Japanese residents for sabotage at Pearl Harbor before, during, or after the raid.[81] Those subsequently arrested as Japanese agents were all white men. "To focus attention on local residents of Japanese descent, actually diverted attention from those who were busily engaged in espionage activity."[82]

It is possible that the absence of a trial on the facts may permit the Court in the future to distinguish or to extinguish the Japanese American cases; for in these cases the defendants did not bring forth evidence, nor require the government to produce evidence, on the factual justification of the military action. Whoever had the burden of going forward, or of proof, government or defendant, the burden was not met.[83] Not even the *Korematsu* case would justify

80. *DeWitt Final Report* at 18; *N.Y. Times,* June 23, 1942, p. 1, col. 4; p. 9, col. 4; id., Sept. 15, 1942, p. 1, col. 3; p. 10, col. 5.

81. See McWilliams, *Prejudice* 144 (1944).

82. Id. at 111.

83. In applying the doctrine of *Mitchell v. Harmony,* the burden of proof in fact falls on the government, claiming the privileges of the emergency. Whatever is said about the presumption of constitutionality of statutes, or the interest of the court in not substituting its judgment on the facts for that of the qualified executive or legislative authority, where the justification for extraordinary behavior rests on a showing of extraordinary circumstances, it will finally be the government's burden to bring in the evidence of emergency or take the risk of not persuading the court. See, e.g., cases cited supra notes 13, 72, and 73.

the exclusion of such evidence, nor the denial of a defendant's request to call the General as a witness. A future case may therefore create a better record for establishing appropriate criteria of judicial control over military conduct, and for applying such criteria to better purpose.

A trial on the factual justification of the curfew and exclusion orders would require the Court to confront *Ex parte Milligan*,[84] which it sought to avoid in all three of the Japanese cases. *Ex parte Milligan* represents an application to a large and common class of semi-military situations of what Chief Justice Stone articulated in the *Hirabayashi* case as a "rule of reason" governing the scope of military power. The military power, the Chief Justice said, included any steps needed to wage war successfully. The Justices in the majority in *Ex parte Milligan* declared in effect that it would be difficult, if not impossible, to convince them that there was or could be a military necessity for allowing the military to hold, try, or punish civilians while the civil courts were open and functioning. And they held further that it is for the judges, not the generals, to say when it is proper under the Constitution to shut the courts or to deny access to them.

*Ex parte Milligan* is a monument in the democratic tradition and should be the animating force of this branch of our law. At a time when national emergency, mobilization, and war are more frequent occurrences than at any previous period of our history, it would be difficult to name a single decision of more fundamental importance to society. Yet there is a tendency to treat *Ex parte Milligan* as outmoded, as if new methods of "total" warfare made the case an anach-

84. 4 Wall. 2 (U.S. 1867). See Frank, "Ex parte Milligan v. The Five Companies: Martial Law in Hawaii," 44 *Colum. L. Rev.* 639 (1944); Klaus, *The Milligan Case* (1929); Fairman, *Mr. Justice Miller and the Supreme Court* c. 4 (1939).

ronism.[85] Those who take this view have forgotten the circumstances of the Civil War. Fifth columns, propaganda, sabotage, and espionage were more generally used than in any war since the siege of Troy, and certainly more widely used than in the Second World War.

*Ex parte Milligan* illustrates the point. Milligan was convincingly charged with active participation in a fifth column plot worthy of Hitler or Alfred Hitchcock. A group of armed and determined men were to seize federal arsenals at Columbus, Indianapolis, and at three points in Illinois, and then to release Confederate prisoners of war held in those states. Thus they would create a Confederate army behind the Union lines in Tennessee. Milligan and his alleged co-conspirators acted in Indiana, Missouri, Illinois, and in other border states. Their strategy had a political arm. The Union was to be split politically, and a Northwest Confederation was to be declared, friendly to the South, and embracing Illinois, Wisconsin, Iowa, Kansas, Indiana, and Minnesota. This plan was not an idle dream. It was sponsored by a well-financed society, the Sons of Liberty, thought to have 300,000 members, many of them rich and respectable; the planned uprising would coincide with the Chicago Convention of the Democratic Party, which was sympathetic to abandoning the war and recognizing the Confederacy.[86]

The unanimous Court which freed Milligan for civil trial was a court of fire-eating Unionists. Mr. Justice Davis, who wrote for the majority, was one of President Lincoln's closest friends, supporters, and admirers. The Chief Justice,

85. Brief for Respondent, pp. 45–48, *Ex parte* Quirin, 317 U.S. 1 (1942); *Ex parte* Ventura, 44 F. Supp. 520, 522–23 (W. D. Wash. 1942). For a moderate view see Schueller v. Drum, 51 F. Supp. 383, 387 (E. D. Pa. 1943). Cf. Frank, supra note 84, at 639.

86. See Klaus, *The Milligan Case* 27–33 (1929).

who wrote the opinion for the concurring minority, was a valiant and resolute supporter of the war, whatever his shortcomings in other respects. The Court had no difficulty in freeing Milligan and facing down the outcry of radical Republicans which was provoked by the decision. The issue dividing the Court in the *Milligan* case was parallel in some ways to the problem presented by the Japanese exclusion program under the statute of March 21, 1942. Congress had passed a statute in 1863 permitting the President to suspend the privilege of habeas corpus in a limited way whenever, in his judgment, the public safety required it, holding prisoners without trial for a short period. If the next sitting of the grand jury did not indict those held in its district, they were entitled to release under the statute.

The statute was in fact a dead letter, although the Court did not consider that aspect of the situation in deciding Milligan's case.[87] Milligan had been arrested by the military. The grand jury had not returned an indictment against him at its next sitting. He had nonetheless been tried by a military commission, and sentenced to death. The minority of the Court urged his release according to the terms of the statute, because no indictment had been presented against him. The Court, however, freed him for normal criminal trial on broader grounds. The controlling question of the case, the Court said, was whether the military commission had jurisdiction to try Milligan. This question was considered without express reference to the statute of 1863, as such, but on the evidence which might justify the exercise of martial law powers either under the statute or otherwise. The only constitutional reason, the Court said, for denying Milligan the trial provided for in the third article of the Constitution, and in the Fifth and Sixth Amendments, is

87. See Randall, *Constitutional Problems under Lincoln* 167 (1926).

that such a trial could not physically be conducted. As long as the courts are open, persons accused of crime and not subject to the laws of war as members of the armed forces or enemy belligerents must be brought before the courts or discharged. *Ex parte Milligan* therefore holds Milligan's trial before a military commission to be unconstitutional, despite the President's action under the first section of the Act of 1863. The factual situation was not such as to justify the exercise of martial law powers, even for temporary detention, and certainly not for trial. Ordinary civilians could be held for military trial only when the civil power was incapable of acting—during an invasion, for example, or during a period of severe riot or insurrection.

It is difficult to see how the *safety* of the country required martial law in Indiana. If any of her citizens were plotting treason, the power of arrest could secure them, until the government was prepared for their trial, when the courts were open and ready to try them. It was as easy to protect witnesses before a civil as a military tribunal; and as there could be no wish to convict, except on sufficient legal evidence, surely an ordained and established court was better able to judge of this than a military tribunal composed of gentlemen not trained to the profession of the law.

It is claimed that martial law covers with its broad mantle the proceedings of this military commission. The proposition is this: that in a time of war the commander of an armed force (if in his opinion the exigencies of the country demand it, and of which he is to judge) has the power, within the lines of his military district, to suspend all civil rights and their remedies, and subject citizens as well as soldiers to the rule of *his will;* and in the exercise of his lawful authority cannot be restrained, except by his superior officer or the President of the United States.

If this position is sound to the extent claimed, then when war exists, foreign or domestic, and the country is subdivided into military departments for mere convenience, the commander of one of them can, if he chooses, within his limits, on the plea of necessity, with the approval of the Executive, substitute military force for and to the exclusion of the laws, and punish all persons, as he thinks right and proper, without fixed or certain rules.

The statement of this proposition shows its importance; for, if true, republican government is a failure, and there is an end of liberty regulated by law. Martial law, established on such a basis, destroys every guarantee of the Constitution, and effectually renders the "military independent of and superior to the civil power"—the attempt to do which by the King of Great Britain was deemed by our fathers such an offence, that they assigned it to the world as one of the causes which impelled them to declare their independence. Civil liberty and this kind of martial law cannot endure together; the antagonism is irreconcilable; and, in the conflict, one or the other must perish.[88]

The Court's dismissal of *Ex parte Milligan* in *Ex parte Endo* requires some analysis. The Court said, "It should be noted at the outset that we do not have here a question such as was presented in Ex parte *Milligan*, 4 Wall. 2, or in Ex parte *Quirin*, 317 U.S. 1, where the jurisdiction of military tribunals to try persons according to the law of war was challenged in *habeas corpus* proceedings. Mitsuye Endo

88. 4 Wall. 2, 127, 124–25 (U.S. 1867).

is detained by a civilian agency, the War Relocation Authority, not by the military. Moreover, the evacuation program was not left exclusively to the military; the Authority was given a large measure of responsibility for its execution and Congress made its enforcement subject to civil penalties by the Act of March 21, 1942. Accordingly, no questions of military law are involved."[89]

The proposition is extraordinary. Under penalty of imprisonment, the orders before the Court in *Ex parte Endo* required that enemy aliens and citizens of Japanese blood be removed from their homes and confined in camps. If found to be "disloyal," they were kept in the camps indefinitely. If found to be "loyal," they were kept in the camps as long as was necessary for the Authority to place them in friendly communities.

The problems of *Ex parte Milligan* are avoided by the simplest of expedients. In *Ex parte Milligan* the Court said that the military could not constitutionally arrest, nor could a military tribunal constitutionally try, civilians charged with treason and conspiracy to destroy the state by force, at a time when the civil courts were open and functioning. Under the plan considered in the Japanese American cases, people not charged with crime are imprisoned for several years without even a military trial, on the ground that they have the taint of Japanese blood. Why does the *Milligan* case not apply *a fortiori?* If it is illegal to arrest and confine people after an unwarranted military trial, it is surely even more illegal to arrest and confine them without any trial at all. The Supreme Court said that the issues of the *Milligan* case were not involved because the evacuees were committed to camps by military orders, not by military tribunals, and because their jailers did not wear uniforms. It is

89. 323 U.S. 283, 297–98 (1944).

hard to see any sequence in the sentences. The Japanese Americans were ordered detained by a general, purporting to act on military grounds. The military order was enforceable on pain of imprisonment. While a United States marshal, rather than a military policeman, assured obedience to the order, the ultimate sanction behind the marshal's writ is the same as that of the military police: the bayonets of United States troops. It is hardly a ground for distinction that the general's command was backed by the penalty of civil imprisonment, or that he obtained civilian aid in running the relocation camps. The starting point for the program was a military order, which had to be obeyed. It required enemy aliens and citizens of Japanese blood to be removed from their homes and confined in camps. As events developed, the general's command imposed confinement for three years on most of the people who were evacuated under it.

There are then two basic constitutional problems concealed in the Court's easy dismissal of *Ex parte Milligan:* the arrest, removal, and confinement of persons without trial, pending examination of their loyalty; and the indefinite confinement of persons found to be disloyal. On both counts, at least as to citizens, the moral of *Ex parte Milligan* is plain. The *Milligan* case says little about the propriety of a curfew, or perhaps even of the exclusion orders as such. The military necessity of such steps is to be tested independently in the light of all the relevant circumstances. The *Milligan* case does say, however, that arrest and confinement are forms of action which cannot be taken as military necessities while courts are open. For such punitive measures it proposes a clear and forceful rule of thumb: the protection of the individual by normal trial does not under such circumstances interfere with the conduct of war.

Much was made in the Japanese American cases of the

analogy of temporary preventive arrest or other restriction approved for material witnesses, the protection of the public at fires, the detention of typhoid carriers, mentally ill persons, and so on.[90] The analogy has little or no application to the problems presented in these cases, except perhaps for the curfew or conceivably the abstract issue of exclusion, as distinguished from detention. The restrictions involved here were not temporary emergency measures, justified by the breakdown of more orderly facilities for protecting society against espionage and sabotage. As interferences with the liberty of the individual, they went well beyond the minimal forms of precautionary arrest without warrant which were permitted by the statute of 1863, discussed in the *Milligan* case; they were closely comparable to the forms of arbitrary action which were actually presented by the facts of the *Milligan* case and strongly disapproved by the Court.

As for Japanese aliens, it is orthodox, though not very accurate, to say that as persons of enemy nationality they are subject only to the government's will in time of war.[91]

90. For temporary restrictions on access to localities see Warner, "The Model Sabotage Prevention Act," 54 *Harv. L. Rev.* 602, 611–18 (1941); Pressman, Leider, and Cammer, "Sabotage and National Defense," 54 *Harv. L. Rev.* 632, 641 (1941). The confinement of alcoholics, psychotic persons, and the like raises different problems. The issue in such cases is not whether persons can be confined in the social interest without trial, but without trial by jury. Ample individual investigation, hearings, and other safeguards are required by way of "due" process of law. Minnesota *ex rel.* Pearson v. Probate Court, 309 U.S. 270 (1940); see Hall, "Drunkenness as a Criminal Offense," 32 *J. Crim. L. & Crim.* 297 (1942); Rostow, "The Commitment of Alcoholics to Medical Institutions," 1 *Q. J. of Studies on Alcohol* 372 (1940). Moreover, the limits to such interferences with individual freedom in the name of protecting society are jealously guarded. Skinner v. Oklahoma, 316 U.S. 535 (1942); see Note, 3 *Q. J. of Studies on Alcohol* 668 (1943).

91. See Comment, 51 *Yale L. J.* 1316, 1317 (1942). Cf. 3 Hyde, *International Law Chiefly as Interpreted and Applied in the United States* §§ 616–17 (2d ed. 1945); De Lacey v. United States, 249 Fed. 625 (9th Cir. 1918).

But the protection of the Fifth and Sixth Amendments extends generally to aliens.[92] Should arbitrary distinctions be permitted in our policy for enemy aliens, distinctions without reasonable basis? Is it permissible to intern all the Japanese who live on the West Coast, but to allow German and Italian aliens, and Japanese who live elsewhere, general freedom? Lower courts have said they would refuse to review executive action directed at the control of enemy aliens.[93] Such a view is far from necessary. The courts go to great lengths to assure reasonable protection to the property rights of enemy aliens, their privilege of pursuing litigation, and the like. It requires no extension of doctrine to propose that their control and custody in time of war be reasonably equal and even-handed. As far as accepted notions of international law are concerned, the "single aim" of specialized enemy alien controls is to prevent enemy aliens from aiding the enemy.[94] The present pattern of discriminatory controls bears no relation to the end of safety.

## V

These cases represent deep-seated and largely inarticulate responses to the problems they raise. In part they express the

92. See Alexander, *Rights of Aliens under the Federal Constitution* 127–29 (1931); Gibson, *Aliens and the Law* 151–52, c. 7 (1940); Oppenheimer, "The Constitutional Rights of Aliens," 1 *Bill of Rights Rev.* 100, 106 (1941).

93. *Ex parte* Graber, 247 Fed. 882 (N. D. Ala. 1918); *Ex parte* Gilroy, 257 Fed. 110 (S. D. N. Y. 1919). However, the premise of these cases is hardly compatible with that of *Sterling v. Constantin*, but rather depends on the proposition that the exercise of executive discretion in military and quasi-military matters is not reviewable, except for fraud, mistaken identity, etc. See also cases cited supra note 13. The statute and regulation involved in those cases applies to any persons, not only to citizens or friendly aliens.

94. See Hyde, loc. cit. supra note 91. As for the status of enemy aliens in court, see *Ex parte* Kawato, 317 U.S. 69 (1942); as to the property of enemy aliens see Symposium, "Enemy Property," 11 *Law & Contemp. Prob.* 1–201 (1945).

Justices' reluctance to interfere in any way with the prosecution of the war. In part they stem from widely shared fears and uncertainties about the technical possibilities of new means of warfare. Such fears were strongly felt everywhere on the Allied side after the German victories of 1940 and 1941. It was common then, and still is common, to believe in a vague but positive way that the restoration of mobility in warfare, and the appearance of new weapons, have somehow made all older thought on the subject of war obsolete. We expected fifth columns and paratroops to drop near San Francisco at any moment. In the panic of the time, it seemed almost rational to lock up Japanese Americans as potential enemy agents.

But the airplane, the tank, and the rocket have not made it necessary to abandon the principles of *Ex parte Milligan*. Whatever the effect of such developments may be on Infantry Field Regulations and the Manual of Arms, they do not compel us to deny suspects the right of trial, to hold people for years in preventive custody, or to substitute military commissions for the civil courts. The need for democratic control of the management of war has not been reduced by advances in the technique of fighting. The accelerated rate of technical advance emphasizes anew the importance of civil control to guard against resistance to novelty and the other occupational diseases of the higher staffs of all armies. And as warfare becomes more dangerous, and as it embraces more and more of the life of the community, the problem of assuring a sensible choice of war policies, and of preserving democratic social values under conditions of general mobilization, becomes steadily more urgent.

What lies behind *Ex parte Milligan, Mitchell v. Harmony,* and *Sterling v. Constantin* is the principle of responsibility. The war power is the power to wage war successfully, as Chief Justice Hughes once remarked. But it is the power to wage war, not a license to do unnecessary and dictatorial things in the name of the war power. The decision as to where the boundaries of military discretion lie in particular cases has to be made differently in different circumstances. Sometimes the issue will arise in law suits, more often in courts-martial, congressional investigations, reports of the Inspector General, or other law enforcement procedures. When a court confronts the problem of determining the permissible limit of military discretion, it must test the question by the same methods of judicial inquiry it uses in other cases. There is no special reason why witnesses, depositions, cross-examination and other familiar techniques of investigation are less available in these cases than in others. As *Mitchell v. Harmony* and many other cases indicate, Mr. Justice Jackson is plainly wrong in asserting that judicial control of military discretion is impossible. Mr. Justice Jackson said:

> The limitation under which courts always will labor in examining the necessity for a military order are illustrated by this case. How does the Court know that these orders have a reasonable basis in necessity? No evidence whatever on that subject has been taken by this or any other court. There is sharp controversy as to the credibility of the DeWitt report. So the Court, having no real evidence before it, has no choice but to accept General DeWitt's own unsworn, self-serving statement, untested by any cross-examination, that what he did was reasonable. And thus it will always be when courts try to look into the reasonableness of a military order.[95]

95. Korematsu v. United States, 323 U.S. 214, 245 (1944). See procedure in *Ex parte* Duncan as described in Frank, supra note 84, at 649; General Wilbur was a witness in the individual exclusion proceedings against one Ochikubo. See *Pacific Citizen*, March 17, 1945, p. 2, col. 1.

The Supreme Court had a real alternative in the *Korematsu* case: it could have remanded for trial on the necessity of the orders. The courts have found no special difficulty in investigating such questions, and there is no reason why they should.

The first and greatest anomaly of the *Hirabayashi, Korematsu,* and *Endo* cases is that they seem to abandon the requirement of a judicial inquiry into the factual justification for General DeWitt's decisions. Despite the careful language of the Chief Justice, these cases treat the decisions of military officials, unlike those of other government officers, as almost immune from ordinary rules of public responsibility. The judges were convinced by the *ipse dixit* of a general, not the factual record of a court proceeding. On this ground alone, the Japanese American cases should be most strenuously reconsidered.

An appropriate procedure for reviewing decisions taken in the name of the war power is an indispensable step toward assuring a sensible result. But the ultimate problem left by these cases is not one of procedure. In these cases the Supreme Court of the United States upheld a decision to incarcerate 100,000 people for a term of several years. The reason for this action was the extraordinary proposition that all persons of Japanese ancestry were enemies, that the war was not directed at the Japanese state, but at the Japanese "race." General DeWitt's views on this subject were formally presented in his Final Recommendations and his Final Report to the War Department.[96] They were reiterated in his later testimony to a subcommittee of the Naval Affairs Committee. After testifying about soldier delinquency and other problems involving the welfare of his troops, General DeWitt was asked whether he had any

96. See supra, pp. 242–44.

suggestions he wanted to leave with the Congressmen. He responded:

I haven't any except one—that is the development of a false sentiment on the part of certain individuals and some organizations to get the Japanese back on the west coast. I don't want any of them here. They are a dangerous element. There is no way to determine their loyalty. The west coast contains too many vital installations essential to the defense of the country to allow any Japanese on this coast. There is a feeling developing, I think, in certain sections of the country that the Japanese should be allowed to return. I am opposing it with every proper means at my disposal.

MR. BATES: I was going to ask—would you base your determined stand on experience as a result of sabotage or racial history or what is it?

GENERAL DEWITT: I first of all base it on my responsibility. I have the mission of defending this coast and securing vital installations. The danger of the Japanese was, and is now—if they are permitted to come back— espionage and sabotage. It makes no difference whether he is an American citizen, he is still a Japanese. American citizenship does not necessarily determine loyalty.

MR. BATES: You draw a distinction then between Japanese and Italians and Germans? We have a great number of Italians and Germans and we think they are fine citizens. There may be exceptions.

GENERAL DEWITT: You needn't worry about the Italians at all except in certain cases. Also, the same for the Germans except in individual cases. But we must worry about the Japanese all the time until he is wiped off the map. Sabotage and espionage will make problems as long as he is allowed in this area—problems which I don't want to have to worry about.[97]

The Japanese exclusion program thus rested on five propositions of the utmost potential menace: (1) protective custody, extending over three or four years, is a permitted form of imprisonment in the United States; (2) political opinions, not criminal acts, may contain enough clear and present danger to justify such imprisonment; (3) men, women, and children of a given ethnic group, both Americans and resident aliens, can be presumed to possess the kinds of dangerous ideas which require their imprisonment; (4) in time of war or emergency the military, perhaps without even the concurrence of the legislature, can decide what political opinions require imprisonment and which ethnic groups are infected with them; and (5) the decision of the military can be carried out without indictment, trial, examination, jury, the confrontation of witnesses, counsel for the defense, the privilege against self-incrimination, or any of the other safeguards of the Bill of Rights.

The idea of punishment only for individual behavior is basic to all systems of civilized law. A great principle was never lost so casually. Mr. Justice Black's comment was weak to the point of impotence: "Hardships are a part of war, and war is an aggregation of hardships."[98] It was an answer in the spirit of cliché: "Don't you know there's a war going on?" It is hard to reconcile with the purposes of his dissent in *Williams v. North Carolina,* where he said that a conviction for bigamy in North Carolina of two people who had been validly divorced and remarried in Nevada "makes of

97. *Hearings before Subcommittee of House Committee on Naval Affairs on H. R. 30,* 78th Cong., 1st Sess. 739–40 (1943). The text of the testimony is given somewhat differently from contemporary newspaper reports in Mc-Williams, *Prejudice* 116 (1944).

98. Korematsu v. United States, 323 U.S. 214, 219 (1944).

human liberty a very cheap thing—too cheap to be consistent with the principles of free government."[99]

That the Supreme Court has upheld imprisonment on such a basis constitutes an expansion of military discretion beyond the limit of tolerance in democratic society. It ignores the rights of citizenship and the safeguards of trial practice which have been the historical attributes of liberty. Beyond that, it is an injustice, and therefore, like the trials of Sacco, Vanzetti, and Dreyfus, a threat to society and to all men. We believe that the German people bear a common political responsibility for outrages secretly committed by the Gestapo and the SS. What are we to think of our own part in a program which violated every democratic social value, yet was approved by the Congress, the President, and the Supreme Court?

Three forms of reparation are available, and should be pursued. The first is the inescapable obligation of the federal government to protect the civil rights of Japanese Americans against organized and unorganized hooliganism. If local law enforcement fails, prosecutions under the Civil Rights Act should be undertaken.[100] Secondly, generous financial indemnity should be sought, for the Japanese Americans have suffered and will suffer heavy property losses as a consequence of their evacuation. Finally, the basic issues should be presented to the Supreme Court again, in an effort to obtain a reversal of these wartime cases. In the history of the Supreme Court there have been important occasions when the Court itself corrected a decision occasioned by the excitement of a tense and patriotic mo-

99. Williams v. North Carolina, 325 U.S. 226, 276 (1945).
100. 18 U.S.C. §§ 51, 52 (Criminal Code §§ 19, 20) (1940); Hague v. CIO, 307 U.S. 496 (1939); United States v. Classic, 313 U.S. 299 (1941). Cf. Screws v. United States, 325 U.S. 91 (1945).

ment. After the end of the Civil War, *Ex parte Vallandig-ham*[101] was followed by *Ex parte Milligan*. The *Gobitis* case was overruled by *West Virginia v. Barnette*.[102] Similar public expiation in the case of the internment of Japanese Americans from the West Coast would be good for the Court and for the country.

## ADDENDUM

In the intervening years since this article was written, steps have been taken to atone for the wrongs done to the Japanese Americans in the name of national security.[103]

On May 20, 1959, the Attorney General of the United States, the Honorable William P. Rogers, convened a ceremony at the Department of Justice to take note of the successful end of the program of restoring citizenship to all but a few of the 5,700 persons of Japanese descent who renounced their citizenship during World War II. The speakers on that occasion were the Attorney General; the Honorable George Cochran Doub, the Assistant Attorney General who had vigorously speeded up both the settlement of property claims[104] and the restoration of citizenship; Edward J. Ennis, Esq., of New York, who had helped to institute the program as an official of the Department of Justice in 1942; and myself, as representative of those who

101. 1 Wall. 243 (U.S. 1863).

102. Minersville School District v. Gobitis, 310 U.S. 586 (1940); West Virginia State Board of Education v. Barnette, 319 U.S. 624 (1943).

103. The history of the episode is reviewed in Morton Grodzins, *Americans Betrayed: Politics and the Japanese Evacuation* (1949), and Dorothy Swaine Thomas, *The Salvage* (1952).

104. Congress passed the American-Japanese Evacuation Claims Act of 1948, P.L. 886, July 2, 1948, 62 Stat. 1231, c. 814, 50 U.S.C. App. 1981–87, under which almost $37,000,000 was paid to over 26,000 claimants for property losses sustained as a result of their evacuation.

had written about the constitutional problems of evacuation.

My remarks were as follows:

This is a day of pride for American law. We are met to celebrate the correction of an injustice. The law has no higher duty than to acknowledge its own errors. It is one of the vital ways in which law draws strength from the conscience of the community, and helps by its example to further the moral development of our people.

The long, difficult, and devoted labors which we honor here express the finest qualities in American life. The government's programs of restitution toward Americans of Japanese ancestry who were removed from the West Coast during the war rest on a premise bluntly put in a committee report of the House of Representatives in 1947: "to redress these loyal Americans in some measure for the wrongs inflicted upon them . . . would be simple justice." Today we confront the fact that as a nation we are capable of wrong, but capable also of confessing our wrongs and seeking to expiate them.

It is not hard to understand the program which was undertaken to remove persons of Japanese blood from the West Coast during the bleak winter of 1942. Pearl Harbor, Corregidor, the Battle of the Coral Seas, and Malaya were heavy on our hearts. Submarines prowled off Norfolk. Tobruk was still to fall. Midway, Stalingrad, and Tunis were far ahead. It was a time of defeat and of fear. Sometimes men act irrationally when they are afraid. While we did not succumb to panic in Hawaii or on the East Coast, we did so in California, Oregon, and Washington. Our sense of panic was institutionalized. Over 100,000 men, women, and children, some 70,000 of them citizens of the United States, were removed from their homes and taken into preventive custody, without indictment or the proffer of charges, on the theory that sabotage and espionage were especially to be feared from those of Japanese blood.

From the beginning, however, the conscience of the nation was engaged. Men were troubled by a persistent sense that the relocation policy was wrong. Our moral concern was soon translated into characteristic programs of action. The famous Nisei regiments which fought so well in Europe symbolized one aspect of that effort. Proposals for change in the relocation program itself soon followed. Despite the weakness, and, as I should say, the error of the Supreme Court's disposition of the problem, the people were not satisfied. They realized that acts can be wrong even though they are constitutionally permissible. No great voting groups or blocs entered the fight. No great political leaders made this cause their own. Nonetheless earnest men and women from all parts of the nation, in Congress and in the executive branch, continued their quiet efforts. The problem has been treated, throughout these sixteen years, without reference to party politics, as a matter of decency, and of decency alone.

I know I speak today for all who respect and revere the law, in congratulating the Attorneys General who have carried the programs of financial restitution through to success, and, even more important, have speeded up and completed the program for restoring citizenship to those who renounced it in the heat of a troubled moment. I especially congratulate the Assistant Attorney General, George Cochran Doub, and his excellent staff. They have made this battle their own, with a fervor which bespeaks their dedication to the highest value of our culture—the conviction that the most exalted office of the state is to do justice to the individual, however small his cause.

I hope that those who have suffered from the actions we took against them during the war have the charity to forgive their government, and the generosity, indeed the grace to find that what has been done to right these wrongs deepens their faith in our common citizenship and in our common democracy.

# 8

## Needed—A Rational Security Program

IN 1947, PRESIDENT TRUMAN established the first program for testing the "loyalty" of governmental employees. His action was a response to the fear and tension which accompanied public recognition of the Cold War. At the time, most of the members of the Yale Law Faculty signed a protest against the premise and the methods of the President's order. Experience has vindicated the soundness of their criticism.

There is a widespread impression that the loyalty-security programs, as they are now known, have been on the wane since the censure of the late Senator McCarthy. The impression is misleading. Although we have been somewhat less agitated about subversives lately, the institutionalized machinery of investigation, screening, hearings, and appeals goes on; and the practice is still spreading.

The loyalty-security programs are not important only because they directly affect the jobs of many millions of workers in government, in the armed services, in defense industries, in schools and universities, and in various "sensitive" jobs throughout the nation. In their present forms these programs also deny basic values of our law. They

First published in 215 *Harper's Magazine* 33 (July 1957).

introduce into the social order, and into the legal system, concepts of guilt without fault which have no place in a society formed under the Constitution and its Bill of Rights, and committed to the faith of freedom.

It should be easier to reach rational conclusions about how to protect the nation's internal security today than it was in 1947. In the first place, the country as a whole knows much more now than it did then about the realities of the Communist movement. The nation realizes now, as only a minority did then, that Communism genuinely threatens the balance of power on which our security as a nation rests—in Asia, in Europe, in Africa, in South America, and in the Middle East. We know that the threat is determined, patient, well-managed, and growing; that it will be pushed into every likely chink in our defenses with carefully calculated force; and that it rests on a massive Soviet industrial base, which is expanding more rapidly than our own. We know that the Communist threat cannot be exorcised by legal action against our weak Fifth Column at home, although that Fifth Column exists and will be used to the limit of its capacities.

In the second place, it should be possible now to reach firmer conclusions than could have been accepted in 1947 about the dimensions of the internal security problem and the consequences of various ways of dealing with it. Thousands of lives and careers have been altered by decisions based on loyalty-security programs. Studies have been made, and books and articles written.[1] The courts have dealt with

1. *Case Studies in Personnel Security,* A. Yarmolinsky, ed. (1955); R. S. Brown, Jr., *Loyalty and Security* (1958); E. Bontecou, *The Federal Loyalty-Security Program* (1953); Association of the Bar of the City of New York, *Report of the Special Committee on the Federal Loyalty-Security Program* (1956); *Report of the Commission on Government Security, pursuant to P. L. 84-304* (1957); E. A. Shils, *The Torment of Secrecy* (1956); C. P. Curtis, *The Oppenheimer Case, The Trial of a Security System* (1955).

important features of their structure, though not yet with their underlying ideas.[2]

The loyalty program launched in 1947 did not represent a new problem in government. The government, like all other employers, has always had procedures for investigating the character and history of its employees and prospective employees. These procedures had developed gradually over many years, and it became explicit policy some twenty-five years ago not to employ Communists or Fascists, or their sympathizers, in the government. Government employees had to take more and more elaborate oaths, and were subjected to more and more searching inquiry, before 'the government could be satisfied as to their fitness to serve. Both during and after the war, investigatory efforts were expanded, in a race to enforce these screening policies effectively, as the federal establishment mushroomed in size.

In 1946 and 1947, however, the contours of the problem changed. It came to be widely suspected that during the New Deal, and during the war, pockets of Communists and their friends had succeeded in penetrating the executive branch of the government. While the evidence of such infiltration on a considerable scale is not wholly convincing, the charge was vigorously propagated and had some foundation. Espionage is an old, old technique of government. And we should take it for granted that Communists will in the nature of their cause seek to lodge themselves wherever they can hope to exert influence—in unions, government departments, radio stations, and schools. Nonetheless, the thought that important or relatively important officials of the government had come close to treasonable activities struck hard and stirred opinion deeply.

2. Greene v. McElroy, 360 U.S. 474 (1959); Peters v. Hobby, 349 U.S. 331 (1955); Cole v. Young, 351 U.S. 536 (1956); Vitarelli v. Seaton, 359 U.S. 535 (1959); Service v. Dulles, 354 U.S. 363 (1957).

# Toward a Theory of Judicial Action

As the reaction gained momentum, the loyalty review procedures were initiated, to provide more security to the government employee as well as to the government, to promote uniformity of standards among the departments, and to give the employee whose loyalty had been challenged an opportunity to answer, to have the protection of a hearing, and to take an appeal.

Since 1947, the political standard by which fitness to serve in the government is determined has been changed twice. The original order of 1947 required a loyalty investigation for every employee and prospective employee of the government. No one was to be accepted for employment, or allowed to continue in employment, if it should be found, "on all the evidence," that "reasonable grounds exist for belief that the person involved is disloyal to the government of the United States."[3] This standard, requiring a positive finding of "disloyalty," was changed in 1951 to provide for dismissal or refusal of employment where, "on all the evidence, there is a reasonable doubt as to the loyalty of the person involved to the government of the United States."[4]

In 1953, the Eisenhower Administration, persuaded that the Truman program was too weak, revised the original Executive Order to make the interests of "national security," rather than "disloyalty" or "reasonable doubt as to loyalty," the test of federal employment. The Eisenhower order established as its standard the rule that no one was to be employed or retained in employment unless his employ-

3. Executive Order 9835, 12 *Fed. Reg.* 1935, March 25, 1947.

4. Executive Order 10241, 16 *Fed. Reg.* 3690, May 1, 1951. Meanwhile Congress had also passed a statute, 64 Stat. 476 (1950), authorizing dismissal "when deemed necessary in the interest of national security," at least in security-connected branches of the government. Cole v. Young, 351 U.S. 536 (1956).

ment "is clearly consistent with the interests of the national security."[5]

A considerable number of studies and reports have given the public some sense of what is involved in many loyalty-security cases: the charges, often vague, and usually concerned with opinion, or the opinions of friends or relatives, rather than conduct; the evidence, often petty, dealing with meetings, subscriptions, radical interests, or unusual behavior, woven into a pattern creating doubt; the personal tragedy of a career and life history near ruin, even where a man has been finally cleared; the loyalty, and occasionally the betrayal, of friends; the prolongation of vague and intangible inquiries in a quasi-judicial form. Reported cases illustrate not only the routine grounds for dismissal—crime, falsehood, misrepresentation, and the like—but also charges which represent fantastic hypotheses about the nature of patriotism and the likelihood of its being betrayed.

Case after case charges a person with friendly association with a relative or friend thought to be a Communist, or a Communist sympathizer, or a member of an organization cited by the Attorney General as being subversive; with appearing on the mailing lists of Communist front organizations or publications; with using as a reference the names of persons "thought to be" or "charged with being" Communist sympathizers of varying degrees, or identified with organizations some of whose directors were charged with being Communist sympathizers; with having protested against loyalty-oath requirements in universities, or contributed to Spanish War Relief, or attended lectures by politically doubtful speakers, or belonged to the Consumers' Union.

The concept of "loyalty" is a test of present or past politi-

5. Executive Order 10450, 18 *Fed. Reg.* 2489, April 29, 1953.

271

cal ideas, ranging from the Communist to the confusingly radical, unorthodox, or eccentric. The notion of "security risk" includes the full ideological spectrum of "loyalty," but it also embraces elements of character weakness, susceptibility to blackmail, alcoholism, and homosexuality. Among the fixed beliefs which prevail in this field is a series of rules of thumb—that persons with relatives behind the Iron Curtain are not to be trusted, since they might be blackmailed; that homosexuals are more subject to blackmail than undiscriminating heterosexuals; and that membership in a certain number of doubtful or subversive organizations, or subscription to a certain number of doubtful publications, is significant evidence of unreliability. Many of the criteria used in enforcing the nonpolitical parts of the "security risk" standard have turned out to be almost more offensive to human dignity than the loyalty test itself. It is hard to imagine a civilized government dismissing a reliable official, with a long and distinguished record of most exacting service, on the ground that years before, when abroad, he had had an affair with a lady. Yet apparently our government has done so. The rule would have an interesting impact if generally enforced.

One of the difficulties in the government's practice has been the way in which these criteria have been applied. No one could deny that what lies behind these words, in some form, and to some extent, has a bearing on sensible decisions as to a person's eligibility for the public service. But they have been enforced in many instances with a foolish literalness, unsophistication, and even hypocrisy. A libertine, a pronounced alcoholic, or a fervent revolutionary could well merit dismissal, for the good of any service, and at almost any level of the service, sensitive or nonsensitive. But it is absurd to fire a married woman as a security risk from an ordinary job in the bureaucracy because her baby arrived a bit too soon after the wedding. The most puritanical New England village takes such events calmly in stride. Should the government have been convulsed into self-righteous action?

The ideas and methods of the federal security programs have spread to vast areas of nongovernmental employment —to defense industries, the military itself, and the maritime industry, to universities which have research contracts with government, to the educational system generally. Professor Brown of the Yale Law School has estimated that formal screening programs of one kind or another directly affect the employment of 13 million persons in the United States, or 20 per cent of the labor force.[6] There is no way of judging how many more millions are under the shadow of this quest for assurance about the reliability of men. The idea of "clearance" has become part of the horizon of expectations of the rising generation.

What have these procedures accomplished? They have dramatized for the country at large the fact that there is a Communist movement, which has eagerly pursued its chosen goals. They have established the weakness of that movement, its successful penetration by counterespionage agents, and its ineffectiveness in labor, in the communications industries, in education, and in the government. The machinery for screening under the various loyalty-security programs has uncovered only one case of espionage, as far as is publicly known, and that indirectly. It has resulted in the ouster from government of several thousand persons and the resignation of many more, though no reliable statistics are available to indicate the proportion of these terminations which involved political issues rather than alcoholism, character defects, or other grounds.

6. Ralph S. Brown, Jr., *Loyalty and Security* (1958).

It has prevented the employment of even larger numbers of persons. Significantly, only a few perjury prosecutions have developed in the wake of several thousand loyalty-security proceedings challenging dismissed employees on the ground that they had made false statements about their politics on entering the government service. In one of the most spectacular of these cases, the government moved for a dismissal because its own officer had misrepresented the facts before a grand jury. Several informants who had brought the accusations which set the machinery into irreversible motion were revealed as neurotic, irresponsible, or corrupt.

These procedures may have prevented harm, through the exclusion from government of potential betrayers of secrets. But, as a practical matter, it is impossible to weigh this possible gain against the undoubted damage done to the morale of the government staff, to the development of science, and to the fabric of law. While the attack on Communists in the trade unions, counterespionage and other police methods, criminal law enforcement, and above all the ordinary processes of public debate have effectively limited the influence of active Communists, the loyalty-security programs have accomplished little in this positive sense.

They have created, however, an atmosphere of fear and insecurity, both in the public service and in other sectors of society, gravely disturbing men's confidence in the fairness of government and in the sense of justice of law. Large numbers of people are now persuaded that there is something seriously wrong with programs that produce such a costly side effect, though there is so far no consensus as to where their weakness lies.

There have been many criticisms of the way in which the loyalty-security programs have functioned and of their effects on the life of the nation. Most of these criticisms accept the premise of the programs and concentrate on the procedures which have been employed. The evidence against a man should be presented to him and to all the tribunals which judge him, the critics urge. He should be able to confront and cross-examine adverse witnesses. The thesis that evidence must be kept secret to protect the government's sources of information has no more place in a loyalty-security hearing, where a man's career and honor are at stake, than in a criminal court. Charges are too broad, and there is no opportunity to test their relevance or sufficiency by moving to strike unusually remote or ridiculous accusations. The person charged should not have to bear the impossible burden of proving that he has led a blameless life and always supported policies which it is now respectable and conventional to have supported. And he should be protected against the harassment and unfairness of having to defend himself against the same accusations over and over again. The government employee being investigated should be allowed to continue on the payroll until his case is settled. He should be helped to find counsel, and his legal costs paid if he is cleared.

These criticisms all have merit. But they do not go to the primary vice of the loyalty-security programs. The root of the matter is not a question of procedure. The fault is substantive. The wrong is to use the authority of the legal system to determine whether or not a man is "disloyal" or a "security risk"—that is, a *potential* criminal. When we embark on this inquiry, we have passed the boundary between the realm of action and the realm of belief, thought, and opinion beyond which no system of law should venture.

Recalling the Dreyfus affair, the Alsop brothers called their book on the Oppenheimer case *We Accuse.*[7] The book

7. Joseph and Stewart Alsop, *We Accuse* (1954).

was a powerful and useful critique of the loyalty-security programs, but the title was mistaken. While the Dreyfus case stirred up a great political outcry, to the everlasting credit of the French people, the case itself was a routine miscarriage of justice—a commonplace accident in the history of law. Oppenheimer's ordeal represents something altogether different. The decision that Oppenheimer is a "security risk" did not rest on forged evidence, or mistaken identity, or lying witnesses, or blind pride. On the contrary, the judgment against Oppenheimer is perfectly plausible, given the premises of the loyalty-security programs. It cannot be called a miscarriage of justice. It is, rather, the kind of judgment to be expected normally from a system of organized injustice—a system of legal procedures through which earnest and sincere judges are required to answer unanswerable questions.

For centuries the law has experimented with the problem of how to find out whether an accused person is guilty as charged: is the court satisfied beyond doubt that the defendant set fire to a given barn, on a given night, in terms of the indictment brought against him? By and large, legal proceedings work reasonably well in answering such questions, at least in the absence of the kind of difficulties which plagued the Dreyfus trials. But how can a tribunal determine, as a matter of law, that a man is a potential criminal?

For centuries also, governments, like other employers, have made executive decisions about hiring and firing. While governments should adhere to high standards of fairness in dealing with their employees, they are entitled to considerable flexibility in their choice of civil servants. Officers of government can and properly do select employees on all sorts of grounds, subjective as well as objective. They must evaluate the man and his record, his promise and the risks which he presents, including the risk that he may turn out to be lazy, dishonest, emotionally difficult, or worse. That is an expected part of any society's machinery for using its manpower.

But it is a totally different matter to put the prestige of the process of law behind a judgment that a person is or may be disloyal to his country, or a security risk—that is, a person likely to commit one of the most degraded crimes we know. As the Supreme Court said, such a judgment is "a badge of infamy. Especially is this so in time of cold war and hot emotions when 'each man begins to eye his neighbor as a possible enemy.' "[8]

It is no wonder, then, that seeking to grapple with mysteries of this order, the five opinions written in the Oppenheimer case each rested on a different premise and a different conception of the matter to be tried. It is hardly surprising that case after case in the loyalty-security programs has turned on the political opinions of the person charged, the magazines to which he subscribed, or on the political and social views and habits of his relatives and friends. Where the law is seeking to determine whether a man is a security risk, these issues are as relevant as anything else.

Most life histories have episodes, or chapters, which would look appalling on the front page of a newspaper or in an FBI security file. There is still point in the old story of the practical joker who sent identical telegrams to the five leading men in his town: "Fly at once, all is discovered," and then found that four left on the next train. And it is routine to discover that the cashier who robbed the bank was a model citizen, a leader of his church, a pillar of the Boy Scouts, and an active and respected member of the community.

In the perspective of psychiatry, moreover, all men have

8. Wieman v. Updegraff, 344 U.S. 183, 191 (1952).

needs, impulses, and drives which, given the right set of circumstances, might lead them into antisocial behavior. And it is equally obvious that many persons who function reliably and adequately—often, indeed, with distinction—have private dimensions which would cause most people to question their judgment—eccentric views about religion or diet, gardening, art, or health, or a buried early scrape or wild oat, which it is usually sensible to ignore. No system of selection, even for the elite of a society, has ever been able to identify the pure in heart.

If the concept of "loyalty-security risk" is not one to which a fixed or determinate meaning can be given—or should be given—by procedures having the authority and sanction of decision by the state, what methods should the government employ to meet its legitimate demand for efficiency, effectiveness, and devotion on the part of its staff?

Some critics, notably Walter Lippmann and C. D. Williams, have suggested that the entire machinery of hearings and determinations be scrapped, and that employment be left to executive discretion. The possible injustice of the boss' decision, they contend, is preferable to the stigma of fully considered official judgments that a man is a loyalty or security risk. This view goes too far. It would weaken, if not destroy, the safeguards of the civil service laws, which have permitted us, not without shortcomings and rigidities, to develop a strong career civil service. And it runs counter to the broader principle that all the citizen's relations with his government should be conducted on a basis of the highest possible standards of evenhanded justice.

As a first step, the selection of government employees and their removal from career jobs should have the kind of procedural safeguards which normally characterize admission to and removal from the bar, the practice of medicine, or the conduct of other licensed callings. The executive decision to hire or fire should be qualified by the interposition of review procedures, as has always been the case in the armed forces, the foreign service, and the civil service. Such procedures of review should be required to meet appropriate constitutional standards of fairness, including adequate notice of specific charges, hearings, and the opportunity to confront the adverse evidence, to present evidence oneself, and to appeal. Existing civil service procedures, which in essentials go back to 1912, provide for hearings of a sort to review the executive's decision as to a man's suitability for continuation in the permanent competitive civil service. Grave doubts have been expressed as to whether such procedures meet modern constitutional standards. They should certainly be reviewed carefully and reformed if found wanting.

Questions of procedural fairness aside, what criteria should govern in handling questions of this order? The basic problem raised by the loyalty-security programs cannot be avoided by giving it a different name or by remitting it entirely to the Civil Service Commission, which has made 90 per cent of the federal dismissals on security grounds, in any event.

One suggestion has been made by the distinguished Special Committee on the Federal Loyalty-Security Program of the Association of the Bar of the City of New York, in its generally excellent Report. The Committee recommended that special personnel security programs should apply to "sensitive" positions and to no others—"sensitive" being defined as positions whose occupants would have access to material classified as "secret" or "top-secret," or would have a policy-making function bearing a substantial relation to national security.[9] For the rest, the federal serv-

9. Association of the Bar of the City of New York, *Report of the Special Committee on the Federal Loyalty-Security Program* 141 (1956).

ice would continue to be protected, as in the past, by laws which forbid the employment of Communists or their active collaborators, and by the general suitability requirements of the Civil Service Commission rules.

For the sensitive positions, the special criterion of employment would be "whether or not in the interest of the United States the employment or retention of employment of the individual is advisable. In applying this standard a balanced judgment should be reached after giving due weight to all the evidence, both derogatory and favorable, to the nature of the position, and the value of the individual to the public service."[10] This test would eliminate the burden of proof under the present order, which requires hearing officials to be satisfied that the employment of the person being studied is *"clearly* consistent" with the interests of national security. It would permit the Security Personnel Board to consider a man's associations, insofar as he was found to be closely identified with, or subject to, significant influence by those with whom he associates. The Committee recommended that evidence elicited from the private and elusive world of ideas be used sparingly and with great care,[11] and that the present Attorney General's list of subversive organizations be abolished, as an indiscriminate tool often wrongly used in personnel procedures throughout the country.[12]

Despite the merit of these proposals, they do not deal completely with the underlying problem. The Committee was on sound ground in stressing that the primary issue should be whether a man reasonably measures up to his job, and that different jobs presuppose different qualifications.

10. Id. at 149.

11. Id. at 152–54.

12. Id. at 154–57. The Committee would recommend the continuance of the list only if substantial revisions of it were undertaken.

But the Report did not carry this principle over to the vast bulk of the cases, which it would leave to be dealt with under the suitability criteria of the existing Civil Service Regulations. The Committee would apparently keep those regulations as they are, even though they require a man to be dismissed if, on all the evidence, there is "reasonable doubt" as to his loyalty—a vague and impalpable criterion which raises all the difficulties we have discussed. These difficulties are different in kind from those presented by the statutory prohibition against the employment of Communists in the government, a practical rule which few would now be disposed to change, despite some of the paradoxes it presents.

Would it not be preferable if the principle suggested by the Committee Report were consistently made the central, and indeed the only, rule for government employment— that is, a man's fitness or suitability for the job in question? This approach would build on the premise that the government is fully entitled to set reasonable qualifications for employment and continued employment—qualifications which deal with every aspect of a man's person, character, and competence relevant to his job. This approach would make the government's right to inquire into a man's beliefs, and his entire history, a function of the requirements of the job he is called upon to do.

For persons already employed, actual performance of their jobs would be the most significant evidence bearing on their qualification for promotion or for continued employment—the only significant evidence for most jobs, and the most important evidence, even for jobs with especially exacting standards. Outside the zone of highly sensitive employment—jobs affecting the national security and policy-making jobs—full field investigations of a man's life would be inappropriate and should not be made. For applicants, a distinction should again be drawn between sensitive and nonsensitive jobs. It is justifiable, at least under present Cold War circumstances, to conduct a full-scale study, including a field investigation, of applicants for sensitive jobs. For others, appropriate inquiry into technical qualifications for the job is indicated. Unless it should appear that the applicant may be barred under the Hatch Act as a member of a political party or other organization which advocates the overthrow of the government, a prolonged search into his life history could not be relevant. If preliminary inquiry raises doubts about the applicability of the Hatch Act, careful consideration of the question should be provided for, perhaps through a procedure comparable to that of the Atomic Energy Commission.

Indeed, I should carry the principle implicit in the Committee's Report even further. In the higher reaches of the civil service, where policy-making is involved, the government is entitled to rely on officials who accept government policy, and not merely on those who accept the Constitution. It has always been routine in the armed forces or the foreign service to transfer officials who strongly oppose the policy of the government to posts where their disagreement would not interfere with effective administration. Such transfers are a sound way of assuring governmental action, without compromising the ideals of a career service. The higher military commander who regards the campaign as wrongly conceived and planned is hardly likely to be the ideal instrument for carrying it out. A convinced isolationist would rarely be an appropriate ambassador to the councils of NATO.

If not overdone, reliance on transfers should become a far more important procedure in dealing with problems of the suitability of personnel than has been the case thus far. There are dangers in such a course, especially in times of political tension. The severity of the sanction of dismissal may prevent action, which might become far too common if timid superiors could get rid of their "risks" by sending them to Botany Bay; and the stigma of transfer might become as real a moral blow to the employee as the stigma of dismissal. Nonetheless there is much to recommend it. If government can take the lead in allaying the sense of panic, which has so seriously distorted common-sense judgment in this field, transfer should not be too dangerous a tool of administrative management. And if we do not dissipate our recent sense of panic, no changes in the rules or procedures will do much good.

Suppose, then, that the government's system for personnel administration is based on the single and valid criterion of a man's personal suitability for a particular job. Suppose further that fair procedures, fully conforming to the constitutional standards applied, say, in disbarment proceedings, are provided for hearing appeals from the decisions of those who must initially decide whether to hire or fire federal employees. These two policies would cut down the number of jobs for which significant political tests for employment were relevant, and would meet the valid procedural criticisms of our experience under the loyalty-security programs of the last fifteen years. Under these circumstances, should we continue to have a separate program, dealing with those cases of suitability for employment which raise questions of a political character? Should there be a separate order, standard, and board or commission to handle this class of cases?

The Special Committee of the New York Bar Association recommended a separate political security program, which might well be in charge of sophisticated men, experts on Communism, who could be expected not to make the vulgar errors which have been such a painful feature of the loyalty-security process thus far. A tight standard might be stated, intended to confine the dismissals of "security risks" to a small number of obvious cases. Nonetheless, the contrary arguments seem stronger. There are advantages in abolishing a separate program of political clearances and in firmly putting all questions about a man's politics into the appropriate context of his personal suitability for a particular job.

The notion of proscribing classes of men for their ideas, their past follies, their private lives, or their relatives is repellent to us. It recalls the policies of the Soviets, who discriminate against kulaks and former members of the Russian middle class, and against their children, too. If eligibility for employment is made once more a matter of individual suitability for particular jobs or classes of jobs, there is little to be gained from keeping or revising the present security and loyalty tests, and much to be gained from starting over.

This nation has been engaged in a long and troublesome exercise—an instinctive and healthy attempt to bring the internal security problem into the law. Among the complex and novel issues of the Cold War, none has been more difficult to resolve than that of devising procedures which would protect government against unreliable or untrustworthy employees, and equally protect government employees against the risks of dismissal by witch hunt. As long as the problem is defined in terms of universal criteria for employment and dismissal—the loyalty or security risk—we are trapped in a dilemma from which there is no visible escape, save a return to the practice of unlimited executive discretion. For the prevailing system requires us to use the prestige of the trial process, with all its historical and psychological power, to make adjudications about the beliefs, opinions, and character of men, and the possibility that they may commit crime. This has been an impossible task, beyond the proper limits of law. But that is what we have been trying to do.

The way out is not to give up the attempt to protect internal security against the efforts of the Communists nor, on the other hand, to abandon the protections of the civil service idea. Defining the problem in terms of an individual's suitability for a particular employment, as I propose we do instead, is not a magic formula which dispels all difficulty. But it maps out an approach which should individualize these problems and make them soluble in terms which protect both the public service and the dignity and privacy of the citizen's life.

An advantage of this approach would be to annul flat rules and presumptions, except for the prohibition against the employment of active Communists. Another would be to require the government to abandon elaborate field studies into an employee's beliefs, and his political and personal history, save for those few jobs where the burden of responsibility requires the government to be thoroughly satisfied as to a man's stability, experience, and personal attitudes. Thus it should stop the dangerous process of accumulating dossiers and do much to end the atmosphere of insecurity and mutual suspicion which has been so damaging a by-product of the loyalty-security programs of the last decade. When the government begins to investigate private lives intensively, it discovers that things are seldom what they seem and that many closets contain skeletons. Once this knowledge is available, it is almost impossible not to use it.

We can evaluate this proposal by considering some of its implications. Under such a standard, there could be no general inquisition into the life histories and political ideas of federal meat inspectors and proofreaders. Perhaps the most severe test for the policy proposed here would be to see how the Oppenheimer case might have been handled under it. Dr. Oppenheimer was in a sensitive position, justifying full inquiry into every aspect of his career and character. The approach proposed here would pose the problem presented by Oppenheimer's record not as the question whether Oppenheimer was a "security risk," but whether his superior acted arbitrarily and without suitable basis in fact in deciding that he lacked sufficient confidence in Oppenheimer's reliability to continue his employment. The question would not be the abstract issue of using the full panoply of semi-judicial inquiry to determine whether Oppenheimer was a probable or likely espionage agent, but the far more limited and tolerable act of taking an administrative appeal from a superior's decision that a member of his staff was not in person or character the kind of man the job required. Most of the same evidence would have been relevant. The fact that Oppenheimer had served well for more than a decade would have been given far greater weight, since the issue would have been his suitability for the job. But that issue would have been altogether different from the question the boards struggled with in vain as the case was actually handled. The end might have been the same, although I should guess otherwise. But the consequences—both to Oppenheimer, to the world of science, and to the law—would have been of a different order.

The moral we should draw from what is now a lengthy and fully disclosed experience with the Communist threat to internal security is twofold: the threat is real, since the Soviet Union is strong, hostile, aggressive, and growing relatively stronger. The fanatic devotees of the Soviet cause are indeed its loyal subjects and may recruit help from those who in any society are willing to engage in the crimes of sabotage or espionage. With equal conviction, we may now conclude that the Communist Fifth Column in the United States is weak and ineffective and well within the control of sound police surveillance. It accomplished little or nothing, by way of sabotage at least, either during the early stages of World War II or during the Korean War. Whatever espionage it conducted, as revealed in several famous cases, was discovered by the accident of Gouzenko's defection or by police methods, not by the universal investigations of the loyalty-security programs.

We should conclude that the process of universal screening was a mistake, and that the rules of exclusion we developed, presuming that people of certain views or habits were more likely than others to commit crime, were wrong. They represent in our law an extension of the dangerous idea behind the relocation program for Japanese and Americans of Japanese ancestry which we carried out during the war: that men can be segregated, penalized, and stigmatized without individual fault because it is widely suspected that they may commit crime. The sound answer, which could satisfy both the legitimate administrative needs of the government and the rights of its employees, should be found by building carefully on the central idea of suitability for the job: that different jobs require different degrees of character stability and different standards of political judgment. Abandoning blanket presumptions of probable guilt, the sensitive areas of government could be assured staffs of appropriate reliability, without making "reasonable doubt of loyalty" a general touchstone for dismissal from the civil service.

Beyond that we need not and should not go. A left-wing employee of the Fish and Wildlife Service might someday put germs in a reservoir. But so might an employee who becomes paranoid, or a civilian.

We can afford the security of freedom. The loyalty-security programs have produced insecurity, not security. They have violated one of the vital ends to which any system of law should be dedicated. As Montesquieu said, "The political liberty of the subject is a tranquillity of mind arising from the opinion each person has of his safety. In order to have this liberty, it is requisite that the government be so constituted that one man need not be afraid of another."[13]

That "tranquillity of mind" for the individual, which Montesquieu rightly saw as an essential goal of government under law, is threatened when exaggerated punishment or repression corrupts society. This is one of the reasons why he opposed loose prosecution for treason and all manner of attempts to fight heresy by legal sanctions.

> The laws do not take upon them [he wrote] to punish any other than overt acts . . . Words do not constitute an overt act; they remain only an idea . . . Words carried into action assume the nature of that action. Thus a man who goes into a public market-place to incite the subjects to revolt incurs the guilt of high treason, because the words are joined to the action, and partake of its nature. It is not the words that are punished, but an action in which words are employed. They do not become criminal but when they are annexed to a criminal action; everything is confounded if words are construed into a capital crime, instead of considering them only as a mark of that crime . . . Whenever this law is established, there is an end not only of liberty, but even of its very shadow.[14]

In seeking to deal with conspiracy, we have through the loyalty-security programs succeeded in punishing heresy, and often mere heterodoxy or confusion.

It is time to call a halt.

13. 1 *The Spirit of the Laws 182* (O. W. Holmes, ed. 1900).
14. Id. at 232–34.

# 9

## *The Price of Federalism*

*I do not think the United States would come to an end if we lost our power to declare an Act of Congress void. I do think the Union would be imperiled if we could not make that declaration as to the laws of the several states.*

—MR. JUSTICE HOLMES

AMONG THE MANY changes in constitutional law wrought by the New Deal Supreme Court, one alone is likely to alter the structure of the environment in which Americans live and work. Eleven years ago the Court upheld the Wagner Act as applied to steel, clothing, and newspaper workers. Thus it abandoned the idea—only a generation old, and never consistently applied—that production was not "commerce," and was therefore beyond Section 8 of Article I of the Constitution, the commerce clause ("Congress shall have power . . . to regulate commerce with foreign nations, and among the several States, and with the Indian Tribes"). The new view restored John Marshall's premise that production and exchange on a national scale constitute a single process, all of which Congress may regulate, and initiated deep changes in the relations between the nation and the states.

Since 1937, the Court has upheld a wide variety of fed-

---

First published in 38 *Fortune Magazine* 164 (1948).

eral regulatory statutes, but it has only begun to consider how far the growth of national power may cut down the authority of the states. So far the Court has been reluctant to deny the states capacity to legislate on the ground that Congress has passed, or could pass, laws in the same field. If the Supreme Court of earlier vintage made of business a no-man's-land that neither the states nor the Congress could regulate, business is now every man's land, with substantial supervision by fifty-one sovereign legislatures. Business finds itself increasingly in lawyers' hands, and a widening system of multiple control often combines the worst features of federal and state regulation.

One great achievement of our constitutional experience has been the creation of a continental economy, with all the freedom and the advantages of specialization that flow from a division of labor on so vast a scale. The protection of the national economy is one of the chief themes of American government, politics, and law. To control a complex modern economy, Congress requires adequate authority. On the other hand, the tradition of federalism has given us the benefit of some discretion for the states to experiment with social legislation at little national risk. And the power of the states to regulate certain aspects of business has constitutional roots almost as deep as the commerce clause.

However, the power of the states over business is necessarily qualified and limited. Everyone agrees in principle that the states should not be allowed to balkanize the United States into fifty tariff-ridden autarchies. Trouble begins, as usual, when one examines particulars. Is it constitutional for Congress to regulate wheat acreage? That depends on whether Congress and the Justices think that the production of wheat is "commerce among the several states." Is it constitutional for a state to limit the number of freight cars on a train? That depends on whether Congress and the courts think that to do so is unduly to burden "commerce among the several states."

The choice between state, national, and multiple regulation affects the balance in our Constitution between the forces of nationalism and of federalism. On this balance the architecture of our economic system in large part depends. The issue goes beyond economics, for the division of authority between state and nation—the internal balance of power in the constitutional system—is the crucial political problem of federalism.

Who is to decide—Congress or the Supreme Court—when a state has overstepped the boundaries of its power? As to that, the Supreme Court's own views have changed more than once, and they are still evolving.

The "leading case" on the commerce clause as a restraint upon the states is *Gibbons v. Ogden*.[1] To encourage Robert Fulton's experiments, New York's legislature awarded him the exclusive right for a period of years to navigate boats "moved by fire or steam" on waters under state control. Congress, however, had passed a general navigation statute under which the steamers of one Gibbons were licensed for the coasting trade as United States flag vessels. When Gibbons ferried passengers from New Jersey to New York, Ogden, a Fulton licensee, sued to stop him. Counsel included such legal lions as Daniel Webster and Thomas Emmet, the romantic Irish nationalist refugee, who hurled at each other quotations from the *Aeneid* in speeches of great color and eloquence.

The circumstances illustrate the characteristic problem of overlapping legislative power in a federal system. Under the New York statute, no one could navigate in New York coastal waters without a license from Fulton, on pain of

1. 22 U.S. [9 Wheat.] 1 (1824).

forfeiture of the vessel. Connecticut and New Jersey had in reprisal enacted statutes that excluded and penalized New York licensees. Had the Supreme Court recognized the authority of New York, the states would have been started on a race of restrictionism. Economic growth would have been restrained and endless material provided for dangerous political conflicts.

Chief Justice Marshall began his opinion with a broad definition. The power of the Congress over interstate commerce, he asserted, is the plenary and absolute power to regulate all aspects of commercial intercourse. "The wisdom and the discretion of congress," he said, "their identity with the people, and the influence which their constituents possess at elections, are, in this, as in many other instances, as that, for example, of declaring war, the sole restraints on which they have relied, to secure them from its abuse."[2] The implication of Marshall's view was that the Supreme Court could not invalidate an act of Congress on the ground that it went beyond the commerce power. And for purposes of the case, he said, commerce included all aspects of navigation.

Marshall thus started his argument from the federal navigation statute. Since the Court read the federal license under that statute as authorizing Gibbons to go into New York waters, the New York statute purporting to control navigation there under local police power was void. New York's broad powers of legislation to encourage health, safety, and science could not be used to control interstate traffic where Congress had prescribed its own rule.

Chief Justice Marshall's opinion was typical of his technique as a judge. Its memorable and lasting effect was his bold conception of the scope of the interstate commerce

2. 22 U.S. [9 Wheat.] 1, 185, 197 (1824).

power. His full statement was hardly necessary to the decision, since few people disputed that actual navigation was a problem of interstate commerce. However, Marshall knew the practical importance of abstraction, and put all his force into staking out his nationalist definition of "commerce among the several states," and of the freedom of Congress to act in this realm. Having accomplished his main purpose, he did not further offend the sensibilities of the Democrats by holding that the New York law was void by force of the Constitution alone; he went on to the Act of Congress of 1793, which did not expressly mention state statutes regulating navigation.

Mr. Justice Johnson, on the other hand, although a friend and appointee of Jefferson and a rebel on the Court against the dominance of Chief Justice Marshall, argued that the federal license was immaterial to the case. "If there was any one object riding over every other in the adoption of the constitution," he wrote, "it was to keep the commercial intercourse among the states free from all invidious and partial restraints."[3] The New York statute, he contended, therefore fell by virtue of the Constitution, even without action in the field by the Congress. And it was the duty of the Court so to hold, without benefit of prior instruction from the Congress.

The Justices divided in the paradoxical way that has always made easy judgments about the Court so dangerous. The Jeffersonian, Johnson, upheld the broadest powers of judicial review and the narrowest possible view of states' rights, while the Federalist, Marshall, rested his opinion on deference to the Congress and on a complete denial of judicial review over acts of Congress, where commerce was concerned.

3. 22 U.S. [9 Wheat.] 1, 222, 231 (1824).

What the Supreme Court should do about state regulation of interstate business where Congress has said nothing
was fully re-examined in 1945 by Chief Justice Stone in
*Southern Pacific Co. v. Arizona.*[4] The Southern Pacific
challenged the validity of a 1912 Arizona statute that made
it illegal to operate trains of more than specified lengths.
The controversy over train lengths has been persistent, the
unions claiming that safety requires limitation, the railroads charging that limitation is featherbedding. Congress,
though repeatedly pressed, has passed no limiting law, nor
can the Interstate Commerce Commission limit the length
of trains except in emergencies. In the *Southern Pacific*
case, therefore, the Court had to face squarely the issue that
Johnson alone saw in *Gibbons v. Ogden:* was the state law
unconstitutional where Congress had refused or failed to
act?

Mr. Justice Black (and intermittently Justices Douglas,
Frankfurter, and Murphy) had tenaciously argued between
1939 and 1941 that the Supreme Court should be neutral
in the contest for authority over commerce. In their opinion
the Court should not declare state statutes unconstitutional
as excessive burdens on the national commerce without
prior direction by the Congress. Justice Black, Justice
Frankfurter, and Justice Douglas had contended that "the
maintenance of open channels of trade between the states"
is far too complex a problem for settlement by the courts.[5]
It was a matter of national concern that could be resolved
only by the Congress. Except where state legislation is "hostile to the congressional grant of authority" (and perhaps
also in cases in which a state law discriminates against the
national commerce), the Court should not invoke the commerce clause as a restraint on the states. Justice Black has

4. 325 U.S. 761 (1945).
5. McCarroll v. Dixie Greyhound Lines, Inc., 309 U.S. 176, 183, 185 (1940).

said repeatedly that for the Supreme Court to attempt a balancing of values—the national interest in uniformity as against the local welfare interest in a particular policy—is to act as a "superlegislature."

By 1945, however, when the *Southern Pacific* case was decided, Justices Frankfurter and Douglas had ceased to fight against the historic assertion of judicial responsibility. Justice Stone led a strong majority (including Justices Roberts, Reed, Frankfurter, Murphy, and Jackson) in holding the train-length law unconstitutional. Justice Douglas dissented, but on relatively limited grounds and without challenging, as did Justice Black, the Court's basic premise. Justice Rutledge concurred separately, a vote that registered his disagreement with Stone's reasoning.

As Chief Justice Stone observed, it has been accepted constitutional doctrine for a hundred years that the Court be "the final arbiter of the competing demands of state and national interests,"[6] at least where Congress has not acted. To be sure, states had been left free where there was no strong national interest in uniformity and no discrimination against or substantial interference with interstate commerce, or where the legislation was strongly concerned with some local issue of health or safety. For example, the states have been allowed, in the absence of a federal statute, to regulate the work of the harbor pilots, to require cabooses on trains, to abolish the potbellied train stove, or to fix the maximum weight and size of highway trucks. But Justice Stone said that a national interest in uniformity should prevail over local regulation even where the latter protected a permissible local interest in safety.

Moreover, Chief Justice Stone contended, state statutes affecting interstate commerce cannot come into court with

6. 325 U.S. 761, 769 (1945).

the normal presumption of constitutionality. Since the burden of the Arizona law fell primarily on out-of-state interests not represented in the Arizona legislature, it could not be treated with the special deference due the products of a fully representative and democratic legislative process. This novel conception of judicial review enlarges the freedom of the Supreme Court to declare state statutes unconstitutional.

Two typical cases illustrate the workings of Chief Justice Stone's conception of the Court as the impartial arbiter of the federal system. The first is *Morgan v. Virginia*.[7] Mrs. Morgan, a Negress, got on a bus in Richmond, bound for Baltimore. While in Virginia she refused to follow the conductor's order to sit in the Jim Crow section and she was convicted of violating a Virginia statute. There is no federal legislation on passenger arrangements for interstate buses, although there is on other bus matters. Indeed, many proposals to eliminate segregation had failed of passage in the Congress. Nonetheless, the Supreme Court released Mrs. Morgan, holding the Virginia statute an undue burden on national commerce in an area where uniformity was essential. Different rules in the different states through which a bus passed would cause inconvenience to through passengers and lead to the confusion and embarrassment of interstate traffic. "To promote and protect national travel," the Court held, "a single, uniform rule" is required.

Under Chief Justice Stone's formula, however, the Supreme Court can uphold as well as strike down state legislation, and this it did in *Bob-Lo Excursion Co. v. Michigan*.[8] Michigan convicted the Bob-Lo Excursion Co. of violating a law by refusing to take Negro passengers on its boats, en-

7. 328 U.S. 373 (1946). See Interstate Commerce Commission Regulation, 26 *Fed. Reg.* 9166–67, Sept. 29, 1961.

8. 333 U.S. 28 (1948).

gaged exclusively in carrying passengers between Detroit and an amusement area in Canada. The case arose when a colored girl, the only one in her high-school class, was asked to leave the boat after her group had embarked. The Court held the Michigan statute applicable even to foreign commerce since none of the considerations requiring uniformity of practice were deemed effective. For all practical purposes, the area is part of Detroit. Application of the statute could not lead to confusion or lack of uniformity, or to any of the other results that the Court found burdensome in the *Morgan* case.

There was a sharp dissent by Mr. Justice Jackson and Chief Justice Vinson, both opponents of state legislation affecting interstate and foreign commerce. In their view, the *Bob-Lo* decision exposed foreign commerce to the risk of burdensome local interference and regulation. They emphasized the uncertainty that results from the Court's technique of weighing state and national interests case by case, after reviewing all the facts. Such practice can provide little guidance for business as to which laws are in effect and which are void. "The commerce clause," Mr. Justice Jackson remarked, "was intended to promote commerce rather than litigation."[9]

State taxation of national business is one of the most frequently litigated problems arising under the commerce clause. Interstate business could hardly be exempted from state taxes, since it depends upon the courts, police, fire brigades, and other services provided by state governments. Business must "pay its way," the Court has said, in all states where it is carried on. But unlimited state taxation of national business could be, and often is, a crippling weapon against out-of-state competition. The tax cases have carried

9. 333 U.S. 28, 43, 45 (1948) (dissenting opinion).

legal reasoning to the extreme limit of verbalism that laymen enjoy attributing to lawyers. Their pattern of decision runs largely along these lines:

First, no state can by taxation deny a person or a corporation from another state the chance to do local business. This is now grounded in part on the proposition that the right to do business throughout the United States is a privilege of national citizenship that no state can abridge. The Supreme Court voided a tax on peddlers and drummers imposed in Virginia, and a South Carolina shrimp-fishing license law that discriminated heavily against out-of-staters. Second, the Court will uphold local taxation of national business if the tax is more or less related to the benefit received. Thus an Ohio corporate franchise tax was upheld against the International Harvester Co., the tax base being a fraction of the value of corporate property and a portion also of the volume of its business. Similarly, a Montana tax was upheld against an interstate moving company that did no local business, as a nondiscriminatory contribution toward maintaining the roads.

On the other hand, state taxes have been invalidated as levied against more than the taxing state's fair share of a company's business. Various formulas are used: the state may not "unduly burden" national commerce, discriminate against it, or tax property "outside" the jurisdiction.[10] The underlying idea seems to be that, in the absence of a directive from Congress, the Court must establish a policy that reconciles and compromises the local interest in taxation and the national interest in interstate business. The difficulties are such that Mr. Justice Rutledge proposed a novel mechanical test to give the states a clear if not ideal rule to live by until Congress could be induced to act. He suggested

10. E.g., Welton v. Missouri, 91 U.S. 275 (1876); Best & Co. v. Maxwell, 311 U.S. 454 (1940).

that the state where goods are sold have the basic power to tax the sale or the proceeds of the sale on a nondiscriminatory basis, allowing the manufacturing state to tax only if it allowed the taxpayer credit for any taxes he had to pay where the goods were marketed.

Despite the scope of the commerce power given Congress by the Court's decisions since 1937, our constitutional practice is still far more federal than national. The Congress has often chosen to add federal to existing state regulation, rather than to create a single national law. State blue-sky laws and the SEC legislation are enforced together, for example, and the Social Security system is built on the principle of state-federal cooperation.

In handling conflicts between state and federal statutes, the Supreme Court's general policy is to allow each as much scope as possible. The policy is not uniformly applied. In the field of labor relations the Court has voided several state laws on the ground that they collide with the policy of the national labor law. In most other fields the Court is disinclined to nullify or to restrict state law in the absence of a fairly positive congressional guide. The Court's policy makes endless litigation necessary and leads to cumbersome and unpredictable results. In the two *Rice* cases, for example, the Court had to choose between state and national regulation of the Chicago Board of Trade and of grain warehouses in the state of Illinois.[11] It decided that both forms of regulation were in full effect until a trial should disclose actual inconsistency, section by section, between the state and the federal statute.

The broadened conception of the commerce clause has brought about important changes in the interpretation of federal statutes, especially the Sherman Act. For example,

11. Rice v. Santa Fe Elevator Corp., 331 U.S. 218 (1947); Rice v. Board of Trade of the City of Chicago, 331 U.S. 247 (1947).

the Supreme Court in 1944 held that insurance companies could be attacked under the Sherman Act for activities deemed in restraint of trade. The Court had for many years upheld state regulation of the insurance business, often saying that insurance was not interstate commerce. And the Sherman Act was passed in 1890, when that narrow reading of the commerce clause was accepted by the Court and by the Congress.

All the Justices who decided that case, including those who dissented, agreed that Congress could, if it wished, take over all or any part of the regulation of the insurance business. The existing pattern of regulation was a historical accident, resting on the interpretation of the commerce clause that had prevailed for many years, and perhaps on the deeper instincts of federalism which that view of the commerce clause articulated. While the insurance case startled the bar, it could hardly have been decided otherwise. It would be anomalous, to say the least, to have one definition of commerce for the purpose of interpreting the Constitution and another for the purposes of the Sherman Act, which was designed to cover the whole constitutional area of interstate commerce.

One of the clearest modern statements of the Court's philosophy in weighing state statutes against the charge of burdening commerce has been made by Mr. Justice Frankfurter, who has long been fascinated by the problems of federalism. "Since Congress can, if it chooses, entirely displace the states to the full extent of the far-reaching Commerce Clause . . . ," he has pointed out, "It needs no help from generous judicial implications to achieve the supersession of state authority."[12]

The essence of Justice Frankfurter's position derives from

12. Bethlehem Steel Co. v. New York State Labor Relations Board, 330 U.S. 767, 777, 780 (1947).

his view of the Supreme Court's limited role in the process of American political life. The Court is an appointed, not an elected, body, and it should interfere with legislative policy only on broad constitutional grounds. The distinction between "legislative" and "constitutional" policy is an elusive question of degree, especially where the constitutional policy of the commerce clause is involved. But Justice Frankfurter's position has the support of practical considerations. The Supreme Court, which has the power to veto but not to draft legislation, could not hope to do as thorough or effective a job as the Congress in liberating the national economy from the restraints, expense, and confusion of our existing system of multiple regulation. Moreover, the Justices, prudently keeping their powder dry, would like not to get too deeply into the detail of continuous controversy over particular problems. By attempting to remit the issue to the Congress, the Court is not abandoning its peculiar historical function of reviewing the validity of legislation. It is simply trying to keep the exercise of that extraordinary power down to a discreet and tolerable minimum.

Despite the appeal of the Court's policy as a matter of political theory, practice would make such a course unrealistic, as Justice Frankfurter himself later recognized. The root of the difficulty is that the Congress in its turn also prefers to avoid unnecessary decisions in politically sensitive areas, and has for generations elected to pass the buck back to the Court. A failure of the Court to decide a case is therefore almost always a decision in favor of the status quo.

If this were the price we had to pay for the federal principle, it would not be too serious a matter. But it is not. In the field of business regulation, deference to the power of the states often mistakes the shadow of pluralism for its substance. The Constitution can tolerate broad changes in the distribution of legal functions without losing its federal character. And in economic regulation, we can safely go a long way toward uniformity of law without imperiling our freedom.

The great purpose of the commerce clause, and one of the dominant motives of the men who drafted the Constitution, was to break down and to eliminate barriers to trade among the states. Yet interstate trade barriers and local limitations on the right to do business have developed on a massive scale during the last generation, particularly stimulated by the depression of the 1930s. Depressions have always encouraged the curious economic policy of becoming richer by producing less and selling it at a higher price. Just as the nations of the world tried to stave off the depression by raising tariffs and imposing import quotas, the states of the union reacted to the pressure by passing laws to protect local industry; to penalize chain stores; to prohibit sales below cost or published prices, or the use of imported material; and by so licensing trade as to keep down the number of competitors. In many states nowadays one needs a license to be a barber, a shorthand reporter, a plumber, a billiard parlor operator, a manicurist, a pedicurist, or a blacksmith. Often such licenses are available only to citizens, and far too often can be obtained only by paying familiar political tribute. Statutes of this order create vested interests that are extremely difficult for legislators to attack. Those who are injured by such restriction are neither mobilized nor particularly conscious of the injury.

Despite several competent studies Congress has been content to sidestep the growing problem. The Supreme Court may, however, be forced by the pressure of cases to take a more affirmative position. Several of its members, notably Justices Vinson, Jackson, and Rutledge, have believed that the protection of the national economy is one of their strongest historical responsibilities. In the absence of congressional guidance, they will almost surely strike down more and more state laws as burdens on commerce. Justice Jackson pointed out with characteristic pungency,

> Our national free commerce is never in danger of being suddenly stifled by dramatic and sweeping acts of restraint. That would produce its own antidote. Our danger, as the forefathers well knew, is from the aggregate strangling effect of a multiplicity of individually petty and diverse and local regulations . . . These restraints are individually too petty, too diversified, and too local to get the attention of a Congress hard-pressed with more urgent matters. The practical result is that in default of action by us they will go on suffocating and retarding and Balkanizing American commerce, trade and industry.[13]

In the long run, the universal power of Congress under the commerce clause cannot easily be reconciled with the continuance of undiminished regulatory authority in the states. It does not, however, necessarily follow that the assertion of national power under the commerce clause must correspondingly destroy the political importance of state government and intensify centralization, for both the national and the state governments now have more to do than ever before. The problem of the commerce clause, and of federalism, is for us twofold: how to do what must be done efficiently and how to do it in ways that satisfy our sense of constitutional propriety. In some areas this standard may mean exclusive federal regulation, in others cooperative federal-state action, in others state jurisdiction unqualified by congressional action. Rigid formulas are a considerable danger, especially on the Supreme Court. Not every deci-

13. Duckworth v. Arkansas, 314 U.S. 390, 397, 401, 400 (1941) (concurring opinion).

sion in favor of a national solution threatens the end of local self-government. The constitutional problem is not how to divide a fixed quantum of governmental authority between state and nation, but how to guide the evolution of government institutions in ways that fulfill the purposes of the federal conception.

The role of positive government—both local and national—has increased immeasurably, and permanently, in American life. The effective exercise of that power is even more essential to the preservation of American democracy than the maintenance in particular areas of a traditional division of function between state and nation. In view of the caution both of Congress and of the Supreme Court in asserting the national power against the power of the states, there is little ground for fearing the disappearance of federalism. The greater danger is that federalism will become a fetish, ultimately weakening the capacity of all governmental bodies to do an adequate and straightforward job.

# Epilogue

MEN DIFFER for a variety of reasons on the problems with which this book is concerned. Disagreements about constitutional problems among the Justices and their critics are drawn from men's differing views of American politics and American history; from their differing views of themselves, their duty, and the Court; their differing evaluation of and identification with one or another of the forces in array before them. In exercising the judicial power with regard to constitutional questions, the judge is not readily confined, even by his habits of learning, his respect for his office, his discipline. It is for this reason that a judge's sense of constitutional policy is so important to his work—quite as important as his ability, character, and judicial temperament. For in the end, given the nature of the judicial power, the judge's feel for the true sources of our public policy cannot help but influence the direction of constitutional development and the growth of the law.

The conclusion to which the essays in this book lead, in my mind, is that we need a more coherent and explicit doctrine of judicial action in advancing the cause of constitutional democracy. The Court, accepting its constitutional responsibilities in good heart, should use its acknowledged powers to further the grand design of the constitutional system: faithfully to enforce the constitutional limitations on the powers of all units of government, and on the community itself when necessary, to protect the individual in a spacious realm of personal liberty, assured by law. This was one of the great goals of the Founding Fathers, which each American generation must rediscover, and reformulate, in terms that meet the particular circumstances of its own experience. All government crowds the individual and confines his zone of freedom. The Founding Fathers intended to establish, and did establish, a government with authority adequate to its tasks—a national government, a republic, a government controlled by the methods of democracy and by a written constitution enforced as law. An affirmative theory of constitutional law, animated by the purposes and values of modern democracy, should not be niggardly in conceding to government the constitutional powers it needs to carry out its political purposes, as long as it remains faithful to the federal plan as it has evolved. But American democracy does not require, and should never require, modes of action that threaten the confident security of the American in his rights.

# Table of Cases

# Table of Cases

# Index

# Index

# Index

# Index

# Index

# Index

# Index

# Index

Richardson, Elliot, 174–82, 188–90

Richardson, James D., 155 n.

Riesman, David, 197 n.

Roberts, Owen J., 215, 224, 230, 295

Rogers, Mr., 232 n., 233 n.

Rogers, William P., 263

Romania, 219

Roosevelt, Franklin D., xxiv, xxix, xxx, xxxvii, 95, 165. *See also* New Deal

Roosevelt, Theodore, xxiii, xxiv, xxxviii, 94

Root, Elihu, xxxviii, 233

Rostow, Eugene V., 4 n., 255 n., 263–64

Rowe, Mr., 199 n.

Rowell, Mr., 204 n.

Rules of law, 8–9, 13–17, 26 ff.

Russia, 182–83, 185, 186, 268, 284, 286; Soviet-American relations, 183

Rutledge, Wiley B., 295, 298, 302

Sabine, George H., 16

Sabotage, 194–266 passim

Sacco, Nicola, 262

Sacks, Albert M., xviii n.

Sandburg, Carl, 204 n.

School segregation, xii, 112

Schwartz, Murray L., 25 n.

Scottsboro boys, 107

Securities Act (*1933*), 132–34

Securities and Exchange Commission, 299

Security risks. *See* Loyalty-security programs

Sedition, 57–58, 69, 70, 103

Sherman, Mandel, 220 n.

Sherman Antitrust Act (*1890*), xx, 43, 299, 300

Shils, E. A., 268 n.

Silving, Helen, 58

Sin, vs. crime, 47 ff., 74

Smith, Mr., 201 n.

Smith, Jeremiah, 116

Smith Act (*1940*), xxxv, 181, 182

Smollett, Tobias G., 57

Social Security, xxviii, 299

Socialism, 70

Socrates, 47

Sons of Liberty, 249

South: efforts of, to circumvent law, 41–44; reaction of, to segregation decisions, 143–46

South America, 268

South Carolina, 298

Soviets. *See* Russia

Spain, Spanish, 232

Spanish-American War, 232

Spencer, Herbert, 78, 159

Spengler, Oswald, 57

Spinoza, Baruch, 47

Srole, Leo, 220 n.

Stanton, Edwin, xxv n.

State courts, criminal cases, 107

States, powers of. *See* States' rights

States' rights, xxvii–xxviii, xxxvii, 96–97, 99–111, 290–304

Stern, Bernhard J., 220 n.

Stimson, Henry L., xxxviii, 212 n.

Stone, Harlan F., 127, 160, 161, 248, 294–96

Stonequist, Everett V., 220 n.

Suffrage, 119

Supreme Court of the United States: popular opinions of, xi–xii; minority opinions, xi–xii; controversy over, xi–xii; social nature of decisions, xiii; in relation to constitution, xix; umpire between states and federal government, xxviii; in light of other governmental bodies, xxx; political power, xxx–xxxi; limitations, xxxi–xxxiii; sphere of activity, xxxiii ff.; two controversies over, xxxv; strict vs. broad construction, xxxvi; liberal and conservative justices, xxxvi–xxxix; anxiety over modes of action, 4; high level of accomplishment, 5–6; criticism of,

316

23 ff., 83–113; political vs. judicial decisions, 24–25; Wechsler attack on, 24 ff.; role of reason in decisions of, 28; inevitable faults in opinions of, 34–36; "neutrality" of, 37–39; classes of questions brought before, 90–93; reasons for controversy surrounding, 91; political element in decisions of, 93–94, 156–61; Federal-State relationships an issue, 96–97, 99-111; policy-making an element, 98–99; interpretation of Congressional authority, 102–03; Fourteenth Amendment cases, 105 ff.; not responsible for kind or number of cases, 109; primary duty, 110; as an instrument of the people's will, 114–46; must make law as well as interpret it, 116; civil rights cases, 124–28; legislative powers, 130–31; role in evolution of constitutional ideal, 141; democratic character of judicial review, 147–92; one of chief agencies for enforcing restraints of Constitution, 154; interpretation of Constitution by, 163–70; judicial independence of, 163–64; prestige, 167–68; accomplishments, 167–70; salubrious effect on democratic forces, 170; element of choice in decisions, 175; limitations on power, 176–77; necessity for restraint, 177–79; upholds Japanese relocation program, 196; and Japanese American cases, 214 ff.; basic hypothesis of the JA cases, 219; underlying issues of JA opinions, 220–31; primary constitutional issues of JA cases, 231–41; rule of proof not satisfied in JA cases, 241–42; justification for JA evacuation not proved, 242–47; pertinence of *Ex parte Milligan* to JA cases, 248–57;

boundaries of military discretion crucial to JA opinions, 258–59; JA opinions sacrificed crucial principle, 261; necessity to repair damage of JA cases, 262–63; New Deal Court, 289; and states' rights, 290–304; commerce cases, 291–304; need for more coherent and explicit doctrine, 305

Sutherland, Arthur E., xvi n., 107, 121 n., 127

Sweden, 121

Swisher, Carl B., 228 n.

Taft, William Howard, 109

Taney, Roger B., xxxvii, 35, 93, 228

Tariff Commission, 120

Tax cases, 298–99

Teapot Dome, xxxviii

Test oaths, 94, 106

Thayer, James Bradley, 148 n., 151 n., 156, 157 n., 158, 159

Thomas, Benjamin P., xxv n.

Thomas, Dorothy Swaine, 263 n.

Thompson, Holland, 220 n.

Thoreau, Henry D., 143

Thurmond, Strom, xxxvii

Tobruk, 214

Tocqueville, Alexis de, 93, 112

Tolan Committee, 193-266 notes, passim

Treason, 57–59, 69, 70

Tripolitania, 214

Trubek, David M., 25 n., 37 n.

Truman, Harry S., 149, 267, 270

Tunisia, 214

Vagts, Alfred, 232 n.

Vallandigham, Clement L., 204 n.

Vanzetti, Bartolomeo, 262

Vinson, Fred M., 297, 302

Virginia, 298

Wagner Act (*1935*), 289

War Department, 204, 259–61

# Index